Aviation CROWOOD **SERIES**

THE TURRET FIGHTERS

Defiant and Roc

Alec Brew

The Crowood Press

First published in 2002 by
The Crowood Press Ltd
Ramsbury, Marlborough
Wiltshire SN8 2HR

British Library Cataloguing-in-Publication Data
A catalogue record for this book is available from the British Library.

ISBN 1 86126 497 6

Acknowledgements

As archivist for the Boulton Paul Association's West Midlands Aviation Archive, which contains the surviving Boulton Paul archives, I have been lucky to have the surviving company records and photographs at my disposal. I have also to thank the many members of the association who have helped me over the years, but in particular former Defiant Squadron personnel: Wg Cdr Eric Barwell, Wg Cdr Christopher Deanesley, Fg Off Fred Barker, Fg Off Fred Gash, Flt Lt John Lauder, Flt Lt Fred Pelham, Flt Lt Frank Lanning, Flt Lt Bryan Wild, Sqn Ldr Edward Wolfe, Sgt Les Allen, Cpl Phil Dimsdale and Sgt Sid Walker.

Other former Boulton Paul employees who have been an immense help include Jack Chambers, Cyril Plimmer, Brian and Jack Holmes, Denis Bolderstone, Harry Law and Bill Pauling.

Les Whitehouse has always been helpful in providing information and illustrations from his own extensive and unique archive of Boulton Paul Aircraft, particularly with regard to the unbuilt turret fighters.

As historian for his former squadron, No. 141, Don Aris has been a continual help, allowing me to borrow many photographs from his very detailed personal history of No. 141, and answering my many questions. Geoff Faulkner has performed the same role as secretary of the No. 264 Squadron Association. Stephen King and Betty Clements allowed me the fruits of their researches into No. 307 Squadron. Russell Brown of the Lancashire Aircraft Investigation Team provided much information about Defiant operations at Blackpool by No. 307 and No. 256 squadrons, and loaned me many photographs. Hywell Evans loaned me the photograph of the No. 456 Squadron Defiant at RAF Valley, which he had used in his own history of aviation on Anglesey.

Ray Sturtivant has provided much information and many photographs of the Roc and of naval Defiants. Del Holyland of Martin Baker Aircraft provided prompt replies to my queries and requests for photographs. Jan Jolie provided much information, and photographs of Defiant operations over the Netherlands. Geoff Hill, restorer of one of the few surviving type A gun turrets, loaned me several photographs, some of which he had acquired from Frank Lanning.

Jenny Woodall loaned me the logbooks of her father, Robin Lindsay Neale, Boulton Paul test pilot, which turned up several previously unsuspected facts.

In the ten years or more that I have spent researching the history of the Defiant and the Roc, there have been many people who have supplied information or photographs, and I am sure I must have missed some from these acknowledgements. Even if, regretfully, I have not included their name, they do also have my thanks.

Typeset by Naomi Lunn

Printed and bound in Great Britain by Bookcraft Ltd

Contents

Introduction

The Boulton Paul Defiant and the Blackburn Roc represent the only operational aircraft to be produced to a novel form of fighting aircraft concept, the turret fighter. The Roc was only used briefly by operational squadrons, and saw very little action, and the much longer career of the Defiant has been surrounded by many myths almost since it first fired its guns in anger. Many of the stories about how the Defiant came about, and how it performed in action, are spurious, but the aircraft undoubtedly carved its own novel niche in British aviation history.

The turret fighter was rather more than just a fighter with a gun turret: it sprang from a fairly simple concept relating to the division of responsibilities in a fighting aeroplane. To put it in simple terms, the pilot should point the aircraft, and a gunner should point the guns. On the face of it there was a great deal of commonsense in this idea, since a pilot could really not be expected to fly his aircraft and aim his guns at the same time, unless the guns were fixed to fire in the direction he was flying. This meant that he could only fire when the target was directly ahead, and it also meant that against a ground target or a slow-moving aircraft he could only fire for a few seconds, and would himself present a no-deflection target for return fire.

If, on the other hand, the guns were fitted to a movable mounting, to be aimed by a separate gunner, they could be brought to bear on the target for a far greater period of time. A gunner would also find it easier to clear stoppages and to reload the guns.

This was the thinking when guns were first attached to aircraft before World War I, and every gun-carrying aircraft that was produced until just after the start of the war featured a two-man crew, pilot and gunner. The main two to enter service in an offensive role with the Royal Flying Corps were the FE 2 and the Vickers Gunbus; these were single-engined pushers in which the pilot sat just behind a gunner in a nose 'turret', the gunner being armed with one or more machine guns that he could aim through the whole of the foward hemisphere.

This first flowering of the turret fighter concept was superseded by the single-seat, fixed-gun fighter. These single-seat 'scouts' were faster and more manoeuvrable, and made short work of the lumbering two-seaters. Only at night, where speed and agility were not so important, were the two-seaters just as useful as the single-seaters.

After the end of the war there was still a feeling in certain quarters that the single-seat fighter had not proved itself against the threat of a large close formation of heavy bombers. Many influential people were convinced that the concentrated defensive fire from the many machine guns in such a formation would prove too much for single-seaters attacking one by one, and presenting a no-deflection target as they aimed their own puny armament of two machine guns. The only answer would be for the fighters to attack in formation, and as the fighter pilots could not be expected to maintain formation and aim their guns at the same time, these responsibilities would have to be divided.

Fourteen years were then to elapse, from the time when the idea of dividing responsibility first emerged, until its realization, when first orders were received for the Boulton Paul Defiant and the Blackburn Roc 'turret fighters' (these were in fact the only ones to go into production). During that time many specifications were issued, several featuring novel armament arrangements, and some prototypes were built, before the definitive turret fighter specification was decided upon.

New generations of turret fighter were planned to follow on the Defiant and Roc, but none was ever built, and the concept died more quickly than the period of time it took to come to fruition.

CHAPTER ONE

The Turret Fighter Concept

During the 1930s, aircraft construction underwent a radical change. The fabric-covered biplane finally gave way to the all-metal monoplane, incorporating innovations such as flaps, variable-pitch propellers and retractable undercarriages. It was the airliner that led the way, in the search for increased speed, first with the Boeing 247 and then with the Douglas DC-2; but new all-metal bombers were also soon to emerge, such as the Martin B-10 and the Tupolev ANT-4.

It was clear that the traditional fighter armament of just two rifle-calibre machine guns would be insufficient to destroy these new bombers as firing passes became shorter, and there ensued intense debate as to how a new generation of fighters should be armed. This led to two basic lines of thought: to some it was simply a case of increasing the number of guns from two to four, six or eight so that the weight of fire on each firing pass would be correspondingly increased; others proposed adding cannon to the fighter's arsenal.

Yet other experts believed that a single fighter attacking a formation of bombers would be unlikely to survive their combined defensive firepower, and fighters would therefore have to attack in formation. However, since from the pilot's point of view aiming and keeping formation were not compatible, fighters would have to be equipped with guns on movable mountings, and these would have to be operated by a second crew member.

Early Gun Carriers

In the early days of arming military aircraft, movable mountings and separate gunners were the only system considered. The first time a machine gun was fired from an aircraft was on 7 June 1912, the aircraft being a Wright Model B of the United States Army; the gunner was Captain Charles de F. Chamdler, and he sat alongside the pilot cradling the Lewis gun on his lap.

The Lewis gun was promoted in Great Britain by the Belgian FN company, and Horatio Barber, formerly of the Aeronautical Syndicate, Hendon, was assigned to design a movable mounting for it. The task of fitting it to a Grahame-White Boxkite for trials was given to twenty-one-year-old John Dudley North, newly employed by Grahame-White Aircraft on the recommendation of Barber, for whom he had formerly worked. North devised a gunner's seat beneath the lower wing, and the aircraft was demonstrated to the British Army at Bisley, with Marcus Manton as pilot, and a Belgian officer, Lt Stillingworth, firing the gun at a 25sq ft (2.3sq m) ground target. Despite 280 hits from 470 rounds fired from an altitude of 400–500ft (120–150m), the Army decided that the Lewis gun was a waste of time.

The first military aircraft that North designed for Grahame-White also featured a machine gun on a movable mounting, but a Colt-Browning in the nose of a two-seat pusher, the Grahame-White Type 6.

The design of this was in response to an Admiralty requirement for an aircraft carrying a gun for offensive purposes, possibly the first such official requirement. Several manufacturers were interested in the possible order that would result, and all the designs they produced featured the same basic layout, namely a single-engined pusher, with a pilot and a gunner in the nacelle in front of the wing, with the gunner operating a machine gun on a movable mounting. The pusher arrangement seemed the only one that could give the gunner a free field of fire in the forward hemisphere.

North's Grahame-White Type 6 was not like the others: it had the engine in the forward nacelle, in front of the wings, with the gunner and pilot in tandem behind it, and the 90hp Austro-Daimler engine's drive shaft ran under the cockpits, and drove the reduction gear to turn the propeller that revolved on the upper longeron of the triangular girder structure holding the tail. A Colt machine gun was sited above the fully enclosed engine on a mounting that allowed it to be moved 180 degrees horizontally and 50 degrees in elevation. The Type 6 appeared at the 1913 Olympia Aero Show, and drew much comment because of the gun; but the aircraft proved to be seriously underpowered. On its only attempt at flight it took several men, who had been holding the aircraft back while Louis Noel ran up the engine,

The Grahame-White Type 6 gun carrier designed by J.D. North in 1913, armed with a Colt-Browning machine gun on a movable mount in the gunner's forward cockpit.

to reverse their effort into pushing, to get the aircraft moving. It accelerated very slowly, and Louis Noel nearly ran out of airfield; he just managed to haul it into the air as the boundary hedge approached, but the Type 6 flopped into the next field, and flight was never attempted again.

Later the same year A.V. Roe built his Type 508 to the same requirement, but with a more conventional engine arrangement. The 80hp Gnome rotary was placed at the rear of the fuselage nacelle, with the two crewmen in the nose. The aircraft was displayed on the Avro stand at the 1914 Olympia Show, but it was also clearly underpowered and there is no evidence that it ever flew, or had a machine gun fitted.

J. D. North's second attempt to fulfil the requirement was the Grahame-White Type 11 warplane; it used the same layout, and was also on display at the 1914 Olympia Aero Show, where it drew much praise for its excellent workmanship. It was fitted with a 100hp Gnome at the rear of the nacelle, like the Avro 508. However, once again it is doubtful that a gun was ever actually fitted, and when flight was attempted the Type 11 was shown to be very unstable, probably due to the short tail moment, and it was abandoned.

Slightly more successful was the Sopwith Gunbus, evolved from a seaplane ordered by Greece. Its appearance resulted

in a follow-up order for six landplane versions powered by a 100hp Gnome Monosoupape and fitted with a single Lewis gun for the gunner in the nose of the nacelle; however, these had not been delivered when World War I broke out. The six aircraft were taken over by the Royal Naval Air Service, and a further thirty were ordered to be fitted with the 150hp Sunbeam Crusader engine; but only seventeen were completed, and few of these ever had their engine fitted. A few

saw service briefly at Dunkirk.

An alternative layout to the single-engined pusher was thought to be a twin-engined aircraft, in which the nose would be free to carry the gunner. This design had the added advantage of doubling the power, an important consideration for lifting a gun and its ammunition as well as two crew-members, and it also made possible the fitment of a heavier weapon than a single machine gun. Vickers began the construction of their FB.7

Technical Information for Early Gun Carriers

	Grahame-White Type 6	RAF FE.2a	Avro 508	Sopwith Gunbus	Vickers EFB 1
Engine	A-Daimler 90hp	Green 100hp	Gnome 80hp	Sunbeam 150hp	Wolseley 80hp
Gun	Colt	Lewis	Lewis	Lewis	Maxim
Span	42ft 6in (12.95m)	47ft 10in (14.57m)	44ft (13.41m)	50ft (15.24m)	40ft (12.19m)
Length	33ft 9in (10.29m)	32ft 3.5in (9.83m)	26ft 9in (8.15m)	32ft 6in (9.91m)	27.5ft (11.4m)
Top weight	2,950lb (1,338kg)	2,680lb (1,216kg)	1,680lb (762kg)	–	2,660lb (1,207kg)
Top speed	70mph (113kph)	80.3mph (129kph)	65mph (105kph)	80mph (129kph)	70mph (113kph)
Climb	340ft/min (104m/min)	–	–	–	450ft/min (137m/min)
to 3,000ft (914m)	8min 10sec	–	–	–	–

The Grahame-White Type 11 Warplane designed by J.D. North in 1914 with the same layout as his Type 6, but initially the pilot occupied the front seat. A gun was never fitted because of the aircraft's unsatisfactory flying characteristics.

after the war began, an unremarkable twin-engined biplane, except for the fact that the gunner in the nose was armed with a Vickers quick-firing one-pounder. A dozen were ordered immediately after the flight of the prototype in August 1915, to be built by Darracq; but the 100hp Gnome Monosoupape engines were in short supply, and no others were available with sufficient power. The two 80hp Renaults fitted to the first aircraft were inadequate, and the aircraft could not meet its specification. Vickers asked for the remainder to be cancelled, and this was agreed by the War Office.

The next Vickers twin-engined fighter was far more compact, though powered by the same 100hp Gnome Monosoupape engines as the first FB.7. Furthermore the FB.8 was armed, not with the one-pounder cannon, but with only a single Lewis gun in the nose, and the appearance of single-engined fighters with interrupter gear permitting forward fire, rather superseded the design. At around the same time, Bristol built their TTA, a much larger twin with two 120hp Beardmore engines and a much heavier armament. The nose gunner had two Lewis guns, and there was a second gunner with a single gun in the dorsal position for rear defence.

World War I Turret Fighters

Only two of the early gun carriers can be considered a success, namely the Royal Aircraft Factory FE.2 and the Vickers Gunbus, and both had long gestation periods.

The Royal Aircraft Factory FE.2

At the Factory the chief designer, Geoffrey de Havilland, did not design a brand-new aircraft as a gun carrier, but instead adapted the FE.2 that had been around in various forms since 1911. It was fitted with a 70hp Renault engine, its undercarriage was strengthened, and it was fitted with a movable mounting on the nose of the nacelle so it could carry a belt-fed Maxim machine gun. By 1914 a new version of the FE.2 was produced with a much more substantial structure, with a redesigned nacelle in which the gunner had a Lewis gun, and the pilot sat 18in (45cm) higher behind him. The aircraft was intended to be powered by the 100hp Green engine, but this heavy unit was later replaced by

the 120hp Beardmore. The aircraft was re-designated the FE.2a, and twelve were ordered at the outbreak of war, the first flying in January 1915. They all saw service in France, and were amongst the few effective gun-carrying aircraft that the RFC had. When it became clear to the military mind that a gun-carrying aeroplane was an essential ingredient of modern warfare, the FE.2 was ordered in large numbers. Slight changes were made to the design as a result of experiences with the FE.2a, and also to ease manufacture; the new version became the FE.2b.

On 4 October 1915 the first FE.2b, 5201, flew for the first time at Mousehold Airfield, Norwich, where it had been built by Boulton & Paul Ltd. The FE.2b was the first effective 'turret fighter', and in fact for a while, official instructions were that it should be referred to as the 'Fighter Mark 1'; but this was rarely done, and it was more widely known, and with some affection, as the 'Fee'. 5201 joined No. 16 Squadron in France on 30 October 1915. The first squadron to be fully equipped with FE.2bs was No. 20, and many units of the new fighter were to operate over the Western Front, providing protection for reconnaissance machines, and partially redressing the imbalance created by the appearance of the Fokker E.111 monoplane. The gunner in the nose was usually equipped with two Lewis machine guns

that could be fitted on a variety of mountings, sometimes being moved from one to another, to face the immediate threat.

The main disadvantage was that the FE.2b was defenceless to the rear, and inevitably the Germans quickly found this out; to counter this threat, a pillar mount was devised so that the gunner could fire back over the top wing. But to do this he had to stand on the box containing spare ammunition drums, and was totally exposed to the slipstream; because of the precariousness of this position he was later provided with a safety cable, one end attached to the floor of his 'turret' and the other to his stout leather belt. More than one wounded gunner is known to have fallen out of his cockpit during combat manoeuvres: for instance, on one sortie the No. 18 Squadron FE.2b flown by Lt Frank Barnard had been attacked by a number of German fighters, and his gunner, Lt F.S. Rankin, had been hit and had fallen from his cockpit. Barnard had climbed into the forward cockpit, leaving the Fee to fly itself, and had somehow hauled Rankin back on board; he had then climbed back into his own cockpit and flown back to base. He tore his arm muscles hauling his gunner back on board, and had to be admitted to hospital; but unfortunately his efforts were in vain, as Rankin later died of his wounds.

The first production FE.2b, serial 5201, built by Boulton & Paul Ltd at Norwich, and flown for the first time on 4 October 1915.

By the middle of 1916 the FE.2b had become outdated as a fighter, though the Fees were nevertheless still able to hold their own. For example, on 18 June 1916 three of them were attacked by the famous Max Immelmann leading seven Fokker Monoplanes; one of the FE.2bs was shot down, but so were two of the attackers, and the rest fled. And on the evening of the same day, Lt McCubbin was flying an FE.2b with a corporal fitter as gunner, when they saw three Fokkers flying below them, and dived to the attack. The Fokkers were engaging another FE.2b, and for a brief time the five aircraft twisted and turned in the sky. But then the pilot of the other FE.2b was wounded, and he spiralled down to make a forced landing behind German lines; and one of the Fokker Monoplanes, flown by Lt Mulzer, landed nearby, out of fuel. The remaining three aircraft continue to battle it out above them.

One of the Fokkers climbed to get above McCubbin, whose gunner opened fire from below with a long burst: the Fokker reared up, rolled onto one wing, and fluttered down like a leaf in autumn, breaking up in the air – first the tail came off, then as the remaining fuselage gained momentum, the wings folded back and broke off. The forward fuselage containing the heavy engine, gun and pilot then inevitably gathered speed and plummeted into the ground, dropping 6,000ft (2,000m) in just a few seconds. This loss was significant because the pilot was none other than the great Max Immelmann, one of the first great fighter pilots.

The FE.2b was to have less success against another of Germany's most famous fighter pilots, Manfred von Richtofen, known as the 'Red Baron' – indeed when Immelmann fell, the 'Red Baron' had already accounted for his first FE.2b. On 12 June he had been one of six pilots of Jagdstaffel 2, led by Oswald Boelke, on a sortie flying the new Albatross D.I. They saw eight BE.2cs of No. 12 Squadron escorted by six FE.2bs of No. 11 Squadron: as they dived to attack, Richtofen chose one of the Fees as his target and opened fire. He missed, as did the return fire from the FE.2b gunner, and they twisted and turned as the FE.2b pilot tried to prevent the German from getting behind, where he was vulnerable. But he must have lost sight of the Albatross, because he levelled out for a moment, and this gave Richtofen the chance he was waiting for, to climb

and attack from underneath, a blind spot for any fighter, with a gunner or not: he opened fire, and the FE.2b jerked and its propeller stopped. Richtofen followed it down to a bumpy landing behind German lines; he landed alongside, and found the British gunner dead, and the pilot dying.

Richtofen was to shoot down a total of twelve of the two-seaters during his career – although the Fee almost took its revenge, because in one combat the Baron was hit in the head by an FE.2b gunner.

Boulton & Paul and the Red Baron

At least nine of the FE.2s shot down by Manfred von Richtofen were built by Boulton & Paul Ltd in Norwich, an interesting first round in the contest between Boulton & Paul-built 'turret fighters' and single-seat German fighter pilots, a contest that was to be resumed with Defiants over Holland and Dunkirk in May 1940.

Victory No.	Date	FE.2 serial	FE.2 Squadron
1	12.6.16	7018	11
3	30.9.16	6973	11
7	3.11.16	7010	?
14	20.12.16	A5446	18
15	27.12.16	6996	25
18	24.1.17	6937	25
27	27.3.17	A5439	25
34	3.4.17	A6382	25
46	22.4.17	7020	11

The FE.2b's Defensive Merry-Go-Round

One tactic adopted by the FE.2b squadrons was also to be adopted by Defiants in World War II: when attacked by single-seaters they went into a tight defensive circle, each covering the tail of the one in front and, with some gunners firing forwards and some standing and firing to the rear, any attacking German was faced with defensive fire from several guns. W.C. Cambray, the C.O. of No. 20 Squadron, described how such actions took place:

The enemy usually collected a formation of six, then perhaps an additional eight, and when there were twenty of theirs to five of ours, they would come close in to attack. I would thereupon fire a red Very light, which told our formation we were going to fight. We would then go round and round in a big circle, each following the tail of the man in front, and always making the whole circle approach gradually closer

to our own lines. Should a Hun dive to attack, the observer of one machine in the circle would fire his top gun, and the observer of the next machine would use his front gun, so that at any given time the attacker would have two guns firing at him.

He went on to describe the close co-operation required between pilot and gunner, and the difficulties experienced when this close co-operation was absent. On one occasion he was flying with a good pilot, but one not experienced in air-to-air fighting. They were attacked from the rear, and he stood to fire over the upper wing, giving instructions to his pilot to take evasive action – and was surprised when the pilot did only a gentle turn. On the second attack he managed to hit the German, who fell away out of control – but again, the pilot had made only a gentle turn. When asked about this on the ground, he said by way of explanation: 'I was afraid I'd chuck you out!' Cambray replied that it was his job to stay in, and that in future, evasive turns were to be rather steeper.

The Germans described the FE.2b's defensive circle as a 'Merry-go-round'. It was during just such a battle between Richtofen's squadron and a squadron of Fees that the 'Red Baron' was hit in the head. The FE.2b squadron circled for fully fifteen minutes as the Germans made darting attacks, and then Captain Woodbridge's gunner fired an accurate burst and grazed Richtofen's head. The German's Albatross went diving to earth, its pilot unable to see; only near to the ground did he regain a hazy vision, enabling him to pull off a shaky landing.

By mid-1916 the Royal Flying Corps was receiving effective single-seat fighters with fixed forward-firing machine guns that were fired through the propeller disc; but the Fee soldiered on as a fighter, as the British were convinced of the effectiveness of a fighter with a movable gun. However, on 6 April 1917 their faith may have been shattered when five crews of No. 57 Squadron, equipped with the FE.2d with the more powerful Rolls-Royce Eagle engine, lost the day against a formation of German two-seaters: the whole FE.2d formation was shot down, the effectiveness of their movable front gun neutralized by the movable rear guns of the German aircraft.

Soon afterwards the FE.2b was converted to a bomber. The substantial lifting properties of its large wing, augmented later with the increased power of the Rolls

A production FE.2d, assembled by Boulton & Paul with nacelles made by Garrett & Sons at Leiston. This Rolls-Royce Eagle-powered version was mostly used as a night bomber.

A production Vickers FB.5 Gunbus with a spigot mounting in the gunner's cockpit to take the Lewis gun.

Royce Eagle engine, made it very effective in the role of night bomber, carrying the war to Germany.

The Vickers Gunbus

The other effective gun-carrying pusher was the Vickers Gunbus, which went through many changes from its first appearance early in 1913 as the Vickers EFB.1 Destroyer (Experimental Fighting Biplane). A two-seat pusher like the others, it was powered initially by an 80hp Wolseley engine, and the gunner was armed with a Vickers-Maxim machine gun able to traverse through 60 degrees both horizontally and in elevation. The EFB.1 was displayed at the 1913 Olympia Aero Show, where the Grahame-White Type 6

was the main rival; but like the Type 6, it made only one attempt at flight, when it crashed.

Even before this, Vickers was working on a new version with a 100hp Gnome engine, the EFB.2. In this, the Vickers machine gun was fitted to a trunnion mounting in the actual nose of the nacelle, but the arcs of movement were limited, and it wasn't easy for the gunner to aim. A third version of the aircraft – which was now widely referred to by the unofficial name of Gunbus – the EFB.3, was prepared for the 1914 Olympia Aero Show, and twelve production aircraft were ordered by the Admiralty, though the order was eventually taken over by the War Office. A substantial redesign was undertaken which emerged as the EFB.5, with the

name 'Gunbus' officially bestowed upon it.

It had become clear that the belt-fed Vickers machine gun, that the company had naturally chosen, was not suitable for such applications, and so they undertook a redesign to accommodate a Lewis gun on a spigot-mounting in front of the gunner's cockpit. Other changes were also made to the aircraft so that it was more suitable for production, and in this form it was re-designated the EFB.4. It then underwent further progressive modifications, to emerge as the FB.5 Gunbus, and was placed into production by Vickers even before an offical order was received, in the full expectation that gun-carrying aircraft would be needed in what would obviously be an imminent war.

The fifty aircraft laid down were indeed ordered by the War Office, followed by over 150 more. The Vickers Gunbus was issued to a number of squadrons early in the war, within the system then prevailing of each squadron having a variety of aircraft in order to fulfil diverse functions. The first three FB.5s had been delivered to Netheravon late in 1914, and two of these were then assigned to Joyce Green – thereby representing the entire aerial defence for London. It was one of these that attempted the first-ever interception of an enemy aircraft over Great Britain, when on Christmas Day 1914 a German seaplane was spotted approaching London up the Thames estuary: Lt M. R. Chidson, with Cpl Martin as gunner, duly took off in the Gunbus, but engine trouble prevented contact being made.

Most of the gun mountings for the Vickers FB.5 were simple pillar or pylon mountings, though four were equipped with the first-ever rotating ring mount – the Vickers Challenger, designed by G. H. Challenger – so that the Lewis gun would revolve as the gunner turned. This mounting pre-dated the more famous Scarff ring, and therefore in some senses must be regarded as the first 'gun turret'.

Once the modern system of squadrons specializing in particular functions had been adopted, No. 11 Squadron was entirely equipped with the Vickers Gunbus, and arrived in France as the first true fighter squadron of any nation. Despite its very modest performance, the Gunbus gave a brave account of itself until supplanted by faster fighters during 1916.

One pilot was awarded the Victoria Cross while flying a Vickers Gunbus. In November 1915, Lt G. S. Insall attacked a

World War I 'Turret Fighters': Technical Information			
	Vickers Gunbus	*FE.2b*	*FE.2d*
Engine	100hp Gnome	160hp Beardmore	250hp RR Eagle
Armament	1 Lewis gun	1–2 Lewis guns	2–3 Lewis guns
Span	36ft 6in	47ft 9in	47ft 9in
	(11.13m)	(14.55m)	(14.55m)
Length	27ft 2in	32ft 3in	32ft 3in
	(8.28m)	(9.83m)	(9.83m)
Height	11ft	12ft 7.5in	12ft 7.5in
	(3.35m)	(3.86m)	(3.86m)
Wing area	382sq ft	494sq ft	494sq ft
	(35.48sq m)	(45.89sq m)	(45.89sq m)
Empty weight	1,220lb	2,061lb	2,509lb
	(553.39kg)	(934.87kg)	(1,138kg)
Loaded weight	2,050lb	3,036lb	3,469lb
	(929.88kg)	(1,377.13kg)	(1,573.53kg)
Top speed	70mph/5,000ft	81mph/6,500ft	94mph/5,000ft
	(113kph/1,524m)	(130kph/1,981m)	(151kph/1,524m)
Climb			
to 1,500ft	5min		
(457m)			
to 3,000ft		7min 24sec	
(914m)			
to 5,000ft	16min		7min 10sec
(1,524m)			
to 10,000ft		39min 40sec	18min 20sec
(3,048m)			
Ceiling	9,000ft	11,000ft	17,500ft
	(2,743m)	(3,353m)	(5,334m)
Endurance	4.5hr		3.5hr

German Aviatik reconnaissance aircraft, but was damaged by groundfire; he landed near to the front lines. But during the night he managed to repair his engine, and returned to his squadron in the morning.

The unfortunate gunner in either the Gunbus or the FE.2b was, certainly to begin with, completely untrained in his duties – indeed, he was usually just a mechanic who had volunteered to go aloft. Most early squadrons did not even have trained armourers to look after the machine guns, let alone gunners trained in air-to-air firing. In return for their bravery in volunteering, these men were subjected to flights in an almost totally exposed position in sub-zero temperatures, their only protection the thin plywood sides of their 'pulpit'. Lt A. J. Insall, a Vickers Gunbus gunner with No. 11 Squadron, later explained what it was like:

It was bitterly cold sitting there, huddled up and entirely passive, with scarcely more protection from the wind of our own making than that afforded to a ship's figurehead facing an arctic gale, and my hands and my feet had some time ago lost all sense of feel, while my knees were just solid areas of bent leg.

The first 'turret fighters', as epitomized by the FE.2b and the Vickers Gunbus – that is, fighters in which a pilot flew the aircraft, and a gunner operated the armament on movable mountings – came about because there was nothing else. The idea of a fixed aircraft gun, aimed by the pilot aiming the entire aircraft, was slow to develop, largely hindered by the fact that the propeller was in the way. Devices to allow a machine gun to fire through a propeller without damaging it were devised before the war by Lt Patlavko in Russia and Franz Schneider in Switzerland, although the French were the first to use such a system operationally.

Raymond Saulnier devised such an interrupter gear in the early months of the war, but because it depended on the reliability of the ammunition, he preferred to use deflector plates fitted to the propeller blades of a Morane monoplane. Finally, on 1 April 1915, Roland Garros became the first pilot to use this idea successfully to shoot down another aircraft, a feat he was to repeat three more times.

As is well known, Garros eventually force-landed behind German lines because of engine failure, thus presenting the Germans with the secret of his success. The direct result was the Fokker Monoplane, equipped with a machine gun with synchronization gear so that it would fire between the propeller blades. This was the first true single-seat fighter, and all the belligerents were soon developing their own equivalents.

By the end of the war, the standard armament for a fighter was two fixed machine guns, sited near enough to the cockpit for the pilot to clear stoppages; the fighter with movable guns had faded from the scene. The exception was the two-seat Bristol F.2b fighter with a fixed, forward-firing Vickers machine gun and a Lewis gun mounted on a Scarff ring for rear defence. This aircraft became an outstanding success once it was flown as if it were a single-seater, with the addition of a rear gun to protect its tail.

The one problem that was not solved before the end of the war was how to stop formations of heavy bombers. The Gotha raids on London had often not even been intercepted, and even when they were, had proved difficult to stop. The Royal Air Force came to believe that '…the bomber would always get through', and decided that the only effective answer was the deterrent effect of having a superior force of heavy bombers of its own. This doctrine of counter-offensive meant that the RAF's heavy bomber force became the most important element in its armoury, almost the very reason for its existence.

Post-War Thinking

After the Great War, ways of countering attacking forces of heavy bombers were still being considered. In 1923 Air Cdr T. C. R. Higgins, director of training and staff duties, examined the problems caused by the Gotha raid on London on 7 July 1917: this raid seemed an ideal example for analysis, though it had not been intercepted at the time. Higgins assessed what would have happened if the Gotha formation had been attacked by a squadron of conventional single-seat fighters. It was the RAF's belief at the time that a bomber's defensive free guns were twice as effective as the fixed guns that armed fighters, and Higgins considered that the attacking fighters would have failed in their attacks because of the bombers' ability to concentrate their fire on each individual attack.

Designs for Effective Fighters

Higgins concluded that what was wanted was a fighter that could manoeuvre in formation next to a bomber formation, and engage it broadside on with heavier weapons than the bomb-laden attackers could carry. He envisaged an intercepting fighter squadron turning in line astern parallel to a bomber formation, so that all their free-mounted guns could fire at once, whereas the bomber formation would only be defended by the guns on the side of the

for a three-seat, twin-engined fighter with a top speed of at least 125mph (200kph), and a landing speed of 50mph (80kph). It was the intention of the Air Ministry that the aircraft would be equipped with two 37mm Coventry Ordnance Works cannon (COW guns), and one defensive Lewis gun in a ventral position, though this was not initially divulged to the two companies that received prototype orders for their proposals. This was to have unfortunate consequences for Bristol Aircraft, who had received an order for one example of their design, the Type 95 Bagshot.

The Type 95 Bagshot

This was a monoplane powered by two 450hp Bristol Jupiter VI engines; though when the designer, Frank Barnwell, learned that it was supposed to carry two COW guns, he realized that it would be too heavy and recommended abandoning the design – but the Air Ministry insisted

that it be built. But Barnwell was proved right, because once flight trials began, it was discovered that insufficient torsional stiffness in the wings caused aileron reversal, and the aircraft was relegated to investigations of this effect.

The Westland Westbury

Its main rival from Westland Westbury was a more conventional two-bay biplane, powered by the same Jupiter VI engines as the Bagshot. Two examples of this were ordered, and the COW guns were actually tested in flight. The rear gun was sited in a station behind the wings and was designed to fire mainly forward and upward over a very narrow arc; however, air tests of the weapon resulted in damage to the aircraft's upper wing surface, which required the fitment of a protective shield. The nose-mounted COW gun was fitted to a much more complicated mounting that allowed it to be fired in any direction.

The sole Bristol Type 95 Bagshot undergoing engine runs. The specified COW guns were never fitted in the nose and dorsal positions of this 'bomber destroyer'.

attack. This concept seemed to have more in common with naval battles, won by the greater weight of broadside, than with aerial combat, and was hotly disputed in certain quarters of the RAF, not least among some members of the wartime Independent Air Force who had seen formations of their own bombers broken up by conventional attacking fighters. Air Cdr Popham of the RAF Staff College also pointed out that Higgin's sketches were two-dimensional, and that a bomber formation would probably be stepped up at different levels so that all their gunners could fire to either side.

Nevertheless Higgins secured the support of the chief of the Air Staff, Sir Hugh Trenchard, a firm believer in the ability of a bomber force to defend itself. The result was the issue of Spec. 4/24, which called

The Westland Westbury, a more successful competitor to the Bagshot for Spec. 4/24, in that it did carry and fire the COW guns, but its performance was not superior enough to the bombers it was designed to intercept.

Technical Information for COW-Gun Fighters

If you were to compare the two COW-gun fighters and a contemporary medium bomber, the Boulton & Paul Bugle shows an unsurprising similarity in size and performance. It also shows why Boulton & Paul were considered likely manufacturers of the type. Although a formation of COW-gun fighters would have outgunned a formation of Bugles, they would have been very lucky to have intercepted them in the first place, with no great performance margin. However, a Bagshot/Westbury might have stood a chance of intercepting the much slower Vickers Virginia night bomber, if it could have found it in the darkness of the night.

	Bagshot	Westbury	Bugle
Engines	450hp Bristol Jupiter VI	450hp Bristol Jupiter VI	435 hp Bristol Jupiter IV
Span	70ft (21.34m)	68ft (20.73m)	65ft ½in (19.82m)
Wing area	840sq ft (78.15sq m)	875sq ft (81.29sq m)	932sq ft (86.58sq m)
Length	44ft 11in (13.70m)	43ft 4.75in (13.23m)	39ft 9in (12.12m)
Height	9ft 6in (2.896m)	13ft 9in (4.191m)	15ft 8in (4.775m)
Weights			
Empty	5,100lb (2,313.36kg)	4,854lb (2,201.77kg)	5,079lb (2,303.83kg)
Loaded	8,195lb (3717.25kg)	7,877lb (3573kg)	8,914lb (4043.39kg)
Top speed	125mph (201kph)	125mph (201kph)	120mph (193kph)
Climb			
to 5,000ft (1,524m)		4.5min	
to 10,000ft (3,048m)			15.5min
to 15,000ft (4,572m)		19min	
Armament	Two COW guns	Two COW guns 1–2 Lewis guns	Two Lewis guns

The first Boulton & Paul P.31 Bittern. This prototype was armed with two fixed Vickers machine guns, but the second aircraft had Lewis guns in revolving barbettes each side of the nose.

Neither of these fighters had much margin of performance over the bombers they would probably have intercepted, and so they were not proceeded with. The Air Ministry did not abandon the idea of fitting the COW gun to fighter aircraft, however, and a new specification, F.29/27, was issued for a single-seat fighter equipped with a single COW gun; but this was to be fixed at an upward angle designed to allow the fighter to attack bombers from below, perhaps silhouetted against the stars. Neither of the aircraft that were ordered in prototype form – the Westland F.29/27 or the Vickers Type 161 – received production orders.

The P31 Bittern

One other specification during the 1920s featured an unusual armament arrangement, designed to counter bombers operating at night. Spec. 27/24 resulted in an order for two examples of the Boulton & Paul P.31 Bittern, unusual for the time in that it was a single-seat, twin-engined monoplane, powered by two 230hp Armstrong-Siddeley Lynx radials. One of the aircraft was fitted with the conventional fighter armament of two fixed forward-firing Vickers machine guns – but the other was novel in that it was armed with two Lewis guns, placed in revolving barbettes on each side of the aircraft's nose, which could move from straight ahead to an upward angle of 45 degrees, the gunsight moving in unison. This meant that the Bittern could attack bombers from below and behind, in an area that was frequently a blind spot.

This attacking technique was pioneered by Albert Ball during 1916, using the characteristics of the Foster rail, on which the Lewis gun was mounted on the upper wing of his Nieuport, to fire upwards into his quarry. Interestingly Ball's father was a director of Austin Motors, and when he returned from his first spell in France, he outlined an 'ideal fighter' that would feature the new Hispano-Suiza V8 engine, and two Lewis guns able to fire upwards in this way. His father took his ideas to the manager of Austin's aircraft department, who happened to be none other than John Dudley North, who had left Grahame-White Aircraft just after the start of the war. North initiated the design of a fighter to incorporate Ball's ideas – though by the time the Austin AFB.1 flew, J. D. North had left to become chief designer of Boulton & Paul's aircraft department, and Albert Ball was dead.

How much influence Albert Ball had on J. D. North's thinking is open to question, but the two men certainly met and discussed fighter armament. Every military aircraft with which North was associated throughout his career, for three different manufacturers, was to feature guns on movable mountings, with the solitary exception of his conventionally armed Boulton & Paul Partridge. Although the Bittern did not go into production, the aircraft with which North will always be most associated, the Defiant turret fighter, would have the same ability to attack bombers from below with the guns in its power-operated turret.

The Search Continues

Although the RAF's attempts at creating a bomber-destroyer in the 1920s had come to nought, and the single-seater with two fixed guns remained supreme, there were still many in the Air Staff who did not believe that such an aircraft would be able to break up well drilled formations of multi-engined bombers. The RAF itself actually had only one squadron of multi-engined day bombers, namely No. 101 Squadron equipped with two flights of Boulton & Paul Sidestrands; but manoeuvres involving this squadron were enough to convince certain influential people that a novel bomber-destroyer was required.

The Sidestrands were equipped with Scarff ring-mounted Lewis guns in the nose and dorsal positions, with another Lewis gun ventrally mounted. They were designed to provide a close formation with all-round defence. In affiliation exercises with the Siskins of No. 111 Squadron during August 1930, it was 'proved that the Sidestrand was a difficult proposition to tackle, and that fighters at present had no attack to meet them'.

Of course there was no way of proving the theoretical accuracy of the bombers' gunners, any more than the Admiralty could prove the effectiveness of the anti-aircraft guns fitted to their battleships. This was to lead to dangerous self-confidence on the part of the Admiralty and the RAF's bomber force.

The 'Bright Ideas Fighter'

Just after these manoeuvres, Wg Cdr A.C. Maund was appointed to head the flying operations of the Air Staff, in charge of formulating the future operational require-ments of the Royal Air Force. Maund was one of those who held a jaundiced view of the potential effectiveness of single-seat fighters. He shared the views of Higgins, that although conventional fighters might be capable of disposing of solitary bombers, they would be ineffective against large formations. He soon proposed that the aircraft industry be asked to devise new forms of fighter aircraft capable of breaking up bomber formations before they reached their target.

In October 1931 he outlined his thoughts in a scheme he placed before the deputy chief of the Air Staff, AVM C. S. Burnett, for a 'Bright Ideas fighter'. He proposed that every aircraft company be circulated with operational requirements drawn up in general terms, inviting tenders to meet these requirements which did not include any recognized conventional form of fighter. He felt the requirements must include the ability to attack in formation to overcome the combined firepower of a bomber formation. It was for this reason that the conventional single-seat fighter had to be excluded, as it was impossible for pilots to keep station on their leader's aircraft whilst aiming the weapons at the same time; the danger of collision was just too great; a recent Court of Enquiry into just such an accident between two Bristol Bulldogs had highlighted this.

The officer commanding the air defence of Great Britain, AM Sir Edward Ellington, consulted the commanders of the twelve fighter squadrons in his command. Five of them felt that in the event of war, the risk of collision was one that should be taken, but only three of them felt that the risk was worth taking for peacetime practice. Ellington therefore concurred with Maund that new fighters needed to have a separate gunner, preferably sited in the nose.

AVM Burnett discussed Maund's ideas with AVM H. C. T. Dowding, then Air Member for Supply and Research. Burnett himself was largely in the camp of those who sought greater firepower for conventional single-seaters, but he was prepared to accede to Maund's suggestion that the industry be asked to come up with new ideas for a fighter aircraft. Dowding thought it unlikely that the industry would think of something that the Royal Air Force itself could not envisage; but his views prevailed, and a memorandum was issued through the service calling for 'suggestions for an improved form of fighting aircraft'.

Entries were to be submitted by 21 November 1932, and the criteria to be met were as follows:

- Fighters flying in formation should be able to open simultaneous fire on bomber formations, and to sustain the fire until the hostile formation were destroyed.
- The armament layout should be capable of deflecting hostile formations away from their course.
- It should also allow the attacking fighters to open fire from as many directions as possible, with the minimum of preliminary manoeuvres.
- The fighters should be able to successfully engage hostile fighters as well as bombers.
- An adequate margin of performance, in top speed, climb and manoeuvrability over contemporary bombers, would be required.
- The ability to operate by day and by night was required, carrying the equipment thought necessary for night-time operations.
- Movable guns should not be obstructed in their freedom of fire by parts of the aircraft, such as the tailplanes.
- The armament fitted should be capable of operation under all conditions.

A large number of entries were considered by a committee chaired by Maund, which met on 10 January 1933. Vague and impractical entries were discarded – this included one design for a twin-engined pusher monoplane with the pilot in a prone position in the nose, as well as others that merely envisaged arming conventional fighters with more guns – until just five serious suggestions were left for consideration. The first of these to be rejected was from Wg Cdr A. A. B. Thomson of the Armaments Branch who suggested an eight-gun, twin-engined biplane fighter, reflecting work already done at Martlesham Heath on testing the effects of increasing fighter armament. The committee rejected Thomson's design because it only carried 200 rounds per gun – in spite of the fact that the weight of the pilot would have to be restricted to 8 stone!

The Power-Operated Gun Turret

The other four entries broadly envisaged one of two layouts: either with a gun turret arranged to cover the whole upper hemisphere, or with a gun turret in the nose to cover the forward hemisphere. The concept of the 'gun turret' was a new one. Because of the greatly increased speeds of modern military aircraft, gunners in open cockpits had been finding it increasingly difficult to train and aim their guns. In the early thirties a few aircraft had begun to

appear with lightweight glazed cupolas over the gun positions, such as the Martin B-10 bomber and the Bristol Type 120 General Purpose aircraft; but these were manually revolved, and were less than satisfactory.

Two companies were working on powered 'turrets'. Boulton & Paul Ltd had been asked by the Air Ministry to investigate ways of protecting the nose gunner of their Sidestrand bomber against the effects of the 140mph (225kph) slipstream, and after much discussion the solution was envisaged to be a fully enclosed glazed

cylinder, revolved pneumatically by the pressure of the barrel of the single Lewis gun on plungers either side of a vertical slot. The gun would be raised and lowered manually, with the gunner's seat connected hydraulically to maintain his sightline.

A mock-up of this turret was finished by June 1933, and the first example would be flown in the nose of a heavily modified Sidestrand before the end of the year, the aircraft being given a new name, 'Overstrand'.

At the same time that Boulton & Paul were working on this pneumatic turret,

The Boulton & Paul pneumatic gun turret as fitted to the nose of the Overstrand, with the single Lewis gun stowed at the top of the gun slot, which is sealed with its zip fastener. This turret featured in early Boulton & Paul turret fighter proposals.

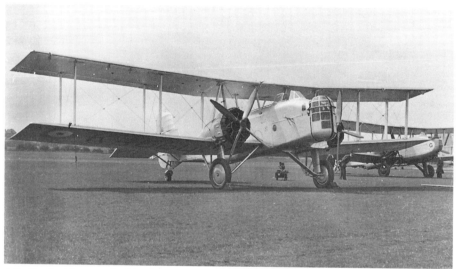

A Boulton Paul Overstrand, with a Sidestrand in the background, the type it was to replace.

The Hawker Demon, the two-seat fighter that came about almost by accident as a fighter version of the Hart, and was to become the first fighter armed with a power-operated turret.

Messrs Nash & Thompson Ltd had been asked to find ways of protecting the rear gunner of the Hawker Demon fighter. The Demon had recently become the RAF's first operational two-seat fighter since the last of the Bristol Fighters had been retired. It came into existence because the Hawker Hart light bomber, that entered service in 1930, had proved to be considerably faster than all existing operational fighters. On the theory of 'set a thief to catch a thief', a fighter version of the Hart had been the obvious solution.

The Hart fighter was armed with two fixed forward-firing machine guns, and a single Lewis gun for the rear gunner, and early in 1932 was ordered into production as the Hawker Demon. The rear gunner found it difficult to aim his weapon against the 182mph (293kph) slipstream, and after various experiments with simple screens, Nash & Thompson were asked to devise a power-assisted mounting.

Archibald Frazer Nash had been designing aircraft armament installations during World War I, but had made his name postwar firstly with the sports cars that bore his name, and then with a crane safe-loading indicator. He had then joined up with his former wartime associate Capt Gratton Thompson to develop a retractable wing-tip flare installation to aid night landings. Awarded the contract to design a new power-assisted gun position for the Demon, these two came up with a hydraulically powered 'turret' that was not fully enclosed, the gunner's only protection being a retracting 'lobsterback' shield.

Although neither of these new 'gun turrets' was operational when Maund's committee assessed the entries for the novel fighter, the concept was clearly known within the Air Force. The committee considered that the most promising layout would be with one of these turrets in the nose of the aircraft, as it was considered that the forward hemisphere was the most important one for fighters. For instance, one proposal, from the AMSR, had envisaged a rear turret in an aircraft that looked rather like a swept-wing, tail-less Hawker Demon. As the pilot as well as the gunner was sited behind the wings, the suggestion ignored the importance the committee placed in visibility in the forward hemisphere, hopefully with both crewmen placed in the nose.

The two proposals that envisaged this layout were Maund's own, for a tail-less single-engined pusher fighter, and that from

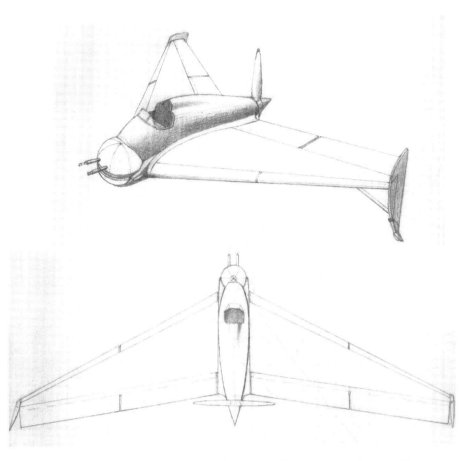

The imaginative sketch provided by Wing Commander Maund to illustrate his ideas for a turret fighter, with both fixed forward-firing guns and a nose turret.

the Directorate of Technical Development (DTD) for a twin-engined aircraft. Both envisaged a crew of pilot and a front gunner, with two fixed forward-firing machine guns in addition to one or two guns in the turret. The DTD's proposal envisaged two Napier Rapier engines, with extended propshafts to the pusher propellers, and a 52ft (15m) span wing. Maund suggested a single 'Merlin' engine, not the later wartime engine, but a Rolls-Royce paper proposal. His spherical front turret was far better thought out than some of the other vague notions, and his proposal included sketches of its basic layout.

The committee could not choose between the designs as they both seemed to have advantages. The single-engined pusher offered a larger field of fire for the gunner and a better performance, whereas the twin-engined aircraft could be of more proven aerodynamic layout. It was recommended that the industry be asked to design experimental two-seat fighters with front turrets, with both designs offered as examples of what was envisaged. Opera-

tional Requirement 9 was framed around this suggestion.

Dowding, whose responsibility it was to implement the committee's decision, accepted it reluctantly. He was of the opinion that such a fighter would be at the mercy of any competent single-seater, and preferred the developments that were going ahead elsewhere to increase the fixed armament of RAF fighters from two to four, and then six guns. Specification F.5/33 was drawn up for a fighter with a front gun turret – but before it was issued to the industry an even more radical proposal emerged.

New Fighter Types

Sir Edward Ellington became chief of the Air Staff in May 1933, and one of his first tasks was to read a review of the previous eighteen months' debate on new fighter types prepared by his deputy AVM E. R. Ludlow-Hewitt, which seemed to place the two-seat front-turret fighter at the bottom of the priority list. Ellington, however, wanted far more urgency in the development of an aircraft where piloting and operating the weapons were separate responsibilities, because he was one of those who believed that fighters would have to attack bombers in unison.

He also felt that a formation of fighters should be able to fight hostile aircraft from either the front or the rear, and envisaged two pilots, one to fly the aircraft and one to man either the front or the rear gun position depending on the tactical situation. As chief of the Air Staff, Ellington's views had to be taken seriously, and a new Operation Requirement 11 was drawn up to outline his concept. From this, a new specification, F.22/33, was drawn up detailing the requirement for a new fighter. Though his idea of having two pilots was not thought sensible, the specification envisaged a fighter with front and rear gun positions armed with single Lewis guns, and manned either by a single gunner who would move between the positions as necessary, or with two gunners. Thus two turret fighter specifications were issued during 1933: F.5/33 for a fighter with a single nose turret, and F.22/33 with nose and dorsal turrets.

Meanwhile elsewhere the RAF had been considering new airborne guns to replace the traditional Vickers and Lewis guns. The contenders were .303in calibre machine guns from various manufacturers, with the Colt-Browning eventually becoming favourite. The Spec F.7/30, which required a fighter armed with four machine guns, eventually led to the production of the Gloster Gladiator, but in 1933 consideration was being given to a fighter armed with six or eight .303in guns.

The new deputy chief of the Air Staff, Ludlow-Hewitt, discussed this new requirement with Sir Edward Ellington, who was still sceptical about the value of single-seat fighters, and was concerned about the growing number of fighter requirements being proposed. Air Cdr R. E. C. Pierse, deputy director of Operations and Intelligence, was of the opinion that the two turret fighter specifications should take preference. They agreed that the single-seater requirement be deferred until the following year, when Spec F.5/34 would be issued, calling for a six- or eight-gun single-seat fighter with a top speed of at least 275mph (440kph).

Westland Aircraft's Pterodactyl Designs

One company that had a head start with Maund's single-engined, tail-less pusher idea for F.5/33 was Westland Aircraft, in as much as they had been developing Geoffrey Hill's tail-less, swept-wing Pterodactyl designs for some years. Their Pterodactyl IV, which first flew in March 1931, was a three-seat, tail-less cabin monoplane with a single Gipsy III engine in a pusher arrangement, and they were actually building a two-seat tail-less fighter, the Pterodactyl V, to Spec F.3/32, though this was with a Rolls-Royce Goshawk tractor engine. It was armed with two fixed forward-firing machine guns, with just a single Lewis gun in the open cockpit at the rear, where the gunner could fire over the complete rear hemisphere. Geoffrey Hill had designed an electro-hydraulic gun turret for the aircraft, with the single Lewis gun mounted on its side to fit the available fuselage width. There is considerable doubt that this turret was ever fitted to the aircraft, beyond perhaps being offered up to the structure to check clearances.

The rear turret gunner on the Pterodactyl V could not fulfil the role envisaged for the gunners of the new turret fighters: he was there for strictly defensive purposes, not offensive, and so this aircraft could not meet the specification.

Westland's F.5/33 proposal, designated the Pterodactyl VI, therefore involved reversing the positions of the engine and crew of the Pterodactyl V. The gunner would also be provided with a fully enclosed gun turret in the nose, but armed with two machine guns, almost certainly to be designed by the company, and the pilot would be sited just in front of the wings with an enclosed cockpit. There would also be a change of engine, with the

troublesome, evaporation-cooled Goshawk giving way to a Rolls-Royce Kestrel. The aircraft was a sesquiplane with endplates on the large, upper swept wing, supported on 'N' struts above the much smaller, unswept lower wing.

Other Designs

Unlike Westland who only seemed to offer an F.5/33 proposal, Bristol Aircraft produced two completely different designs for the two specifications. Their Type 140 for F.5/33 was a two-seat fighter with a spherical nose turret, powered by a single Bristol Perseus 665hp radial in a pusher arrangement. Their Type 141 was a three-seater with nose and dorsal turrets, powered by two Bristol Aquila 600hp radials. Armstrong-Whitworth Aircraft produced twin-engined designs for both specifications, though each was quite different. Their A.W.32 was to Spec F.22/33, and was powered by two of the proposed Armstrong-Siddeley Double Genet Major engines. It had a span of 48ft (14.6m), a length of 39ft (12m), and a wing area of 335sq ft (31sq m). The all-up weight was 6,500lb (3,000kg), and the estimated top speed at 13,000ft (4,000m) was 255mph (410kph).

The A.W.34 was to Spec. F.5/33, and was to be powered by two Armstrong-Siddeley Terrier engines. It had a slightly smaller span of 47ft (14m), but a larger wing area of 350sq ft (32.5sq m).

Gloster Aircraft also produced two related twin-engined designs for each specification, though they were a company that had almost exclusively produced single-engined aircraft throughout their history. The F.5/33 proposal envisaged two Bristol Aquila engines just like the Bristol Type 141. Just down the road at Yate,

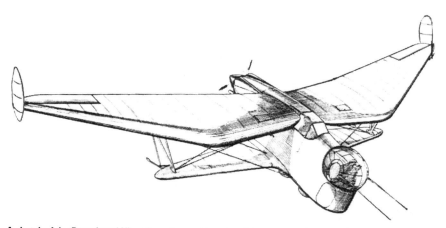

A sketch of the Pterodactyl VI, with engine and turret positions reversed to meet Spec. F.5/33.

Parnall Aircraft also produced an F.5/33 design (though no details survive), as did Fairey Aircraft, who also produced a related F.22/33 proposal.

Boulton & Paul Designs

In Norwich, Boulton & Paul had the advantage of being the only aircraft company that actually had a gun turret under development, the pneumatic nose turret for the Overstrand (Type 1). It followed that this turret featured heavily in their proposals, but they were also designing new pneumatic turrets, including one glazed in only its upper half (Type 2), but also armed with only a single Lewis gun.

The Boulton & Paul P.76 proposal for F.5/33 featured a single Overstrand turret in the nose and, like most of the other companies, also specified twin fixed machine guns; but unusually the P.76 featured twin Vickers guns in the rear fuselage fixed to fire upwards at an angle of 45 degrees. This was the upward firing arrangement pioneered by Albert Ball, and with which so many of J. D. North's fighters were equipped. The P.76 was offered in two quite different versions, powered either by two Napier Rapier V 350hp 'H' inline engines in an airframe with a span of 47ft 6in (14.5m), or by two Bristol Pegasus IV 700hp radial engines in a much larger airframe of 58ft 6in (17.83m) span.

(Right) Boulton Paul P.76 to Spec. F.5/33.

(Below) Equipment layout in the Boulton Paul P.76. Note the upward-firing Vickers guns in the rear fuselage.

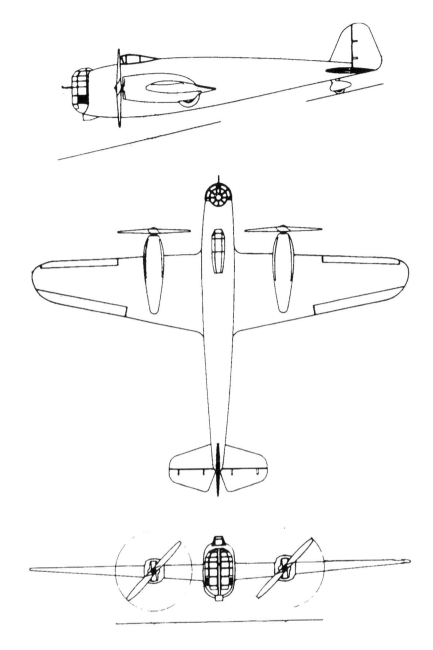

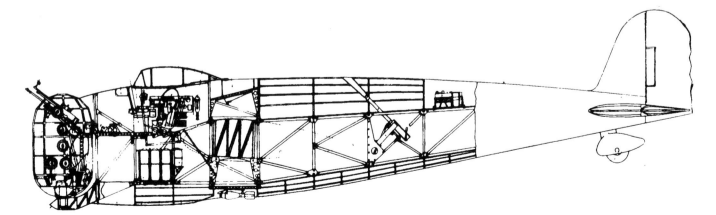

Technical Information Boulton & Paul P.74 and P.76						
	P.74A	P.74B	P.74C	P.74D	P.76A	P.76B
Engines 2 x	350hp Rapier	350hp Rapier	700hp Pegasus	700hp Pegasus	350hp Rapier	700hp Pegasus
Turret armament	2 x Type 1	Type 1 & Type 2	2 x Type 1	Type 1 & Type 2	1 x Type 1	1 x Type 1
Fixed armament	nil	nil	nil	nil	4 x Vickers	4 x Vickers
Span ft (m)	48 (14.6)	48 (14.6)	60 (18.3)	60 (18.3)	47.5 (14.5)	58.5 (17.8)
Length ft (m)	39.3 (12)	39.3 (12)	48 (14.6)	48 (14.6)	39.5 (12)	44.5 (13.5)
Wing area sq ft (sq m)	350 (32.5)	350 (32.5)	530 (49.2)	530 (49.2)	340 (31.6)	520 (48.31)
Top speed at 15,000ft	195mph 314kph	203mph 327kph	226mph 364kph	232mph 373kph	217mph 349kph	247mph 397kph
Service ceiling	25,000ft (7,620m)		27,500ft (8,382m)		29,000ft (8,839m)	
Loaded weight lb (kg)	6,147 (2,788)	6,147 (2,788)	9,035 (4,098)	9,035 (4,098)	5,797 (2,630)	8,780 (3,983)

The Boulton & Paul P.74 to F.22/33 was closely related to the P.76, with the same power options, in similar airframe sizes, all with a Type 1 Overstrand turret in the nose but with a choice of either the Type 1 or the new Type 2 turret in the dorsal position. Versions with the Overstrand turret in both locations had a very narrow rear fuselage, rather in the manner of the Handley Page Hampden, but attached beneath the turret. With the smaller Type 2 turret they had much broader rear fuselages, enabling higher top speeds to be estimated because of the better aerodynamic characteristics.

The P.74A and P.74B with the Rapier engines had a span of 48ft (15m). The P.74A, with two Overstrand turrets, had a top speed of 195mph (314kph) at 15,000ft (4,500m), and the P.74B, 203mph (327kph). The Pegasus-engined P.74C and P.74D were much larger, with a span of 60ft (18m). The P.74C was estimated to achieve 226mph (364kph) at 15,000ft, and the P.74D the best of all the four layouts, 232mph (373kph). Clearly the drag and weight of two turrets rather than one

would affect performance quite considerably.

None of the proposals for the two specifications met with much enthusiasm, as they did not seem to offer much of a performance margin over the bombers then under development. Indeed, Sir Edward Ellington himself seemed to think none of them would be more useful than a fighter adaptation of one of the new bombers designed to Spec B.9/32 (Wellington and Hampden), in the way the Demon was developed from the Hart. It was clear that the problem would have to be re-thought.

The Turret Fighter goes into Service

In the meantime, the two-seat 'turret' fighter was actually going into service. The first production Hawker Demon, of an initial batch of seventeen, had flown in February 1933, and the type replaced Bristol Bulldogs in No. 23 Squadron. Further orders were placed for the aircraft, totalling 108, to equip Auxiliary Air Force squadrons. The last fifty-nine of these were subcontracted to the newly independent

firm of Boulton Paul Aircraft Ltd. Boulton & Paul Ltd had sold off its aircraft department to an investment group, and although it continued for a while in the same premises at Mousehold Airport, Norwich, it was soon to move to a brand-new factory at Wolverhampton.

The prototype Frazer-Nash FN.1 'lobsterback' turret was first tested in a Demon late in 1934, and was approved for service use. Although the gunner was not completely enclosed, as was usual in later turrets, the FN.1's folding windshield did offer a high degree of protection, and there was a heating system for the gunner's head, hands and feet, as well as his gun. Nash & Thompson took over Parnall Aircraft at Yate to manufacture the turret, and to develop and manufacture further hydraulic turrets. Demons equipped with the FN.1 did not go into service until 1936, by which time all Demon production was centred on Boulton Paul Aircraft from their Wolverhampton factory.

The operation of the Demons in service with No. 23 Squadron, albeit with only Scarff ring-mounted rear guns, brought about a change in thinking on future turret-fighter proposals. It was noted that Demon pilots tended to fly their aircraft like single-seaters, using their two fixed front guns as the primary weapons. This was the method used by the two-seat Bristol Fighters in World War I to achieve success, but it went against the philosophy espoused by the turret-fighter enthusiasts. In September 1936, No. 74 Squadron submitted a report on the two-seat fighter tactics it had devised in Malta. They envisaged the Demons making normal front gun attacks, in a manner that allowed the rear gunners to get in a burst of fire as well. But Dowding's comments on the tactics highlighted the fact that they neglected the principal advantage offered by a two-seat fighter, of flying on a parallel course to the enemy and concentrating the attacker's fire on one point, perhaps from a blind spot.

It had already begun to be proposed that the new turret fighter specification should not require fixed forward-firing guns, on the basis that it was undesirable to split the armament. This was despite the fact that most of the turret fighter proposals to date, from Air Force or industry, had included one or two such guns in addition to their turrets.

Group Captain A. T. Harris, deputy Director of Plans, suggested that a single-

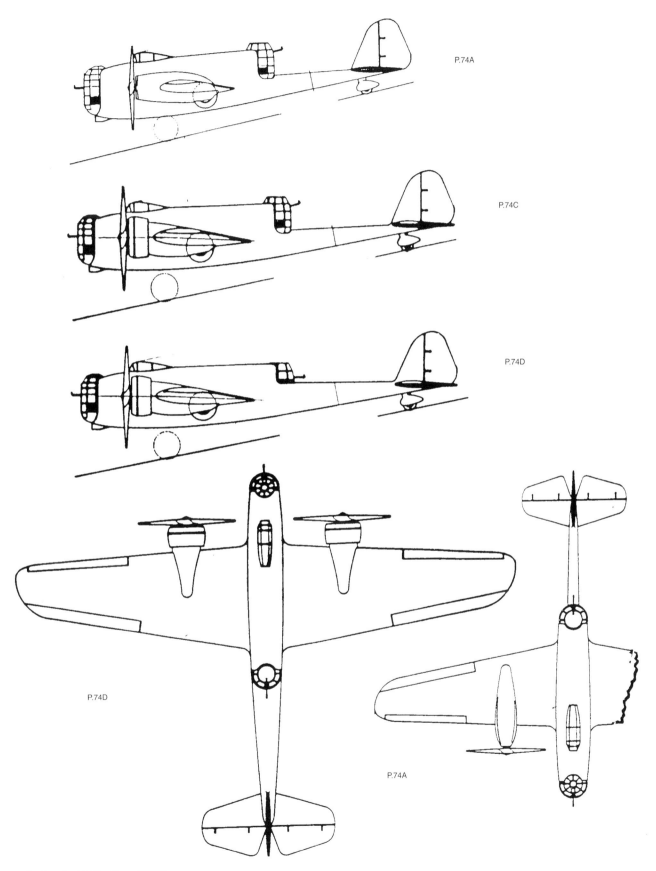

P.74A

P.74C

P.74D

P.74D

P.74A

The Boulton Paul P.74 to Spec. F.22/33.

engined two-seat fighter could have sufficient performance. There was also a change in the thinking behind the earlier preference for a front turret, in the belief that a turret mounting four machine guns able to fire over the upper hemisphere would confer the ability to attack from below and behind, below and in front, or on the flank of a bomber formation. This would enable the turrets of a large formation of such fighters all to be trained on the enemy while flying in formation.

These tactics were just those proposed by Higgins in 1923. They were supported by AVM C. L. Courtney, who replaced Ludlow-Hewitt as deputy chief of the Air Staff in 1935. He felt the new fighter did not need a downward-firing capability, but did need beam and rear firing. Ellington continued to argue that if fighters were to dive on formations of bombers, they would need the ability to fire downward, but Courtney was able to demonstrate that a fighter diving on a bomber actually needed upward fire not downward fire, otherwise the pilot would not be able to see the aircraft he was attacking.

Ellington conceded this point, as well as the need not to split the armament by having fixed as well as movable guns; and thus the principle of the new fighter having all its armament concentrated in a dorsal turret was finally arrived at. The new turret fighter specification was discussed by the Operational Requirements Committee.

A Hawker Demon equipped with the Frazer-Nash FN.1 gun turret, but with a gun camera replacing the normal Lewis gun, for training purposes.

The minutes do not mention any discussion of the absence of front guns, but Wg Cdr C. H. Heath, who was head of the Air Ministry's Armament Branch, and was present, later wrote that certain former fighter pilots who were at the meeting expressed strong opinions about the lack of front guns, and the tactics that were being proposed for the new aircraft. Specification F.9/35 was duly approved on 20 May 1935. Later in the year, Spec. O.30/35, for a naval equivalent of F.5/35, was also issued; and thus the design processes that brought about the Boulton Paul Defiant and the Blackburn Roc were set in motion.

Hawker Demons awaiting delivery outside Boulton Paul Aircraft, Pendeford, Wolverhampton, in 1936. Almost overnight the company had become the country's foremost producer of two-seat turret fighters.

CHAPTER TWO

Specification F.9/35

The new specification was issued to the industry on 26 June 1935, together with Spec. F.10/35 for the new eight-gun single-seat fighters being developed by Hawker and Supermarine. Companies attempting to design the new turret fighter found that the aircraft's required performance was to be remarkably close to that of the single-seaters, despite having to get airborne with a second crew member and a power-operated turret (though this requirement was partly alleviated by having to carry only half the number of guns).

Top speed at 15,000ft (4,500m) was to be 298mph (479kph) as opposed to 315mph (507kph) for the single-seaters. Time to 15,000ft was only to be a minute more, at 5.5 minutes, and the service ceiling was to be only 2,000ft less, at 33,000ft (10,000m). Endurance was to be the same for each type, namely 1.5 hours at 253mph (407kph) for the turret fighter, and at 267mph (430kph) for the single-seater. The aircraft was to be fitted with a power-operated turret able to fire over the whole of the upper hemisphere, and over as much of the lower hemisphere as possible. The requirement was that it should be suitable both as a day and as a night fighter, and should be able to carry eight 20lb (9kg) fragmentation bombs for army co-operation sorties.

The SAMM AB.7

The firm of Boulton Paul Aircraft already had an ace up its sleeve. On a sales visit to France, J. D. North, the managing director and chief engineer, had been approached by the French company Societe d'Applications des Machines Matrices (SAMM), whose chief engineer, Antoine de Boysson, had designed an electro-hydraulic turret armed with four Darne machine guns, the SAMM AB.7. The company had been unable to interest the French government in this design, the latter being wholly pre-occupied with fitting the Hispano 20mm cannon to aircraft, and encouraging

SAMM to develop a movable mounting for this weapon; a mounting that was to emerge as the AB.15. Knowing of Boulton Paul's Overstrand turret, SAMM therefore approached North, who went to see the AB.7.

He knew immediately that it was superi-or to his own designs, which were limited to twenty revolutions before their pneumatic reservoir was exhausted, whereas the AB.7 had its own hydraulic motor, drawing only electric current from the parent aircraft. It was also armed with four belt-fed machine guns as specified in F.9/35. On his return to Great Britain, North urged the Air Ministry to purchase the French turret, but though Gp Capt C. Hilton Keith agreed that the SAMM turret represented a considerable advance on anything yet produced, they declined, believing that such items should be sourced in the United Kingdom. With the issue of Spec. F.9/35, North immediate-ly saw the value of the French turret and sought a licence agreement for its manufac-ture. Boulton Paul beat another of the major British aircraft companies to this deal by twenty-four hours. An agreement was signed on 23 November 1935, for the pur-chase by Boulton Paul of two complete AB.7 turrets, for 150,000 francs less 10 per cent. At the same time an option was signed on a licence to manufacture them, with suit-able modifications for British requirements, and to exploit the relevant SAMM patents to produce a full range of turrets for aircraft and anti-aircraft purposes.

The expiry date of the option was 25 April 1937, and on the 22nd, Boulton Paul purchased the rights to the SAMM system for 250,000 francs, plus legal expenses, giv-ing them the rights to sell their version of the turret throughout the Empire and Com-monwealth, paying a royalty of £50 only for the first 125 turrets. Total payments to SAMM were to amount to just £8,501.

Designing the Airframe

With the design of an actual turret

secured, Boulton Paul set to work with a degree of urgency to design an airframe around it; this was given the project num-ber P.82. Construction of their Overstrand had been completed at Norwich, and though they were starting the manufacture of the Hawker Demon, which would soon be moved to their new factory in Wolver-hampton, they were anxious to secure orders for another of their own designs. To alleviate the drag of the turret, a great deal of use was made of Boulton Paul's own 4ft (1.2m) wind tunnel, in which 1/15 scale models were extensively tested. After detail design began, a 1/13 scale model was tested in the same tunnel, before the preparation of a 1/10th scale model for the National Physics Laboratory tunnel, where a 1/5th scale model of the rear fuse-lage and tail was also tested. Speed was of the essence in the design process, because although Boulton Paul had the only suit-able turret in existence, other manufactur-ers had other things to their own advan-tage.

For instance, Hawker Aircraft already had a suitable airframe for F.9/35 on the drawing board. They were building the prototype of a light bomber, the Henley, which itself used the outer wings, tailplane and same Merlin engine as their Hurri-cane. The prototype Hurricane would fly for the first time on 6 November 1935. The design of the centre fuselage of the Henley was altered to accommodate a four-gun turret in place of the Henley's sin-gle rear Lewis gun. Nash & Thompson were entrusted with the design of a new, hydraulic, four-gun turret, with the guns in pairs above one another on each side, in the manner of the SAMM AB.7. A retractable fairing would be raised to streamline the turret when it was not in use, only being lowered during action.

Fairey Aircraft were also able to adapt an existing airframe, the Battle light bomber, equipped with a four-gun turret of indeterminate origin, and of course pow-ered by the same Merlin engine.

Bristol Aircraft also adapted an existing

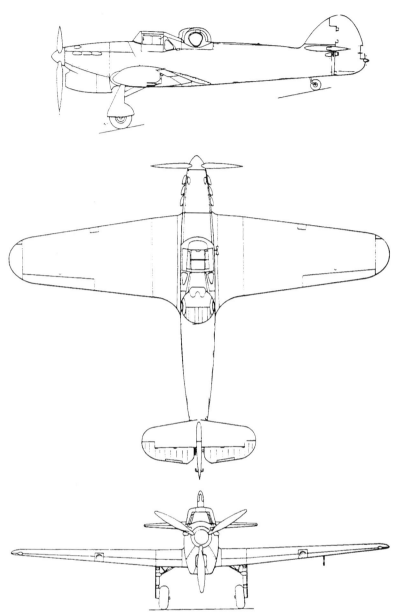

The Hawker Hotspur.

design: their Type 146, single-seat, Mercury-powered fighter that was under construction to Spec. F.5/34. This was an all-metal monoplane with the required armament of eight guns – though all the designs being built to this specification had already been overtaken by events elsewhere at Hawker and Supermarine. Bristol adapted this design as the Type 147, to take a remotely operated four-gun turret of their own design. The gunner would sit back to back with the pilot, on a swivelling seat, operating the low-profile turret mechanically by two hand-wheels. Changes gave the Type 147 a slightly increased span of 40ft (12m), and a fuselage 3ft (1m) longer than that of the Type 146, at 40ft (12m).

The Type 147 was to be powered by the 890hp Perseus X engine, which would give it a top speed of 280mph (451kph); but Bristol also offered the aircraft with a new engine on their drawing boards – the Hercules, that would have given it a top speed of 315mph (507kph).

Armstrong-Whitworth offered a version of their F.5/33 design, the AW.34, powered by two Armstrong-Siddeley Terrier engines. To achieve the required performance, the span was to be reduced from 47ft (14m) to 39ft (12m), reducing the wing area from 350sq ft (32.5sq m) to 259sq ft (24sq m). The length of the revised design was to be 37ft 3in (11.4m). The aircraft was to be fitted with a dorsal four-gun turret of its own design. Armstrong-Whitworth were developing their own gun turrets, manually operated nose and tail units designed for the AW.23 bomber/ transport and fitted to the early Whitleys, and the Anson dorsal turret.

Gloster also offered a version of their

The Fairey F.9/35 contender was based on the Fairey Battle, and will therefore have looked something like the Battle prototype from the front.

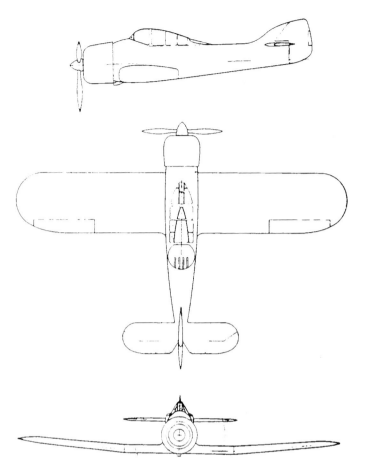

The Bristol Type 147.

previous F.5/33 twin-engined design, powered by 625hp Bristol Aquila radials, but with fixed, forward-firing armament as well as a four-gun dorsal turret, probably the new Boulton Paul turret.

Supermarine began to design a contender, their Type 305, which was based on the Spitfire wing and tailplane but with a new, deeper and wider fuselage. The radiator for the Merlin engine was moved to beneath the engine, from the wings, and the company envisaged a four-blade propeller. The dorsal turret was a low profile, remotely operated design, with a cupola like a shallow dome, and a second, glazed cupola of equally low profile for the gunner, between the turret and the pilot's cockpit. The turret and the gunner were linked electro-mechanically, revolving together, but the gunner's seat did not tilt with the elevation of the guns. The guns could revolve through 360 degrees, and be elevated from horizontal to 90 degrees. The top of the gunner's cupola could be tilted up to form a windscreen, so the gunner could stand up and thereby enjoy a greater degree of all-round visibility: in his normal seated position his eyes were level with the fuselage upper surface. Supermarine stated that it was hoped to accommodate the bombs required by the specification in the wings, presumably where the guns had been sited in the Spitfire wing, with a suitable 'ejector mechanism'.

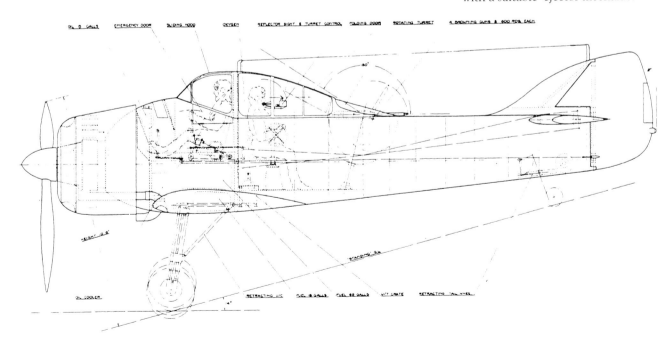

The layout of the Bristol Type 147's crew and remotely controlled turret.

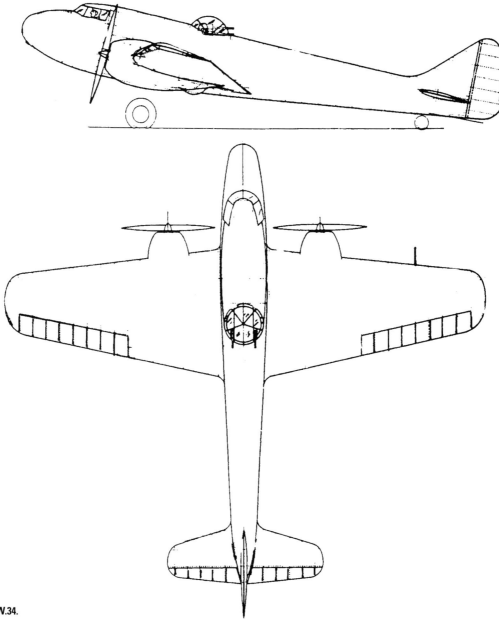

The Armstrong-Whitworth AW.34.

Technical Information for the Supermarine Type 305	
Engine	960hp Rolls-Royce Merlin
Span	37ft (11.3m)
Length	30ft 6in (9.3m)
Wing area	242sq ft (22.5sq m)
Loaded weight	5,650lb (2,563kg)
Top speed	315mph at 15,000ft (507kph at 4,500m)
Service ceiling	30,000ft (9,000m)

The remotely operated turret, like that for the Bristol Type 147, would have been far from simple to design. Such turrets caused endless trouble when other manufacturers attempted to produce them later during the war. When Frazer-Nash were approached in March 1936, they thought the gun mounting as designed was not rigid enough, and that the guns should not be remotely operated.

Supermarine then designed a second version of their turret fighter, in which the four Brownings in the turret were replaced by four Lewis guns; but the gunner remained in his separate compartment, though this was given glazed side panels to improve his view.

Supermarine's parent company, Vickers, submitted an almost identical turret fighter to Spec. F.9/35, the main difference being in the tail, which had a much smaller fin above the fuselage, thereby improving the field of fire for the guns, and a second fin beneath the tail, the two fins being linked by a single rudder behind the tail.

Even before these designs had been submitted, Vickers-Supermarine were advised by the Air Ministry that they should stop work on their turret fighters to concentrate on the new Warwick heavy bomber and getting the Spitfire into production.

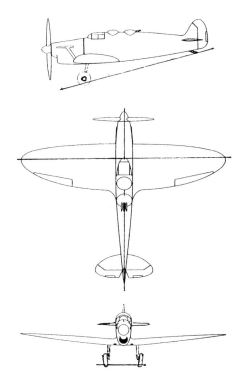

The Supermarine Type 305.

Designs prepared for Spec. F.9/35	
Armstrong Whitworth AW.34	2 x Armstrong-Siddeley Terriers
Bristol Type 147	1 x Bristol Perseus
Bristol Type 147	1 x Bristol Hercules
Boulton Paul P.82 (Defiant)	1 x Rolls-Royce Merlin
Fairey F.9/35	1 x Rolls-Royce Merlin
Gloster F.9/35	2 x Bristol Aquila
Hawker F.9/35 (Hotspur)	1 x Rolls-Royce Merlin
Supermarine Type 305	1 x Rolls-Royce Merlin
Vickers F.9/35	1 x Rolls-Royce Merlin

Constructing the Prototype

Such was the importance of the turret fighter in the Air Ministry's future plans, that in October 1935 funding for the prototype construction of five of the designs was approved. Hawker and Boulton Paul were the favoured designs at this stage, the former because of their proven track record as fighter manufacturers, and the latter because of the SAMM turret. Two of the Hawker design were to be ordered, serialled K8309 and K8621, and two of the Boulton Paul P.82, serialled K8610 and K8620. Two were also ordered from Fairey as a back-up, and given serials K8622 and

K8623, and one of the larger Armstrong Siddeley F.9/35, to be serialled K8624. In addition, one prototype of the revised Gloster F.5/33 project was also ordered to a new specification, F.34/35, and allocated the serial K8625.

The original specification was revised somewhat when the prototypes were ordered, with, in particular, greater fuel tankage being required. However, the changes did not result in any major alteration either to the design of the Boulton Paul P.82 or to the performance estimates, except those affected by the increase in weight.

A second turret fighter was already

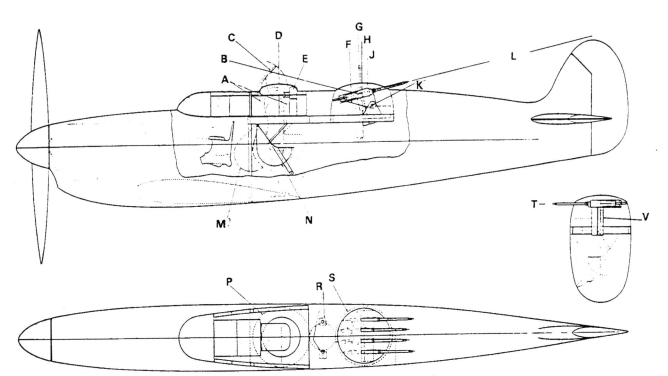

The fuselage layout of the Supermarine Type 305 with its remotely operated low-profile turret.

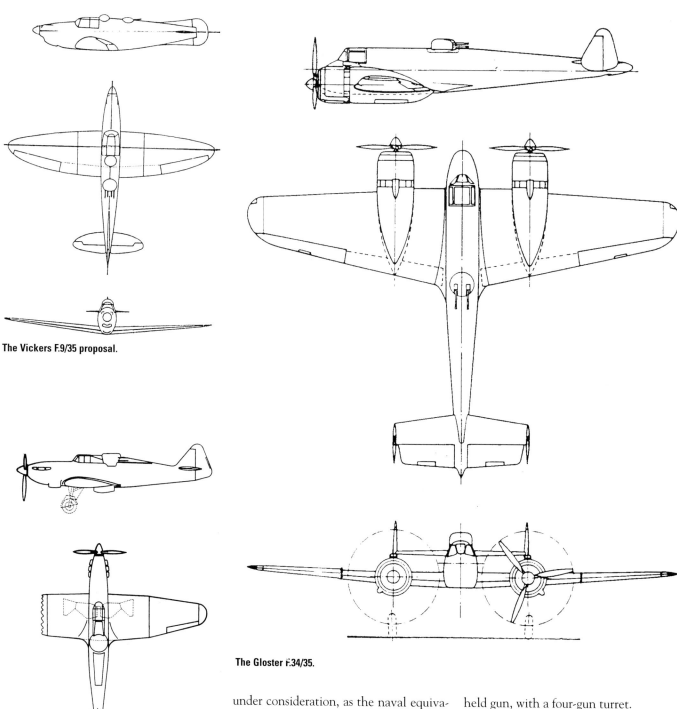

The Vickers F.9/35 proposal.

The Boulton Paul P.82.

The Gloster F.34/35.

under consideration, as the naval equivalent of the F.9/35 designs. A new specification, O.30/35, had been issued on 31 December 1935 calling for a turret fighter suitable for use on aircraft carriers. Blackburn Aircraft were already constructing the prototypes of the Fleet Air Arm's first operational all-metal monoplane, the two-seat Skua, which would serve in the dual role as a fighter and dive-bomber. It was a relatively simple matter for their chief designer G. E. Petty to replace the rear observer's position, with its single hand-held gun, with a four-gun turret.

At Boulton Paul they completely redesigned the P.82 as the P.85, but with the new Bristol Hercules HE-1SM radial as an alternative to the Merlin of the P.82. The engines were set lower, presumably to give a better view over the nose for carrier operations, and the radiator in the Merlin-engined version was sited under the nose, making room for the struts of the optional float undercarriage that was specified. Racks were provided for two 250lb (113kg) bombs and eight 25lb (11.3kg)

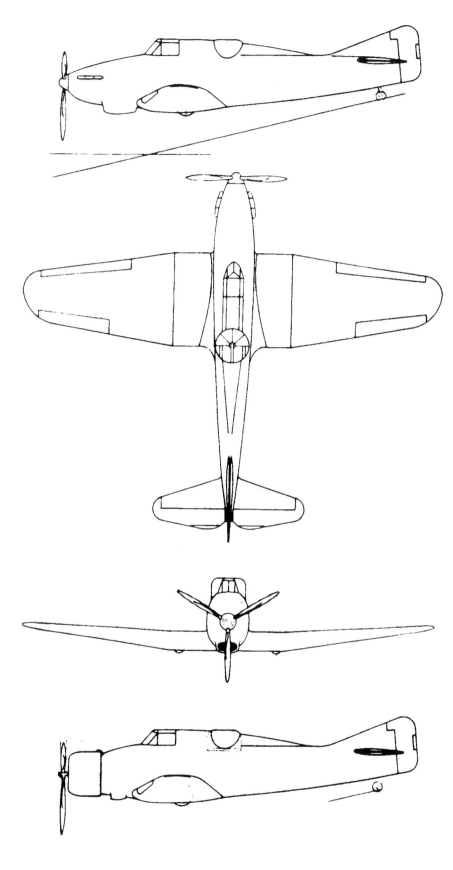

The Boulton Paul P.85.

bombs. There would be stowage for a dinghy in the upper rear fuselage.

The wing centre-section of the P.85 was narrower than that of the P.82, presumably for wing-folding requirements, which meant the inward retracting undercarriage of the P.82 had to be changed to a rearward retracting arrangement; but the span of the P.85 was still greater, at 42ft 6in (13m), as against 39ft (12m) for the P.82 then envisaged. The fuselage was also longer, at 38ft (for the Merlin-engined landplane), as against 33ft (11.6m) for the P.82, though this was later to grow by 2ft (60cm).

The top speed of the Hercules-powered version was 312mph (502kph) at 15,000ft, and for the Merlin-engined version 308mph (496kph). The floatplanes were much slower, of course, at 263mph (423kph) and 258mph (415kph), respectively. A dual-control training version of the aircraft was also outlined, with the turret replaced by a second pilot's seat with an open cockpit.

At Hawker Aircraft they were preoccupied with getting the Hurricane into production and building the first prototype Henley light bomber, on which their new turret fighter was based. But waning official enthusiasm for the Henley slowed up development on that aircraft, and therefore the Hawker turret fighter as well.

At Boulton Paul there was no such delay. Drawings of the SAMM AB.7 turret had been received, and were rapidly converted to imperial measurements and specifications. Wooden mock-ups of both the P.82 and the new turret were completed by

Technical Information for the Boulton Paul P.85			
	Landplane	*Landplane*	*Seaplane*
Engine	Hercules	Merlin	Hercules
Span ft (m)	42.5 (12.95)	42.5 (12.95)	42.5 (12.95)
Length ft (m)	37 8in(11.48)	38 (11.58)	39 9in (12.12)
Height ft (m)	12 (3.66)	12 3in (3.73)	13 9in (4.19)
Wing area sq ft (sq m)	318 (295.4)	313 (290.8)	318 (295.4)
Top speed at:			
5,000ft (1,524m)	290mph (466kph)	269mph (433kph)	246mph (396kph)
10,000ft (3,048m)	307mph (494kph)	308mph (496kph)	258mph (415kph)
15,000ft (4,572m)	312mph (502kph)	308mph (496kph)	263mph (423kph)
Rate of climb at:			
5,000ft (1,524m)	3,250ft/min (991m/min)	3,200ft/min (975m/min)	2,640ft/min (805m/min)

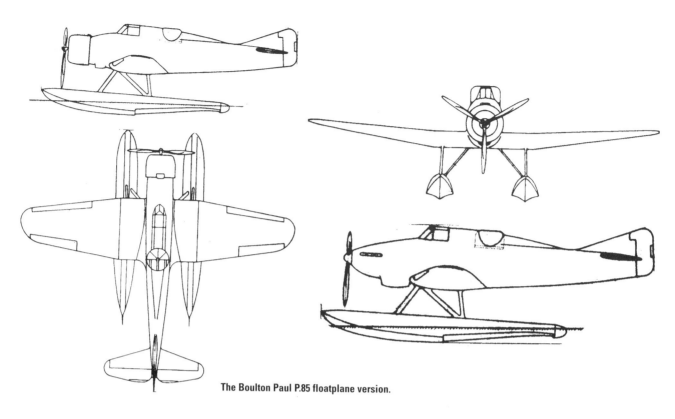

The Boulton Paul P.85 floatplane version.

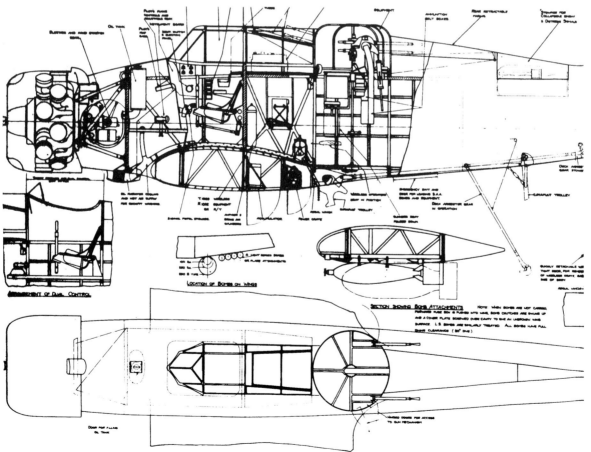

Fuselage layout of the Boulton Paul P.85.

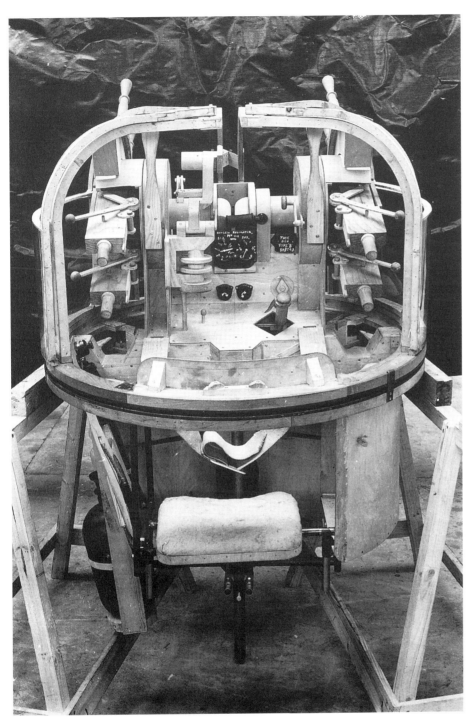

Wooden mock-up of the Type A turret at Norwich in 1936.

The wing of the Boulton Paul P.82 under construction at Norwich in 1936. The P.82 mock-up is to the left.

Turret Fighter Armament

In 1935 it became apparent that the Hispano-Suiza company in France had developed an excellent new 20mm cannon, with a better rate of fire than other designs. It was being developed there as a motor-cannon, mounted between the banks of a Hispano-Suiza V12 engine. The Air Ministry inspected the weapon and chose it as the future armament for the RAF, encouraging Hispano-Suiza to open a new factory in Great Britain to produce it. A new specification was issued, F.37/35, calling for a single-engined fighter capable of at least 350mph (560kph), and armed with four of these weapons.

It was logical to suggest that just as this new fixed cannon fighter would replace the eight-gun F.10/35 fighters, the replacement for the as yet unbuilt F.9/35 turret fighter would be an aircraft armed with the Hispano cannon in one or more turrets. The Air Staff suggested an aircraft fitted with a turret that mounted four 20mm cannon, and able to fire straight ahead, for which a front turret was possibly demanded. This went back to the concept that had been overturned in producing F.9/35.

When the Operational Requirements Committee met to discuss it, two layouts were suggested: either a two/three seat aircraft with two turrets each mounting two 20mm guns, in nose and dorsal positions; or an aircraft with a single dorsal turret with four of the guns. Specification F.18/36 was outlined in March 1936 for the latter type, but also with a single fixed forward-firing machine gun. By June, consideration was given to cancelling all the F.9/35 designs altogether in favour of this new fighter.

February 1936, and the assistant director of Research and Development (Armaments) came to Norwich for the final mock-up conference on the 28th. The turret was to be modified to take four Browning machine guns: this was to be the new standard weapon of the RAF. On the mock-up they were fitted with articulated cocking handles. It was decided at the meeting that a stand should be designed for the turret, to support it when it was removed from the aircraft, and that this should be made rigid enough to test-fire the guns. Construction of the first components of the prototype commenced on 21 March – the same month that a new specification was issued, outlining the replacement for the new turret fighter.

The Boulton Paul Prototype

In view of this, Boulton Paul pressed on with the construction of the P.82 prototype with all haste, and the system of construction they devised aided this considerably. The light alloy skin of the aircraft was drilled and riveted to stringers on the flat and was then wrapped round the structure, which itself consisted of a large number of separate major components. For instance, the sides of the lower rear fuselage were constructed separately, with the skin attached to tubular rib structures. The sides were then bolted together at the bottom, and at their upper sides were joined by a corrugated alloy deck. The upper fuselage was formed entirely of plywood, which aided the construction of retractable fairings sited on either side of the turret. These helped to streamline the turret, but retracted as the guns passed over them, as cams operated pneumatic rams.

Aerodynamically the advantages of an elliptical wing were well known, but constructing such a wing was not easy, as Supermarine were discovering with the Spitfire. Boulton Paul devised a wing of basic elliptical shape but modified into two linear tapers, for ease of construction. The heart of the aircraft was the wing centre section, carrying the inward-retracting undercarriage, and on top of which sat the fuselage; in fact the upper surface of the wing formed the pilot's cockpit floor. The outer wings, of a slightly greater taper, were then bolted on. There were almost no forming processes in the whole structure, and very little double curvature.

When the director of Technical Development arrived at Norwich in September 1936 to view the first SAMM AB.7 turret, just arrived from France, he was pleasantly surprised by the progress made in the construction of the P.82 prototype and the techniques being used. A great deal of work was done in Boulton Paul's own 4ft (1m) wind tunnel in the streamlining of the aircraft, to try and overcome the penalty of the weight of the turret. Apart from the retractable turret fairings, the inward-retracting Dowty undercarriage was entirely enclosed in the wing by doors, the lower half of the wheels being covered by flaps hinged to the leg. The tailskid was also retractable, and flush riveting was used throughout. By September the engine mounting had already been delivered by Rolls Royce, but Boulton Paul were still awaiting the Dowty undercarriage.

The first ground-firing tests of the AB.7 turret took place at Orfordness on 17 October 1936, and the turret's designer, Antoine de Boysson, attended though he was not allowed to see details of the aircraft for which it was intended. At about this time, no doubt with the new cannon fighter in mind, Boulton Paul ordered an example of the SAMM AB.15 pedestal mount for the Hispano cannon.

Towards the end of 1936 the last of the company's personnel who were prepared to make the move to the new factory at Wolverhampton transferred from Norwich, and construction of the P.82 prototype was moved to a new experimental shop alongside the new drawing office. One man who would not make the move was the company's chief test pilot since 1925, Sqn Ldr C. A. Rea, who stayed in Norwich and formed his own company. He was replaced by Flt Lt Cecil Feather, formerly a specialist armament pilot at the Aircraft and Aircraft Armament establishment at Martlesham Heath. It was Feather who made the first flight of a Boulton Paul-built Hawker Demon at the new site on 21 August 1936. A total of 106 Demons would be built at Pendeford over the next eighteen months.

The first flight of the prototype P.82 had been scheduled for 4 March 1937, but despite two shifts being instituted, things were not going as swiftly as planned. This was disguised whenever there was a visit from the Royal Air Force, with panels and parts being fitted to the aircraft temporarily, to give the appearance of more progress having been made than was in fact the case. Of course, having to remove them all again afterwards only slowed things up even more.

In March the Armstrong-Whitworth's twin-engined F.9/35 design was cancelled. Designing and building a large new airframe, to be powered by a new engine that was never in fact built, and armed with a brand new, complicated power-operated turret, was always going to be a major task, but with Armstrong-Whitworth fully stretched in bringing the Whitley into production, and trying to find time to build the four-engined Ensign for Imperial Airways, the turret fighter was also always likely to be a non-starter. The Gloster F.34/35 design and the back-up Fairey F.9/35 design had already been cancelled, so that left just Hawker and Boulton Paul vying for production orders for the RAF's turret fighter, and Blackburn and Boulton Paul for the Fleet Air Arm's equivalent. The Gloster turret fighter design was later reworked by the company as a single-seat Taurus-powered fighter with five fixed 20mm cannon to Spec. F.9/37, but although promising, it was only built in prototype form.

Boulton Paul had designed a competent contender for the fixed cannon fighter Spec. F.37/35, namely their P.88 powered by either a single Hercules or a Rolls-Royce Vulture; but in March 1937, prototype orders went to Westland for their design, which became the Whirlwind. Much was therefore riding on the two turret-fighter projects.

Into Production

Decision day for all concerned was 28 April 1937, and it was with great relief that the company received a production order for the P.82, for eighty-seven aircraft with the serials L6950–L7036. The aircraft was then given the suitably aggressive name Defiant. Hawker Aircraft were still clearly favoured however, as they received orders for 389 of their aircraft (serials L3643–L4031), named Hotspur, to be built by Avro. The order for the naval turret fighter went to Blackburn, with 136 Rocs ordered. Commonality with the Skua was clearly an important factor in the choice of the Roc, for the P.85 differed rather more significantly from its RAF brother. The Fleet Air Arm was able to plan joint squadrons of Skuas and Rocs, thus two versions of one type to fly and maintain. Even so, with performance estimates for the P.85 giving it a top speed almost 100mph (160kph) higher than the Roc, the decision does seem extraordinary. The only detrimental feature of the P.85 design was the width of the aircraft with the wings folded, namely 15ft 3in (4.65m), which was rather more than the Navy's preferred 11ft (3.35m).

Blackburn were far too busy with production of the Shark, and the development and production of the Skua dive bomber/fighter, 190 having been ordered off the drawing board in 1936, and the prototype of which had just had its first flight, on 9 February 1937. In December 1936 they had also received orders straight off the drawing board for 442 Botha torpedo bombers, and preparations for the mass production of this was likely to take up all

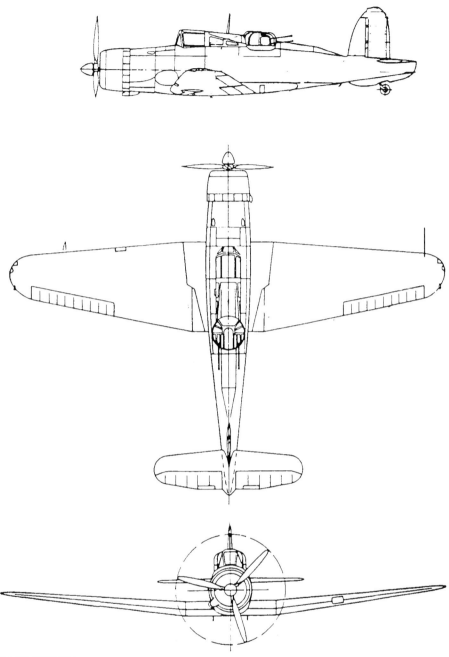

The Blackburn Roc.

was issued for the cannon turret fighter, to Operational Requirement 50. It now required a twin-engined, two-/three-seat aircraft with four Hispano cannon in a power-operated turret. Top speed and cruising speed were to be at least 370mph (595kph) and 320mph (515kph) at 35,000ft (10,668m), respectively. It was to be able to maintain altitude on one engine up to 15,000ft (4,572m). Good manoeuvrability and low-speed handling, as well as steadiness as a gun platform, were also essential.

Boulton Paul's design, the P.92, was a shoulder-wing aircraft, to be powered by 1,760hp Rolls-Royce Vulture engines. The fuselage was kept very slim because the cannon turret was set between the wing spars with a low profile, 13ft (3.96m)-diameter cupola of light alloy. The gunner would sit between the breeches of each pair of cannon, with a small, 3.2ft (0.97m) glazed dome housing his head and gunsight. The cannon barrels were lowered into slots in the cupola when not in use, and automatically covered by shutters. Outboard of the cannon there was provision for a pair of .303 Browning machine guns on each side, and there was a small bomb-bay aft of the turret.

The P.92 was an all-metal aircraft with stressed skin construction throughout. The fuselage was designed to be made up of easily subcontracted sections that would be bolted together: the forward fuselage/cockpit, the centre fuselage, two rear fuselage sides, and the tail. The wing consisted of the all-important centre section containing the turret, and the two outer wings.

Armstrong-Whitworth's design to F.11/37 was rather more radical, being a twin-engined pusher with Merlin engines. It had a tricycle undercarriage, and the four-cannon turret was mounted just behind the pilot, though it could only fire in the forward hemisphere. With less power than the P.92, it had much smaller dimensions, with a span of 43ft (13.11m) and a length of 43ft 3in (13.18m).

Gloster Aircraft's F.11/37 proposal followed the basic layout of the company's earlier turret-fighter proposals, with two engines, a pilot seated ahead of the wing, and a turret aft of the wing, as well as twin fins and rudders. The aircraft had much more powerful engines, however, with either Rolls-Royce Vultures, Armstrong-Siddeley Deerhound III, twenty-one cylinder 1,425hp triple-banked radials, or

available factory space. The detail design and production of the Roc was therefore sub-contracted to Boulton Paul, who were in any case supplying the four-gun turret. They gave the aircraft their own project number: P.93.

Boulton Paul were thus in the peculiar position of building prototypes and laying down adjacent production lines for two entirely different turret fighters. With the benefit of hindsight it would have seemed more sensible for the Air Ministry to have

rationalized production by cancelling the Roc and letting the P.85 Sea Defiant go ahead after all, especially as Boulton Paul's Design Department was already working on the potential Defiant replacement.

A Modified Specification is Issued: F.11/37

On 26 May 1937 a modified Spec. F.11/37

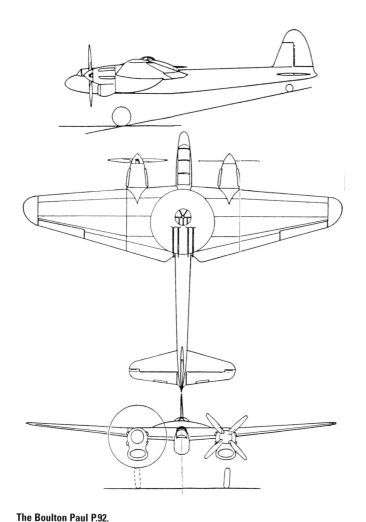

The Boulton Paul P.92.

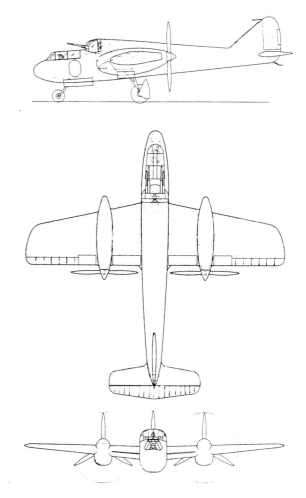

Armstrong-Whitworth F.11/37 proposal.

Bristol Hercules VI radials. The turret was fully retractable, the top being flush with the fuselage upper surface when retracted, and Gloster also offered it with two 23mm Madsen cannon as an alternative to the four 20mm Hispano-Suizas.

A bomber version of the same airframe was also designed, but with a different fuselage, able to carry 3,000lb (1,360kg) of bombs or a 2,000lb (907kg) torpedo.

Other companies also offered F.11/37 proposals. Supermarine drew up their Type 320, also a twin Vulture-powered aircraft, and there were submissions from Bristol, Short Bros and Hawker.

Testing the Defiant

By May, the wings of the Defiant prototype were being mated to the fuselage. A third wing had been built for structural testing, and in December 1937 this had been despatched to Farnborough along with the

foreman of the Experimental Department, Ted Parkinson. He watched with trepidation as the design load was applied to the wing he had made, through hydraulic cylinders strapped to a beam. The wing-tip was lifted about 12in (30cm), but thankfully nothing failed, and on release of the load it returned to within $^1/_4$in (6mm). Ted returned about a week later when the wing was taken to the limit and beyond, finally giving way with a terrific bang that shook the room. But Boulton Paul's impressive method of construction had been proven.

Air Firing Trials

The SAMM AB.7 turret, to be re-designated the Boulton Paul Type A Mk.I, was fitted to the modified nose of Overstrand K8175 for air firing trials from 3 July to 28 August 1937, against a Hawker Hart towing vertical and horizontal flag targets. The performance of the turret was entirely

Technical Information for the Gloster F.11/37	
Span	63ft (19.20m)
Length	45ft 6in (13.87m)
Height	13ft 10in (4.21m)
Wing area	565sq ft (52.49sq m)
Loaded weight	17,100lb (775.6kg)
Fuel capacity	280gal (1,273ltr)
Top speed (Vultures)	378mph at 15,000ft (608kph at 4,572m)
Climb	8.7min to 25,000ft (7,620m)

satisfactory. The Armament Department, headed by H. A. 'Pop' Hughes, was producing two new versions of the turret: the Type A Mk.IID for the Defiant, and the Mk.II8 for the 8 oc, that differed only in the non-conductive inserts in a cylinder specially devised to prevent the gunner hitting parts of his own aircraft. Electrical contacts passed over the drum as the turret was moved, stopping the electrical firing of the guns when they were pointed at the tail or other obstructions. The device cut out the left or right pair of guns as appropriate.

The Browning guns were sited in pairs above another on each side of the turret. The gunner operated the turret with a single control handle, with a firing button on the top. He sat on a backless seat, with his feet in the stirrups of simple footrests or a swivelling bar. Entry to the turret was through two sliding doors behind his seat; this was also the normal way to get out of the turret, though escape could be made through a hatch in the bottom of the fuselage. Either way it was a tight squeeze for a gunner to bail out, and was found to be virtually impossible with a normal parachute; eventually a special low-profile 'parasuit' was developed, worn on the gunner's back.

The Defiant prototype was not to be fitted with the turret initially, though a mock-up was installed to check clearances. Tests of the Dowty undercarriage revealed a number of problems concerned mainly with the hydraulic oil emulsifying. George Dowty visited the factory several times himself, but the problem was eventually cured by Duckham's coming up with a new oil. There were no further failures on the prototype, though the undercarriage was tested through several hundred operations.

The First Engine Tests

The first engine runs of the Defiant prototype, K8310, were made in July. The turret position was faired over, and ballast would be carried for the first flight. On 11 August 1937 the Defiant, still unpainted, was brought out onto the apron at the back of the new Boulton Paul factory. The engine was run up to the satisfaction of Joe Plant, the 8 olls-8 oyce representative, and a few adjustments were made. Cecil Feather then took the aircraft down the grass taxiway to the airfield for some high-speed taxiing trials, before returning to the factory. The aircraft was serviced, and then Feather returned to the airfield and took off. The first flight was cut short when an oil seal broke in the propeller hub, and Feather landed with oil stains despoiling the shiny metal of the nose; but when he went to report, he said: 'The aircraft flew

The prototype P.82 Defiant, K8310, on the apron at Pendeford before its first taxiing tests and flight. Note the lower wheel-flaps that were later replaced by centreline doors.

The prototype Defiant on the grass at Pendeford ready for its first flight. Unpainted and without turret, it still retains the original retractable tailskid.

neutrally, and appears to handle very well. I hope the next prototype and the production aircraft will be as good.'

A number of changes were thought necessary before the aircraft was delivered to Martlesham Heath. The retractable tail-skid originally fitted was replaced by a wheel, and the hinged flaps that covered the lower half of the wheels when retracted were deleted. The Hurricane prototype had had similar hinged flaps, but they were constantly damaged by dirt and stones flung up by the wheels. The Defiant was fitted with a novel curved brush just behind the main wheels, which brushed dirt off the tyre as the undercarriage retracted. The flaps would later be replaced by doors mounted on the centre-line, and operated by a single vertical Dowty hydraulic ram. Trouble with the Dowty undercarriage continued, as it would often not lock up. At first the electrical pump was replaced by a Lockheed Mk.IV engine-driven pump, but further problems meant the Dowty shock absorbers were also replaced by Lockheed Airdraulic units.

The Prototypes are put through their Paces

The Defiant prototype was delivered to Martlesham Heath on 7 December, where it was put through its paces until the 23rd. The aircraft was found to be very pleasant to fly, with a sprightly top speed of 320mph (515kph) without the drag of the turret. It could climb to 10,500ft (3,200m) in only 7.5min. On the down side, the aircraft was criticized for having no cockpit heating, and the operation of some of the controls was not liked. The unpainted wing was often slippy, and a non-slip mat was obviously needed. Nevertheless the Defiant had proved itself satisfactory for service use, and this resulted in a further order being received in January 1938 for another 202 production aircraft, partly in response to the cancellation of the Hawker Hotspur that was slipping even further behind schedule. In addition, all the factories in the Hawker-Siddeley group were at full stretch, with new aircraft of many different types being ordered in large numbers.

The first prototype Hotspur, K8309, was completed in the summer of 1938, and its first flight, at Brooklands, was on 14 June, ten months after the Defiant. The deep fuselage of the original design, with retractable fairings to streamline the turret, had been dropped, and the pilot's cockpit canopy now sloped down steeply to the upper fuselage immediately in front of the turret. The original arrangement of the guns in the turret had also been altered: instead of being in pairs one above the other as in the Boulton Paul Type A, they were arranged in an arc across the turret, in the manner of the Frazer-Nash FN.13 tail turret then being designed for the Sunderland.

For the first flight the Hotspur carried only a ballasted wooden mock-up of the turret, which was never in fact to be built. In addition the Hotspur had provision for a Vickers machine gun in the nose, synchronized to fire through the propeller, though as the outer wings were basically Hurricane units it would have been perfectly practical to have fitted up to eight Brownings there. Trials at Martlesham showed that it was about 20mph (30kph) faster than the Defiant, probably due to its lighter loaded weight, and had pleasant flying qualities.

The Hawker Hotspur with the dummy turret fitted.

Hawker Hotspur Technical Information	
Span	40ft 6in (12.34m)
Length	32ft 10.5in (10.01m)
Height	13ft 10in (4.21m)
Wing area	261.6sq ft (24.3sq m)
Empty weight	5,800lb (263.08kg)
Loaded weight	7,650lb (347.04kg)
Top speed	316mph at 15,800ft (508kph at 4,816m)
Landing speed	85mph (137kph)
Climb	10.85min to 15,000ft (4,572m)
Service ceiling	28,000ft (8,534m)

The mock-up turret was soon removed, and the rear cockpit was faired over. The aircraft was then used for a number of flap and dive-brake trials in connection with the similar Hawker Henley. It was delivered to Farnborough in 1939 where it continued its experimental work.

On 12 February 1942, Flt Lt W. D. B. S. Davie, with Mrs Gwen Alston as observer, was carrying out gliding tests in a Hotspur, fitted with a variable drag flap. At the end of one glide a fire broke out in the carburettor, which prevented the engine picking up. Davie raised the undercarriage, which had been lowered for the test, and succeeded in making a belly landing at Hartford Bridge Flats. Davie and Mrs Alston were unhurt, and the Hotspur was declared repairable; however there was little point to the latter expense, and the aircraft was scrapped.

The last of 106 Hawker Demons left the Boulton Paul factory in 1937, but the company was busy with large subcontract orders: for Blackburn Shark spars, complete Saro London wing sets, Blackburn B2 wings, and Fairey Seafox tailplanes. The armament department was developing a complete range of electro-hydraulic gun turrets based on the SAMM principle, and these were being considered for fitment to most of the bomber designs emerging in the late 1930s.

An assistant test pilot had been engaged in 1936 to help Cecil Feather with the test-flying of the Hawker Demons: George Skelton, born in Australia, but who had learned to fly in South Africa where his family had moved. He joined the Royal Air Force in 1930, and flew Bristol Bulldogs with No. 32 Squadron at Kenley, and then Westland Wapitis with No. 30 Squadron in Iraq. In 1936 he was promoted to flight lieutenant and placed on the Reserve Class C, so that he could join Boulton Paul.

Boulton Paul test pilot, George Skelton, who became an operational Defiant pilot with No. 264 Squadron during the war.

Setting Up the Production Lines

In 1937 a factory extension that increased the floor area by 80 per cent was begun, to make room for the new production lines for the Roc and the Defiant. As the Roc was very similar to the Skua, which had already flown, there were to be no prototypes, the first three production examples serving this role. Boulton Paul's detailed re-design involved the widening of the centre fuselage to take the Type A Mk.IIR turret, with the same retractable fairings on each side as on the Defiant. A tiny wireless cabin was sited between the pilot's cockpit and the turret, the wireless equip-

ment to be operated by the gunner. In addition the wings were re-rigged with 2 degrees of dihedral, instead of having the upturned tips of the Skua. The aircraft was of all-metal construction, and skinned in flush-riveted Alclad throughout. Boulton Paul's production effort was helped by General Aircraft being subcontracted to make the entire tail of the aircraft, that company also supplying some Skua rear fuselages.

Some Specification Details

The Roc was powered by an 890hp Bristol Perseus XI radial with a three-blade propeller. With a span of 46ft (14m) and a length of 35ft 7in (10.84m), it was slightly larger than the Defiant; it had an all-up weight of 7,950lb (3,606kg). From the outset it was designed with pick-up points for floats, a requirement of many naval aircraft up to that time. However, the first flight of the Roc was still nearly a year away.

The prototype Defiant was fitted with a non-slip mat on the wing, and with a heater for the pilot's cockpit drawing hot air from the oil cooler, with all draughts in the cockpit being sealed off. The turret was heated by air taken from the glycol radiator, and gunners were also later to wear electrically heated clothing. For a while the turret cupola was fitted for aerodynamic trials, and then in February 1938 the SAMM AB.7 turret was finally fitted to K8310. The turret was the same one that had been tested in the Overstrand, but now had intercom and oxygen systems fitted, as well as a new type of gun adjuster and an emergency outside hood release.

Other changes to the airframe included the removal of a central strut fitted to the pilot's windscreen: there was no need for a gunsight on the aircraft, but pilots had objected to the strut right in front of their field of view. Thus the two flat surfaces of the first windscreen were replaced by a single curved Plexiglass unit. A further strange feature of the Defiant was that the pilot was provided with a normal gun button and could fire the guns, provided they were locked in the forward position, although there was no synchronization gear to protect the propeller. On at least one recorded example during the war, a Defiant pilot on a non-operational flight over the Irish Sea slid back his canopy and rested his elbows on the canopy rail while the guns were pointed forward in this way,

A close-up of the turret fitted to the prototype, showing that the pilot's canopy could be slid over one of the gun barrels if the turret was in this position.

The first prototype with the turret finally fitted, ready for flight outside the flight sheds at Pendeford.

nd by mistake touched the firing button nd the guns fired. The shot ripped though he elbows of his flying jacket, but luckily lid not touch his arms, which could easily have been shot off.

Another slight problem with the design as that if the pilot's canopy was slid back en the guns were pointing forward, but iightly to one side, the canopy actually ent over one of the barrels, so that one in could then fire through the sliding .ood.

The total weight of the turret including gunner and 2,400 rounds of ammunition was 815lb (370kg), raising the total weight of the aircraft to 7,500lb (3,400kg).

After these tests the aircraft then went for armament trials at Orfordness, but new performance trials were delayed by trouble with the Merlin 1 engine.

In March 1938 Boulton Paul received a contract for the construction of three prototypes of their P.92 turret-fighter project. Two were to be powered by the Rolls-

Royce Vulture engine, and one with the new 2,055hp Napier Sabre. The four-cannon turret was now designated the Type L, and the company's machine-gun turrets then envisaged – apart from the Type A for the Defiant and Roc – were the Type C two-gun nose turret, the Type E four-gun tail turret, and the Type K retractable two-gun ventral turret. The Type L turret was also being considered as the defensive armament for a future 'ideal bomber'.

In April the stress office began work on stressing a two-seat trainer version of the Defiant. The turret was to be replaced by a second pilot's seat on a raised structure, giving the instructor his own windscreen. But the dual-control Defiant was never built because the pleasant flying qualities of the fighter made it an easy process for new pilots to convert to flying it.

The Department of Technical Development agreed in April that the first production Boulton Paul-built Type A Mk.IID turret would go to the Royal Aircraft Establishment for electrical tests, and the second example would be fitted to the second prototype Defiant, K8620. This was supposed to fly a month after the first prototype, but was delayed because it was being brought up closer to production standards, with modifications deemed necessary from test-flying K8310. It would also be fitted with the revised Merlin II engine, which it was hoped would cure the reliability problems.

Orders and the Workforce

On 5 May 1938, the Air Council Committee on Supply questioned Boulton Paul about expected deliveries of the two turret fighters. The company stated that they expected to complete all 136 Rocs by November 1939, though none had yet flown, and they complained that Roc production was being held up because they had to wait for modifications to be approved on the Skua before they could be instituted on the Roc. They also claimed that they would have delivered 450 Defiants by March 1940, at which point the production rate would have been around fifty per month. They also pointed out that they only had orders for 289 Defiants at the time, and so a further 161, with serial batches in the 'N' range, were immediately ordered, to give the 450 total.

Around 600 Norfolk men had moved with the company from Norwich, but the company had begun recruiting further

A rare air-to-air picture of the prototype K8310, with the turret finally fitted and other changes including the fixed tailwheel replacing the tailskid.

Roc final assembly with the complete tails, built by General Aircraft, being attached to the fuselages.

many other workers, such as tyre fitters from the nearby Goodyear factory, were also attracted to the high wages offered by Boulton Paul. It was found in particular that the bonuses offered on Roc wing production were very generous, and new workers had to be told to slow down, so that this was not made too obvious.

As production built up, the company had to scour further afield to find skilled men, in competition with the rest of the expanding aircraft industry; eventually it was obliged to open a training school in Cannock, and to bring in men from as far afield as Scotland.

Performance Testing the Prototypes

The prototype Defiant, K8310, was sent to Martlesham Heath in October 1938 for performance tests with the turret fitted. The weight and drag of the turret were found to have reduced the top speed to 303mph (487kph) at 15,000ft (4,572m), and it took 20.1min to reach 20,000ft (6,096m). The Hurricane Mk.1 had a top

skilled men even before the move was complete. This was one of the reasons that Wolverhampton had been chosen for the new factory, as there was a large local pool of skilled engineering workers, not least because of the recent closure of many of the town's motor manufacturers, such as Sunbeam, Star and AJS. Furthermore,

Roc wing production, which is said to have produced high bonus payments.

committee of supply, the Fifth Sea Lord expressed the opinion that the Roc should be cancelled, as it would obviously be useless as a fighter. This was not done, however, because the production line was already in full operation, though the first aircraft had not yet flown, and it was felt that cancellation would disrupt the build-up of Boulton Paul's labour force and facilities, which would be needed for the Defiant. Also, Boulton Paul had already begun design work on the changes needed to make the Roc a target-towing aircraft, as far back as April 1938. The Roc's major second-line role in the future war was mapped out almost from the moment it was ordered, and Sea Gladiators were also ordered to make up the Fleet Air Arm's front-line fighter strength.

The first Blackburn Roc, L3057, was finally ready for flight on 23 December 1938, and the Blackburn test pilot Fl Lt H. J. Wilson came down from Brough to take it up. Wilson would become famous after the war when he broke the world air-speed record, flying a Meteor. Unlike the first Defiant, the Roc was flown with its Boulton Paul Type A Mk.IIR turret fitted from the outset. The aircraft was then flown up to Brough for Blackburn's trials, and to Martlesham Heath in March 1939, where it was joined by the next two aircraft, L3058 and L3059, for performance and armament trials.

speed only 15mph (24.1kph) higher, but took only 11.7 minutes to reach 20,000ft (6,096m).

The pnuematic rams that automatically raised and lowered the fairings on either side of the turret as it revolved were supplied from the same pneumatic reservoir as the brakes. The pilot's gauge showed a pressure drop of 10lb/sq in on each revolution of the turret, which could not be replenished quickly enough from the engine-driven compressor. It was feared, therefore, that if the turret were revolved too much, the brakes would be ineffective on landing; and so it was suggested that the gunner be supplied with a button to lower and fix the fairings down at the beginning of an engagement, leaving them down throughout. There would be a reduction in top speed of up to 6mph (10kph), but this was thought acceptable.

In October 1938 at a meeting of the

A view of Roc production, showing how crowded the factory was, with thirty-eight Roc centre fuselages visible in this picture (out of 136 produced altogether).

A Roc rear fuselage being built in its assembly jig.

The Roc was found to be a pleasant aircraft to fly and, like the Skua, could be held in a steep dive by the generous dive brakes. As expected, its performance was dreadful, with a top speed of only 223mph (359kph) at 10,000ft (3,048m), and a service ceiling of 18,000ft (5,486m). It did have a very useful endurance of six hours, however.

After the first aircraft, all initial Roc test-flying was undertaken by Cecil Feather and George Skelton. The fourth aircraft, usually regarded as the first production machine, L3060, was delivered to Brough in March in connection with the plan to fit the Roc with floats. The next two aircraft went to Worthy Down the following month for their handling notes to be prepared.

The prototype Blackburn Roc, L3057, awaiting its first flight on the apron at Pendeford.

The Defiant second prototype, K8620, outside the flight sheds, with the prototype Blackburn Roc behind it. It has further changes to K8310, including ejector exhausts, a window between the pilot and gunner, and the retractable wireless aerial fitted.

Production Rocs, L3077 and L3084-6, outside the flight shed. The factory is being camouflaged ready for war, but the aircraft are still produced in silver finish.

The first prototype, K8310, but with further changes that make it more akin to production aircraft.

The second Defiant prototype, K8620, finally flew for the first time on 18 May 1939. The aircraft had many of the production modifications deemed necessary after test flights of the first aircraft, including a VDM De Havilland spinner instead of the Rolls-Royce unit, stub exhausts, and a small window in the fixed panels between the pilot's canopy and the turret. It was also fitted with a retractable underfuselage wireless aerial mast, just in front of the tailwheel.

At an early stage it had been realized that the normal aerial position above the fuselage could not be used because of the turret. One mast was therefore sited between the undercarriage bays, and a retractable one just in front of the tailwheel. This mast extended automatically as the main undercarriage retracted. From K8620 onwards, the tailwheel was no longer retractable, and the entire Dowty hydraulic system was replaced by one from Lockheed, including the main undercarriage legs.

Performance Trials K8620 and L6950

Top Speed

Altitude		6.5lb boost (2.95kg)		12lb boost (5.44kg)	
feet	metres	mph	kph	mph	kph
2,000	610	250	402	283	455
5,000	1524	261	420	294	473
10,000	3048	279	449	312	502
15,000	4572	297	478	305	491
20,000	6096	295	475	–	
25,000	7620	274	441	–	

Ceiling	28,100ft	(8,565m)
Take-off run	315yd	(288m)
Distance to rest over 50ft (15.2m) screen	560yd	(512m)

Climb

Altitude		Time in mins	Rate (ft/min)		T.A.S	
Feet	metres		ft/min	m/min	mph	kph
1,000	305	0.7	1,435	437	177	285
2,000	610	1.4	1,455	443	179.5	289
3,000	915	2.1	1,475	450	182.5	294
5,000	1,524	3.4	1,515	462	188	302
6,500	1,981	4.4	1,540	469	192	309
10,000	3,048	6.7	1,610	491	202.5	326
13,000	3,962	8.6	1,415	431	207	333
15,000	4,572	10.1	1,240	378	209	336
18,000	5,486	12.8	980	299	211.5	340
20,000	6,096	15.1	805	245	213	342
26,000	7,925	27.0	285	87	220	354

Top speed using 100 octane and increased boost

Altitude		Standard		Using 100 octane and increased boost	
Feet	metres	mph	kph	mph	kph
1,000	305	247	397	279.5	450
2,000	610	250.5	403	283	455
3,000	915	254	409	286.5	461
5,000	1,524	261	420	294	473
6,500	1,981	266.5	429	299	481
10,000	3,048	279	449	312	502
13,000	3,962	290	467	308.5	496
15,000	4,572	297	478	305.5	491
16,500	5,029	302.5	487	303	488
16,600	5,060	303	488	-	-
18,000	5,486	300	482	-	-
20,000	6,096	295	475	-	-
23,000	7,010	284.5	458	-	-
26,000	7,925	266.5	429	-	-

delivered during July, all going straight to maintenance units.

The first production Defiant, L6950, made its initial flight on 30 July, and was used to test the racks for eight 25lb bombs as specified. It was delivered to the A & AEE on 19 September 1939 for performance trials.

The only production Defiant delivered from Pendeford before the start of the war was in fact the third, L6952, which went to the Air Fighting Development Unit at Northolt on 22 August; L6951 went to the Central Flying School, Upavon, on 5 September, two days after Neville Chamberlain's fateful speech declaring that 'this country is at war with Germany'.

Defiant's Successor: the P.92

Work on the P.92, the cannon turret fighter that was to replace the Defiant, was progressing in Boulton Paul's experimental department. The company had tested a model of the aircraft in its own 4ft (1m) wind tunnel with satisfactory results, but a 2/7th scale model with a 17ft 10in (5.4m) wingspan was tested in the RAE's 24ft (7.3m) wind tunnel from March to September 1939. Two 15hp electric motors turned the propellers. This had tended to suggest a stability problem at slow rates of pitching, which would call for a different wing plan. In addition, movement of the long cannon barrels affected the stability, and raising them 45 degrees and revolving them through 135 degrees seemed to increase the drag of the aircraft by as much as 35 per cent.

A second model to 1/7th scale was made, with a new, more swept-back wing plan, moving the mean chord relative to the centre of gravity. This model was tested in the National Physics Laboratory wind tunnel, and showed entirely satisfactory stability characteristics. To resolve the problem completely it was decided to build a half-scale flying model of the P.92, and to use the new wing plan of the 1/7th scale model.

The P.92/2, as it was called, was subcontracted out to Heston Aircraft who designated it their J.A.8, and it was given the serial V3142. It was powered by two 130hp Gipsy Major II engines, with the nacelles matching the shape of those of the proposed Vulture engines as closely as possible, so that cooling air had to be ducted in from the fairings. The undercarriage

Production of the Roc began to pick up, with three more delivered to Worthy Down in May and five in June, four of them to Worthy Down, where five Rocs had been assigned to 800 Squadron, and three to 803 Squadron. The other production machine went to the A & AEE for armament trials. There were six Rocs

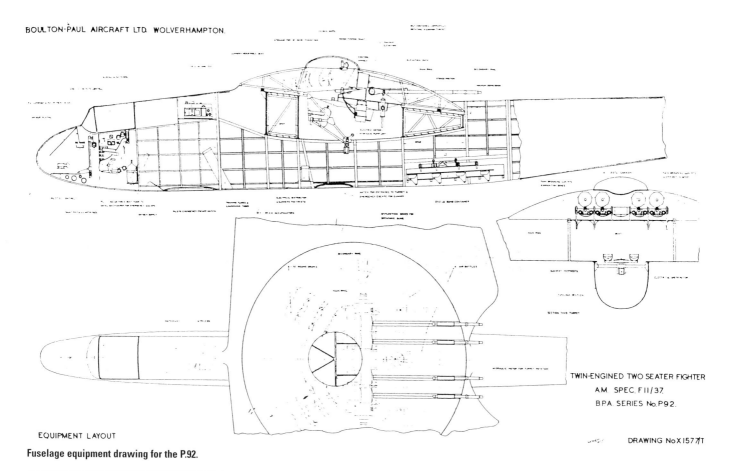

BOULTON-PAUL AIRCRAFT LTD. WOLVERHAMPTON.

TWIN-ENGINED TWO SEATER FIGHTER
A.M. SPEC. F.11/37.
B.P.A. SERIES No. P.92.

EQUIPMENT LAYOUT

DRAWING No X 1577/T

Fuselage equipment drawing for the P.92.

The P.92/2, V3142, after it had been completed by Heston Aircraft. It is parked on the compass-swinging ring at Pendeford.

Boulton Paul P.92 and P.92/2 Technical Information

	P.92	P.92
Engines	2 x 1,710hp Rolls-Royce Vulture II	2 x 1,920hp Napier Sabre
Propeller dia.	13ft 6in (4.11m)	13ft 6in (4.11m)
(3-blade)		
Power unit weight	7,880lb (3,574kg)	7,380lb (3,348kg)
(oil and 292gal)		
(oil and 1,327ltr)		
Dimensions		
Span	65ft 10in	65ft 10in (20.06m)
Length	54ft 4in	54ft 4in (16.56m)
Height (tail down)	13ft 10in	13ft 10in (4.21m)
Wing area	706sq ft	706sq ft (65.6sq m)
Loaded weight	21,000lb (9,525kg)	20,000lb (9,300kg)
Performance		
Top speed		
at sea level:	299mph (481kph)	
at 15,000ft (4,570m):	355mph (571kph)	370mph (595kph)
	(4,000rpm)	(3,000rpm)
at 30,000ft (9,145m):	352mph (566kph)	
Cruising speed		
at 15,000ft (4,570m):	300mph (482kph)	315mph (507kph)
Climb at sea level:	2,000ft/(610m/)min	2,600ft/(792m/)min
at 11,000ft (3,350m):	2,200ft/(671m/)min	
at 15,000ft (4,570m):	2,150ft/(655m/)min	2,600ft/(790m/)min
at 30,000ft (9,145m):	1,050ft/(320m/)min	
Time to 11,000ft		
(3,350m):	5.5min	
to 15,000ft		
(4,570m):	7min	6min
Service ceiling:	38,000ft (11,580m)	
Take-off run:	280yd (256m)	
Distance to clear 50ft:	470yd (430m)	
Normal range:	450 miles – 292gal	
	(724km – 1,327ltr)	
Fuel for 2,000 miles:	778gal (3,537ltr)	823gal (3,741ltr)
(3,218km)		

	P.92/2
Engines	2 x 130hp Gipsy Major II
Dimensions	
Span	33ft 1.5in (10.09m)
Length	27ft 6in (8.38m)
Height	7ft 7.5in (2.32m)
Wing area	354sq ft (33sq m)
Loaded weight	2,778lb (1,260kg)
Performance	
Top speed	152mph (245kph)
Cruising speed	135mph (217kph)

was fixed for simplicity, and the 'turret' was initially just a plywood dome. The whole aircraft was built of wood, and there was some difficulty building a spar of sufficiently narrow dimensions at the wing-tip. Because it was difficult to find a half-size pilot, the front fuselage had to be bulged somewhat to accommodate a normal-size one, because the full-size aircraft was so slim. Even so, the pilot had to virtually sit on the cockpit floor of the aircraft.

Bailing Out of the P.92

On both the P.92/2 and the full-size aircraft there was clearly going to be a problem if the pilot had to bail out. He was seated very near to the tips of the propeller blades, and on the full-size aircraft there would be the additional problem of the four long cannon barrels that could form an obstacle behind him, depending on where they were pointing.

On the P.92/2 it was arranged for the pilot to bail out by collapsing the back of his seat with a special handle; the seat was, in any case, sited virtually on the cockpit floor. He would then push out a panel in the fuselage side and wriggle out through the opening. On the full-size aircraft it was arranged that the pilot's seat would tilt back through 110 degrees, and the pilot would slide out through a hatch on the underside of the fuselage, upside down. Boulton Paul built a mock-up of this arrangement and it was tested by J. D. North himself, falling into a net rigged beneath – though unfortunately the net was not taut enough, and the great man banged his head on the concrete floor. The foreman in charge of the test was summoned to the managing director's office after he returned from sick leave, expecting the worst. But all North said was: 'Well, it worked, didn't it ?'

P.92 Layout

The gunner entered his turret through a hatch on the underside of the fuselage, which also served as his emergency escape hatch. Just behind this was a compartment for a 230lb (104kg) bomb container.

The P.92 also had room for a navigator seated in tandem behind the pilot, though an observer's cockpit was not designed into the aircraft at the outset. The area just behind the pilot only contained the flare chute and the radio. With the aircraft having a potential range of 2,000 miles (3,220km), a navigator would normally be necessary, but airborne interception radar (AI) had already been demonstrated to Air Marshall Hugh Dowding in June 1938. Nevertheless, Dowding was firmly of the opinion that the pilot would not be able to operate the AI, not least because doing so would destroy his night vision. It therefore seemed certain that an observer would later be added to the P.92, and that he would also become the radar operator; and with the nose and wings of the P.92 conveniently free of guns, the radar aerials would be easy to site. All turret fighters were envisaged as both day and night fighters from the outset.

The company also built a mock-up of the centre section of the P.92, incorporat-

The P.92 centre-section mock-up.

ing the turret. The cannon were armed with thirty-round drums, and it was the gunner's job to reload them with new drums, which were hung on four overhead rails so that he could just slide them into position. There were three spare drums for each cannon, giving 480 rounds in all. The company also designed and built a cannon fire selector, allowing the gunner to fire any or all of his guns. The four machine guns outboard of the cannon contained their ammunition in boxes.

Early Tests

With a cupola of 13ft (4m) diameter, it was clearly important that the centre section of the wing be as rigid as possible, as any movement would distort the turret ring, causing it to jam. The vibration of four cannon being fired would also not help. Early tests of this structure in June 1939 resulted in failures, and caused a redesign with extra stiffening.

The SAMM AB.15 pedestal mounting for the Hispano cannon was also tested in the nose of the Overstrand, which had been used for air tests of the AB.7 turret. The work Boulton Paul did with the Hispano cannon, in the air and in their gun butts, proved very valuable for all the manufacturers who would be using it. A standard Defiant turret was also adapted to take a single cannon, sited on the starboard side, when the turret was pointed aft, with the gunner on the other side.

This turret was then fitted to the Defiant prototype, K8310, and was sent to the A & AEE for trials on 9 July 1939. The cannon could be elevated 88 degrees and depressed 10 degrees, which was slightly more than the Type A turret machine guns. At the trials it was found that the 5ft

A mock-up of the P.92's gun turret with the four cannon fitted.

also have implications for the Type L turret for the P.92. The A & AEE's engineers designed fixed fairings to attach to the barrel to alleviate this drag, but they broke up in the air. H. A. Hughes, at Boulton Paul's armament department, designed floating fairings that automatically adopted the optimum position in the airflow, and those worked better than the A & AEE's examples when tested on both the Defiant and the Overstrand. However, they were still not completely satisfactory.

Adapting to the New Generation Turret Fighter

Despite all the work being done by Boulton Paul with the P.92, the preferred layout for a new generation turret fighter was still being discussed. In 1939 the Air Staff again perceived a requirement for a turret fighter with the ability to fire at considerable angles of depression, which again seemed to indicate the need for a nose turret. This seemed to be the same old argument, but it was once more overturned by the possibility of using the Boulton Paul Type L cannon turret in the new 'ideal bomber'. A new ASR F.2/38 was therefore drawn up with a dorsal turret like the P.92, a specification redrafted the following year as F.26/39. However, the project was dropped in October 1939.

Two new naval fighter specifications were also issued in 1939: F.8/39 for a fixed gun fighter, and F.9/39 for a new turret fighter, clearly to provide the Fleet Air

The cannon-fire selector box designed by Boulton Paul for the P.92 turret.

(1.5m) cannon barrel produced a greatly increased drag on the turret when revolved in the slipstream, an increase of up to 87 per cent at maximum speed. The standard turret's motor, which was still fitted, could not cope with this, and it would

Rivet failures on a section of the P.92 turret ring under test.

The SAMM AB.15 Hispano cannon mounting in a special nose position of an Overstrand.

Overstrand K8175, in the Boulton Paul flight shed with the AB.15 cannon mounting in the nose.

Arm with a rather more effective aircraft than the Roc. Blackburn naturally offered designs for both of these specifications: their B.33 project for N.8/39, and B-31 for N.9/39. Westland Aircraft offered a design with a single Bristol Taurus engine.

One of the few other designs submitted against the turret fighter specification was from Gloster, who offered a single-engine design with the basic Defiant/Roc layout, powered by either a Bristol Hercules or a Napier Sabre engine. A four-gun Frazer-Nash turret was sited immediately behind the pilot's cockpit. The Blackburn wing-folding mechanism as used on the Roc and Skua was adopted, reducing the overall width of the aircraft for stowage in a carrier hangar to 11ft (3.35m).

Both N.8/39 and N.9/39 resulted in only paper projects. They were combined the following year in a new specification for a two-seat naval fighter which would produce the Fairey Firefly. There were to be no more naval turret fighter specifications, so the Blackburn Roc was to be unique.

The Defiant prototype, K8310, at Boscombe Down, crudely camouflaged, and fitted with a standard turret adapted to take a single 20mm Hispano cannon; it was designated the Type F turret.

**Technical Information for the Gloster
F.9/39**

Dimensions
Span	50ft (15m)
Length	39ft 1in (11.9m)
Height	16ft 2in (4.9m)
Wing area	396sq ft (36.8sq m)
Loaded weight	10,000lb (4,540kg)

Performance
Top speed	321mph at 17,000ft
	(516kph at 5,180m)
Climb	2.2min to 5,000ft (1,525m)
	11.1min to 20,000ft (6,100m)
Endurance	6hr

A production Roc, L3158, outside the factory in March 1940. It later served with No. 771 Squadron at RNAS Hatston.

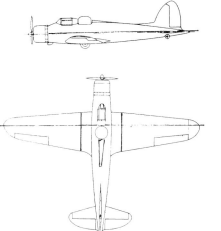

The Gloster F.9/39.

The Defiant prototype, K8310, being demonstrated at the Royal Aeronautical Society garden party in 1939.

By the outbreak of war, Boulton Paul had delivered just thirty-one Rocs and the solitary production Defiant, L6952, to the AFDU. This was shortly joined by L6951, and the two Defiants were then engaged in air fighting trials against, not bombers as might have been expected, but No. 111 Squadron's Hurricanes. It was not thought that the Defiant would ever face single-seat fighters in action, as they were designed to break up bomber formations attacking Great Britain, which was out of range of Germany's sole single-seat fighter the Bf 109. Thus the Defiant's predictably poor performance against the Hurricanes, with their much lower wing loading, and power loading, did not seem too important at the time.

More important trials took place at

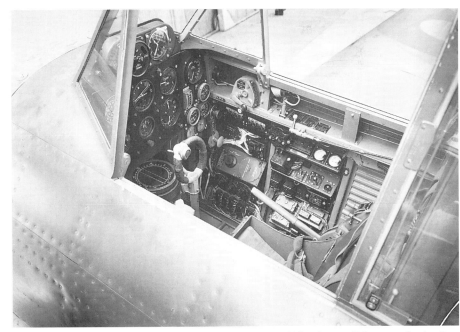

A Defiant cockpit, showing that the pilot had a gun button: he could fire the guns if they were fixed to fire forward.

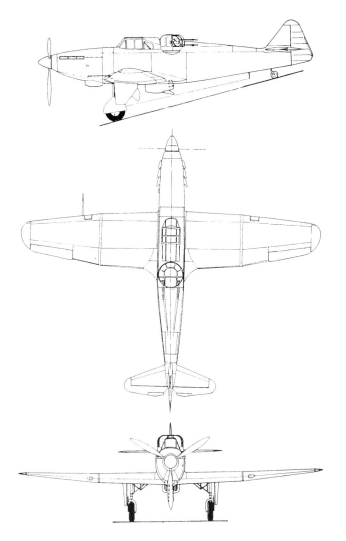

Defiant Mk I.

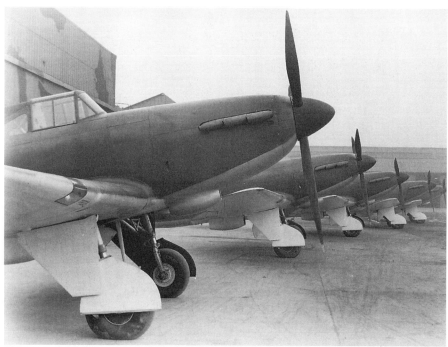

Boscombe Down on 20 September when the fourth production aircraft, L6953, was flown in mock combat with a Blenheim IV, the fastest bomber in RAF service. It was found that the Blenheim pilot could not lose the Defiant, no matter what drastic manoeuvres he undertook. By suddenly diving he could gain a respite, but once he levelled off the Defiant was able to pull alongside and then close in. The only difficulty the Defiant crew experienced was at very low altitude, where the pilot would have to lower a wing so that the gunner could bring his guns to bear. Boulton Paul technicians at Boscombe were able to give the guns 7 degrees of depression by losing 7 degrees of elevation, and this helped, but the final report indicated a preference for the guns to be able to bear as near as possible to the line of flight – in other words, so that the Defiant could make a conventional fighter attack.

It was clear that fighter pilots would be hard to shift from their conventional view of fighter tactics, which is why Spec. F.9/35 had specified no fixed forward-firing guns. It has been said that the Defiant was seen as a Hawker Demon replacement, but no Demon squadron was re-equipped with the new turret fighter. The Demon had been a stop-gap replacement for the single-seaters that had been unable to catch the Hart, and was replaced by the RAF's newest single-seaters, the Hurricane and the Spitfire.

The Demon, though fitted with the FN.1 turret, was not a 'turret fighter'. It was flown and fought like a single-seater, with conventional tactics. Entirely new tactics would have to be worked out for the operational use of the Defiant and Roc, possibly in conjunction with single-seaters, so that large bomber formations could be attacked from several directions at once, bringing a huge weight of fire to bear, while splitting the defensive fire. The unit entrusted with devising the new tactics would be No. 264 (Madras Presidency) Squadron, reformed at Sutton Bridge on 30 October 1939, as the first Defiant Squadron.

Production Defiants outside the factory just after the start of the war.

CHAPTER THREE

The Blackburn Roc in Service

As the war began, a number of Rocs went to training squadrons to prepare crews for their introduction to service. No. 758 FRU Telegraphist Air Gunners' Training Squadron at Eastleigh received its first in November 1939, and No. 774 Armament Training Squadron initially had three Rocs on a turret conversion course at Worthy Down, also from November 1939. In the same month No. 759 Fighter School and Pool Squadron at Eastleigh received the first of five Rocs.

As related previously, eight Rocs had gone to Worthy Down before the outbreak of war, five for No. 800 Squadron and three for 803 Squadron. These two squadrons had been equipped with Skuas earlier in the year, for service on the Navy's newest aircraft carrier, *Ark Royal*. The Rocs did not join the Skuas aboard the carrier, which operated in the North Sea just after war broke out. One of 803 Squadron's Skuas was the first British aircraft in the war to shoot down a German

aircraft, a Dornier Do 18 flying boat. The *Ark* then took her Skuas to the South Atlantic, leaving the Rocs to be reassigned to other units from Worthy Down, before the year's end. No Roc was ever deck-landed on a carrier, let alone served on one, though No. 769 FRU, the deck-landing training squadron, did have a Roc, L3114, from August to November 1940.

One of No. 803 Squadron's Rocs was lost on an operational patrol: on 23 October 1939, Plt Off L. R. Tregillis and Naval Artificer R. E. Eason took off on a fighter patrol over the sea, off Wick in Scotland in Roc L3063. They failed to return, reason unknown.

The only other two operational squadrons in the Fleet Air Arm to actually operate Rocs were two other Skua squadrons, Nos 801 and 806. Both had been re-equipped with Skuas before the war began, No. 801 Squadron aboard HMS *Furious* and No. 806 at Eastleigh.

No. 806 Squadron received five Rocs, L3101-3 and L3105-6 on 8 February 1940, with L3118 joining them during April. On 26 May the squadron was moved back to Worthy Down, and each day was moved forward from there to Detling, from where they gave cover to the Dunkirk operations as a fighter unit of Coastal Command. Their main role in these operations was the dive-bombing of German heavy coastal batteries. Tragically, on the first day of this operation three Skuas were mistaken for German aircraft by RAF Spitfires and shot down, though the crews managed to ditch the aircraft and were saved. By the end of June the squadron had given up its Rocs, and shortly afterwards its Skuas, and in July became a Fairey Fulmar squadron.

Five Rocs – L3117, L3128, L3135, L3160 and L3161 – joined 801 Squadron at Hatston in the Orkneys in June 1940, and the squadron was almost immediately moved to Worthy Down to replace No. 806, also operating from Detling in Kent to cover the Dunkirk evacuation, completed on 4 June. The squadron continued to operate across the Channel, and the

A production Roc, awaiting its first test flight at Pendeford just after the start of the war, with no guns as yet fitted to the turret.

A row of five production Rocs awaiting test flights, and showing two different camouflage styles. The first in the line is L3105, which first went to No. 806 Squadron at Worthy Down.

Head-on view of a production Roc, showing the split white/black camouflage used on the undersurfaces early in the war.

Sub Lt Stanley Gordon Orr with an 806 Squadron Roc probably at Detling, from which operations were flown over Dunkirk. He became one of the Fleet Air Arm's highest-scoring fighter pilots, with twelve victories by the end of the war.

Rocs must have been involved in this because one is reported to have been shot down during an attack on a gun battery at Cap Blanc Nez, near Calais on 21 June; Sqn Ldr A. V. M. Day and his gunner F. Berry were both killed.

Before two months were up, No. 801 Squadron had also given up its Rocs, and once again became an all-Skua unit. Thus the very short operational career of the Blackburn Roc was over. No. 801 Squadron continued to operate its Skuas until August 1941, when it acquired Sea Hurricanes. This was largely because the Skua was barely viable as a fighter aircraft, being far too slow and under-armed – and

the Roc was even slower, and was never any use at all as an operational aircraft. There were very few enemy aircraft that it could even catch – and yet steps were taken to adapt it for a role that made it even slower: as a floatplane fighter.

The Roc as Floatplane

As indicated earlier, the Roc was designed from the outset to operate from floats, as were many Fleet Air Arm aircraft up to that time. The first and third Rocs, L3057 and L3059, were sent to Blackburn Aircraft's factory at Dumbarton in October

1939 to be fitted with floats. These were adapted from the Blackburn Shark floats, Alclad units mounted on 'N' struts and a single front strut, with a spreader bar. The floats were equipped with water rudders operated by the aircraft's normal braking system. The wheel wells were covered over by metal plates.

In November 1939, L3059 was tested at Helensburgh where the M.A.A.E. had just moved from Felixtowe. Directional instability was found, and on 3 December the aircraft crashed just after take-off. The other aircraft was modified with an extra fin below the fuselage, and this greatly improved matters, making turns at low altitude far less hazardous. Another Roc, L3060, was also sent to Brough to be fitted with floats as a replacement for L3059, but there is some doubt that this was actually done, as it ended its days after a wheels-up landing at Farnborough in January 1940.

If the Roc was hopeless as a fighter in its normal form, with floats it was even worse. Its top speed was only 193mph (311kph) at 10,000ft (3,048m), and 170mph (273kph) at sea level; initial climb was 1,130ft/min (344m/min), and service ceiling 14,400ft (4,389m). The aircraft that the Roc floatplane might conceivably have faced in an operational environment was the Arado Ar.196 reconnaissance seaplane: this had similar performance, but with twin 20mm cannon amongst its armament, it would have been a deadly opponent.

No. 805 Squadron was formed at Donibristle in May 1940 to operate as a Roc seaplane fighter squadron, with a planned

Roc L3059, shortly after its conversion to a floatplane. It displayed directional instability and crashed.

complement of eighteen Rocs. After a Roc conversion course the squadron moved to Lee-on-Solent, but was then disbanded, after existing for only a few weeks.

Improving the Landplane Roc

Desperate attempts were made to improve the landplane Roc's performance by fitting a better propeller. An 11ft 6in (3.5m) diameter Skua unit was tried instead of the normal 12ft (3.7m) diameter de Havilland Type 5/8. With this, sea-level climb in fact deteriorated to 600ft/min (183m/min) from 710ft/min (216m/min), but it improved at 5,700ft (1,737m) from 830ft/min (253m/min) to 1,000ft/min (305m/min), and 1,900ft (579m) was added to the service ceiling. A special propeller with a Skua hub and the blades normally fitted to the Tiger engines of an Armstrong-Whitworth Whitley was also

tried, but this, too, was ineffective.

The majority of Rocs went straight to Fleet Requirements Units and training squadrons. As previously related, Boulton Paul had completed the stressing calculations for the redesign of the aircraft for target towing even before the first one had flown. Many Rocs were soon serving in this role, usually with the turret removed, while others served as targets for trainee fighter pilots, and ground gunners. This did not always preclude enemy action, as some of these units were in the line of fire during the Battle of Britain, such as No. 759 Fighter Pilot Training Squadron at Eastleigh, and No. 2 Anti-Aircraft Co-Operation Unit at Gosport.

Rocs in Combat

On 13 June 1940, L3146 of No. 2 AACU attacked an enemy aircraft over the

ranges, but with inconclusive results; however, it was hit by two bullets from return fire. This particular Roc had an eventful career, after this brief brush with the enemy. On 3 June 1942, operating at Roborough, it suffered a brake failure while taxiing and collided with a parked Fairey Battle. Then on 16 September 1942, landing at Detling, the tailwheel strut snapped off; and on 16 October while undertaking low-level photography over the Thames estuary an engine fire caused the pilot, Fl Lt D. W. Ashby, to ditch in the water. He and his observer, Fl Sgt Brown, were rescued.

On 16 August 1940, German Ju 87 dive bombers attacked Gosport and two Rocs, L3131 and L3162, were damaged in the attack, though both were later repaired. The commanding officer then sited four of his Rocs around the airfield with the turrets permanently manned as anti-aircraft posts, thus putting the Roc's lack of speed to its best advantage.

A Notable Engagement

A well known engagement involved a 2 AACU Roc, L3085, and Plt Off D. H. Clarke, who had painted a red 'Saint' (the Leslie Charteris character) in a red-framed yellow diamond on each side of the rear fuselage of his 'own' Roc. On 26 September he was sent out to search for survivors in the water 15 miles (24km) south-west of St Catherine's Point. With Sergeant Hunt in the gun turret – which, unusually for 2 AACU Rocs, was fully armed – he took off in the late afternoon. As he instituted a square search in the area indicated, he noticed what he thought was a Swordfish also searching about 3 miles (5km) away.

After about forty-five minutes of fruitless search in the gathering gloom, he suddenly noticed that the Swordfish, now only half a mile away, was in fact a twin-engined floatplane. Out of curiosity, wondering what it was, he flew towards it: and then suddenly realized it was a Heinkel He 59, a German aircraft probably on the same air-sea rescue task as himself. Unsure as to whether he should open fire on an aircraft on such a humanitarian mission, he flew across its nose with Hunt training his turret on it.

As he did so the German nose gunner opened fire with his 7.9mm machine gun, and Hunt returned fire, his tracer pouring into the Heinkel's fuselage. After the pandemonium and shock of his first action,

Roc L3084, later to undergo trials as a floatplane.

Clarke swung on a parallel course, and re-established communications with Hunt, whose intercom lead had been pulled out. The Heinkel turned for France, skimming the waves. Happily the twin-engined biplane was even slower than the Roc, with a top speed at sea level of only 137mph (220kph), and Clarke was able to gain on his adversary; although he was still faced with the problem of having to drop a wing to enable Hunt to open fire, even though his propeller was skimming the wave-tops.

At 300yd range he dropped a wing, and Hunt opened fire with another broadside. The Heinkel replied from all three gun positions, nose, dorsal and ventral, a single machine gun in each, but Clarke had to lift the wing after only a few seconds to avoid side-slipping into the sea, causing the last few rounds of Hunt's burst to shoot harmlessly up into the air. The two aircraft continued these brief exchanges of fire for about twenty-five minutes, until the coast of France was looming up. Both aircraft were hit, and one of the Heinkel's gunners stopped firing; but just as Clarke was about to turn away, the Roc was hit in the engine.

It faltered, and Clarke switched to the reserve 17gal (77ltr) tank, pulling up and away. Just as he thought he might have to ditch, the Perseus picked up, and he nursed the damaged aircraft back to Gosport. But before he could taxi in, the engine stopped, out of fuel. Clarke claimed the Heinkel as 'damaged'.
On his return his groundcrew found two incendiary bullets in the main fuel tank, above which he sat. They had entered low down in the petrol, which extinguished them; slightly higher, in the explosive fuel/air mixture above, and the Roc would have been 'missing in action'. This action was almost certainly the nearest the Blackburn Roc ever came to destroying a German aircraft in combat.

Rocs for Finland

The Roc almost found its way into the Finnish Air Force during the Winter War, fighting the Russians. When Russia invaded Finland on 30 November 1939, freed to act by Stalin's non-aggression pact with Hitler, there was a huge amount of sympathy in the West for the Finns. On the 21 February 1940, agreement in principle was reached to supply thirty Gladiators,

twenty-eight Gauntlets, twenty-four Blenheims, seventeen Lysanders, twelve Hurricanes and thirty-three Rocs. The French were also to supply a variety of aircraft.

The Blenheims of No. 600 Squadron had their newly installed AI radar stripped out, and the squadron was ordered to Finland. A total of twenty-three Blenheims actually reached Finland, one crashing on the way, and the thirty Gladiators were also delivered.

The Rocs began to assemble at Aston Down on 6 March, where they had Finnish markings applied, as well as their Finnish serials RO-118 to RO-150. They were to be delivered by air to Finland, with five scheduled to leave on the 9 March, and thereafter five every four days. By 9 March nine Rocs had left for Scotland, but had encountered bad weather and were stuck at Squires Gate, Blackpool. Already 3,000lb (1,360kg) of equipment for the Rocs had left Perth by air. By 12 March some of the Rocs had reached Dyce Airfield, Aberdeen, amongst them RO-143 and RO-150 – but it was too late.

The Finns fought a desperate defence of their country, inflicting humiliating reversals on the mighty Red Army; but by March 1940 the writing was on the wall, and on the 12th the Russo-Finnish Treaty was signed, ceding huge tracts of Finland to her aggressive neighbour. The Rocs had not been delivered in time, though it is hard to see that they would have greatly

affected the outcome. All the aircraft were returned to Fleet Requirements Units.

Rocs for the Anti-Aircraft Gunners

The Rocs' role was now to provide targets for the anti-aircraft gunners of His Majesty's ships and Fleet Air Arm fighters. The Fleet Requirements Unit that used the greatest number of Rocs was No. 771, based at Twatt and Hatson in the Orkney Islands, and serving the fleet at Scapa Flow. A total of forty-four Rocs were to pass through its hands, exactly twice as many as No. 776 at Speke, Woodvale and Stretton, serving the ships operating out of Liverpool, which only had a total of twenty-two Rocs. The other largest users were No. 759 FRU at Yeovilton and Eastleigh with twenty-one, and No. 772 FRU at Machrihanish in Argyl with twenty in all. A total of twenty-one United Kingdom-based Fleet Requirements Units operated at least one Roc during some point in their lifetime.

No. 2 Anti-Aircraft Co-Operation Unit at Gosport provided targets for anti-aircraft gunners on ships and land, right along the south coast. In this capacity it used a total of twenty-two Rocs at various times.

Life was not always easy flying low-level dummy attacks on anti-aircraft gun

A Fleet Requirements Unit Roc, converted to a target tug, with the observer's open cockpit where the turret used to be.

positions, or simulating the dive-bombing attacks of its cousin the Skua. A 2 AACU Roc, L3143, suffered an engine failure while climbing away after a simulated dive-bombing attack on Hayling Island, forcing Sgt B. St Travell to ditch in the sea, from where he was rescued. A 771 Squadron Roc from Twatt, L3159, suffered a similar fate: after a simulated diving bombing attack it suffered an engine failure, followed by a forced landing on Ronaldsway. Another 771 Squadron Roc, L3177, ditched in the sea after a destroyer shoot and engine failure. There were three men on board and they all perished.

Some Rocs seemed to suffer more than their fair share of accidents. One such was L3171, operating with 771 Squadron: for instance, on 20 October 1942 it hit a pile of sand when touching down at Twatt. Then on 16 June 1943 it was being taxied too fast with low brake pressure, and hit a parked Albacore; and on the 29th of the same month it was taxied into a parked lorry. Even transfer to 776 Squadron at Stretton did not improve its luck, and while taxiing at Speke on 26 October 1943 it ran into a van parked on the perimeter track. This accident was the final straw, and subsequently no one bothered to repair poor old L3171.

Rocs Abroad

Many of the Rocs served abroad with Fleet Requirements Units in the Carribean, Africa and the Middle East. In these areas they were all operated without their turrets, serving largely as target tugs. Eight Rocs found their way to Piarco in Trinidad, one of them being L3130 that had been force-landed at Squires Gate, in a storm, on its delivery flight back on 23 January 1940, and had overshot through a hedge. On its repair in May 1942 it was shipped to Trinidad, and while it was there it had a Walrus gun mounting fitted, for reasons unknown.

A dozen Rocs went to Dekheila in Egypt, and a couple to Wingfield in South Africa. No. 777 Fleet Requirements Unit in Freetown, Sierra Leone, had three Rocs, and flew these in formation for a photograph that has been reproduced many times. In Bermuda, some of the five Rocs that were delivered operated with either wheels or floats. The use of the floatplane version as a target tug was investigated at Helensburgh between March and

An FRU Roc, L3086, at Dekheila, Egypt.

September 1942, with L3174 fitted with floats, and with a wind-driven winch in place of the turret. There was a metal container carried under the fuselage containing the target sleeves.

Boulton Paul had delivered the last of the 136 Rocs on 19 August 1940, and there had, of course, been no more orders, not least because Boulton Paul needed the production capacity to produce large numbers of the far more successful Defiant.

Blackburn Roc Squadrons	
No.725 – Eglinton L3071, L3074, L3097, L3134, L3139	No. 770 – Crail L3062, L3088, L3118, L3131, L3152, L3171
No. 754 – Lee-on-Solent L3058	No. 771 – Twatt/Hatston L3062, L3071, L3073, L3074, L3077, L3078, L3079, L3080, L3083, L3085, L3087, L3089, L3091, L3093, L3096, L3097, L3098, L3104, L3118, L3121, L3128, L3139, L3141, L3142, L3150, L3151, L3152, L3153, L3156, L3158, L3159, L3165, L3166, L3167, L3170, L3171, L3174, L3177, L3178, L3185, L3186, L3187, L3190, L3192
No. 755 – Worthy Down L3165	
No. 757 – Worthy Down L3104	
No. 758 – Eastleigh L3091	
No. 759 – Yeovilton/Eastleigh L3061, L3070, L3073, L3075, L3092, L3094, L3095, L3097, L3104, L3109, L3113, L3114, L3115, L3117, L3118, L3135, L3136, L3142, L3150, L3155, L3159	No. 772 – Machrihanish L3062, L3071, L3073, L3074, L3080, L3083, L3084, L3093, L3097, L3102, L3110, L3114, L3121, L3124, L3129, L3135, L3142, L3149, L3156, L3159
No. 760 – Yeovilton L3099, L3100, L3105, L3109, L3111, L3121, L3125, L3139, L3140	No. 773 – Bermuda L3069, L3092, L3100, L3109, L3140
No. 761 – Yeovilton L3092	No. 774 – Aldergrove/St.Merryn L3061, L3065, L3066, L3067, L3076, L3090, L3138, L3140, L3164, L3169, L3176
No. 764 L3099	
No. 765 – Lee-on-Solent L3058, L3091	No. 775 – Dekheila, Egypt L3086, L3123, L3132, L3138, L3148, L3149, L3155, L3157, L3162, L3163, L3183, L3184
No. 767 – Arbroath L3078, L3135	No. 776 – Speke/Woodvale/Stretton L3058, L3066, L3075, L3078, L3080, L3087, L3117, L3118, L3119, L3124, L3150, L3160, L3164, L3167, L3169, L3171, L3174, L3175, L3178, L3189, L3190, L3192
No. 769 – Donibristle L3066, L3070, L3078, L3079, L3080, L3081	

Blackburn Roc Squadrons *continued*

No. 777 – Freetown, Sierra Leone
L3067, L3090, L3165

No. 778 – Lee-on-Solent/Arbroath
L3084, L3085, L3141, L3162

No. 782 – St.Merryn
L3071

No. 787 – Duxford
L3079

No. 789 – Wingfield, South Africa
L3127, L3141

No. 791 – Arbroath
L3062, L3071, L3092, L3093, L3118, L3129, L3134,
L3136, L3150, L3160, L3161

No. 792 – St.Merryn
L3064, L3065, L3075, L3079, L3094, L3110, L3113,
L3134, L3137, L3180

No. 793 – Piarco, Trinidad
L3076, L3106, L3116, L3125, L3130, L3163, L3176,
L3191

No. 800 Fighter Squadron – Worthy Down
L3061, L3064, L3065, L3066, L3067, L3068

No. 801 Fighter Squadron
L3117, L3128, L3135, L3160, L3161

No. 803 Fighter Squadron – Worthy Down
L3062, L3063, L3064, L3080, L3081, L3083, L3116

No. 805 Fighter Squadron – Donibristle
L3136, L3164

No. 806 Fighter Squadron – Donibristle
L3065, L3075, L3101, L3102, L3103, L3105, L3106,
L3118, L3154, L3156

No.2 Anti-Aircraft Co-Operation Unit – Gosport
L3062, L3071, L3072, L3075, L3082, L3085, L3089,
L3108, L3109, L3126, L3127, L3129, L3131, L3143,
L3146, L3149, L3162, L3172, L3173, L3175, L3179,
L3190

A formation of three Rocs from RNAS Donibristle in November 1939. That coded 'E' is L3114, and 'O' is L3118.

A Blackburn Roc fitted with a 70gal (3201) ferry tank beneath the centre-section.

A Roc target tug, L3086, at Dekheila in Egypt.

54

CHAPTER FOUR

The Defiant Day Fighter

The squadron entrusted with bringing the Defiant into service was No. 264 (Madras Presidency) Squadron, that re-formed at Sutton Bridge on 30 October 1939 under the command of Sqn Ldr Stephen Hardy. The squadron had flown Short Type 184 seaplanes during World War I, but was dissolved shortly afterwards.

To begin with, No. 264 had no Defiants, and had to make do with a few Miles Magisters, three of which – N3857, N3867 and N3868 – arrived on 8 November. These were augmented with a few Fairey Battles until the first three Defiants – L6959, L6960 and L6961 – arrived on 9 December, with six more arriving by the end of the year. Many of the pilots were new to monoplanes with retractable undercarriages, and this period gave them a chance to get used to such modern features.

Take, for instance, Plt Off Eric Barwell, an RAFVR pilot: he arrived on 20 December, but Sqn Ldr Hardy advised him that he needed more training, and he was sent to No. 12 Group Fighter Pool at Aston Down for a month of flying Harvards. On his return he was taken up by A Flight commander Flt Lt Nicholas Cooke for a couple of flights in a Magister, and then one flight in a Battle. After a flight in the Defiant gun turret with Cooke at the controls, he was finally let loose in the new fighter.

By the end of the year, fourteen pilots had flown the Defiant solo, and twelve of these were deemed competent; the other two were assigned to more practice-flying on Battles. When the gunners arrived, the first thing that was done was to split them into two groups, those over and those under 5ft 8in (1.7m) tall, to determine how comfortable the turret could be made. The parasuit designed for the Defiant gunner meant that the seat-back padding could be removed, which improved the amount of room he had by a couple of inches.

A high proportion of the air gunners were New Zealanders trained at the Air Observer's School at Ohakea in New Zealand. At the time, many of the air gunners were only leading aircraftmen or corporals; the order to make all aircrew at least sergeants did not come until the end of May 1940.

The squadron had moved to Martlesham Heath on 7 December and, as with most new aircraft, the Defiant suffered various teething troubles. First, the Merlin engine was still not entirely reliable, and despite the change to Lockheed units, there continued to be problems with the hydraulic system. The whole squadron was grounded for a week on 28 January, while Rolls-Royce and Lockheed technicians sorted them out.

Trials and Training

During these first few months the squadron learned how to operate their new aircraft, forming pilot/gunner teams, practising the formation flying that was essential to the turret-fighter concept, and firing at targets in the Wash. On 15 February, the first night-flying training began, the turret fighter having been envisaged as a night fighter as much as a day fighter from the outset. Barwell was to fly a leisurely eight hours during February, but this was to increase the following month when Hardy was replaced as CO by Sqn Ldr Phillip Hunter. Born in Chesham, Hunter had joined the RAF in 1931, and in February 1933 was posted to No. 6 Squadron in Ismailia, which was then just changing its Bristol F.2B fighters for Fairey Gordons. On his return to the UK he joined the RAF College Cranwell, and then moved to the Central Flying School in Upavon in March 1937. It was Hunter who set about devising tactics for No. 264 Squadron to use on operations.

At Northolt they had already tried flying a section of three Defiants against Blenheims from No. 25 Squadron, and formulated a scheme for a Defiant squadron to attack simultaneously from each flank and from below, in sections of four aircraft.

Sqn Ldr Phillip Hunter leading A Flight of No. 264 Squadron in Defiant N1535.

did not let his speed drop below 160mph (257kph). He had his squadron practise a defensive circle, or a spiral down to low level, for those occasions when they might be attacked by a large force of Bf 109s, something which did not seem very likely at the time, because German single-seaters were out of range, and there was no apparent likelihood of the Defiants being sent to France.

The squadron also practised dive bombing and ground strafing at Orfordness, a role for which the aircraft was equipped, with light duty bomb racks, but which nonetheless seemed to be contrary to the basic concept of the turret fighter. Clearly the design had been seen as a possible army co-operation aircraft, and in January 1940 one Defiant, L6968, was sent for trials with the School of Army Co-operation at Odiham.

The Lysander was the standard army co-operation aircraft and represented the accepted thinking of the time, of low speed, short landing and good visibility. Before the rude awakening of the Blitzkrieg, when the Lysander's terrible vulnerability over the front line was exposed, the higher speed and better defensive armament of the Defiant was obviously being considered.

The six Defiants of No. 264 Squadron's A Flight, which undertook the Defiant's first successful operational sortie, over Holland.

The Squadron is Operational

In mid-March 1940, No. 264 Squadron was declared operational. Then based at Wittering, they operated forward detachments to Bircham Newton, for convoy patrols. During the same month No. 141 Squadron at Grangemouth, up to then equipped with Blenheim IFs, received their first Defiants. By the end of May they were fully equipped with their new aircraft and began working up as the second Defiant squadron, many of their aircraft being delivered to them by No. 264 Squadron pilots.

Deliveries from Boulton Paul had been slow to build up, with only six in December, despite a labour force of 2,900 and two shifts operating. Of course they were also building Blackburn Rocs at the rate of sixteen per month, and were facing mounting difficulties with gun-turret production: every time they increased their productive capacity, new orders for turrets would come in. These had been received for the Lockheed Hudson, the forthcoming Handley Page Halifax and the Armstrong-

One of the Defiants used, L6951, had come from the Central Flying School, and the other two directly from Boulton Paul.

No. 264 Squadron now became involved in tactical trials, five aircraft moving to Martlesham Heath and Northolt, thus enabling Hunter to lead a section of four Defiants against various bombers. Six Hampdens from Nos 49 and 144 Squadrons, and three Blenheims from 604 Squadron provided the targets, and later Wellingtons also joined in. The aim was to find the best way to attack various bombers, and to work out a tactical plan.

They came up with three distinct attack plans: overtaking on a parallel course, converging on a beam attack, or diving across the noses of a bomber formation – the latter had to be from at least 1,000ft (300m) above to help the Defiant's poor acceleration. Hunter still believed the best Defiant section would be three aircraft, the standard RAF section, which was handier to operate than four, and could still be split either side of a bomber. The squadron practised the various attacks, co-ordinating approaches from different directions to split the defensive fire of a bomber formation, while bringing all the weight of fire of No. 264's gunners to bear at the same time. With practice, synchronized attacks were found to be quite easy.

There remained the problem of what tactics to utilize if the Defiants were faced by Bf 109 fighters. To investigate how the aircraft handled against a single-seater, Hunter arranged with Fg Off Stanford Tuck of No. 65 Squadron to attack in his Spitfire at any point as Hunter flew his Defiant on a steady course from Northolt to White Waltham. Tuck bounced the Defiant, and a turning fight ensued that lasted ten minutes.

During the dogfight Hunter's gunner expended all his cine gun film; he was often able to fire at the Spitfire across the arc of the turning circle, whereas Tuck, on the other hand, never had the chance to bring his guns to bear, and did not expend any cine gun film. On one occasion Hunter even managed to get on the tail of the Spitfire and slightly below, so that his gunner could fire.

This showed Hunter that in a turning fight the Defiant could defend itself against single-seaters, provided the pilot

The light duty bomb-racks fitted beneath the wing of a Defiant.

A Defiant being tested with bomb-racks; however, they were never used in action.

The three Boulton Paul test pilots mainly responsible for Defiant testing: left to right: Robin Lindsay Neale, Colin Evans, and chief test pilot, Cecil Feather.

Whitworth Albermarle. A new turret factory was under construction, integral with the rest of the main building at Pendeford.

At the start of the war, George Skelton was recalled from his duties as assistant test pilot and rejoined the RAF, being transferred to No. 264 Squadron as B Flight commander. His place was taken by Robin Lindsay Neale, a well known pilot in the light aircraft community during the 1930s, and a director and pilot for Dart Aircraft. He had joined the RAF at the start of the war, and from 23 October until 18 December flew Rapides and Ansons from Bagington. He was released to take up the post of assistant to Cecil Feather on 1 January 1940. He had his first flight in a Roc, in L3136 with Skelton, on the 3 January, and soloed the following day. His first flight in a Defiant, also with Skelton in L6969, was on the 9th. He was a skilled and flamboyant pilot, well liked by everyone in the company.

Joining the company at the same time was Flt Lt Colin Evans, who had completed a short service commission with the RAF and then become a flying instructor. He served as a test pilot with Boulton Paul until joining Fairey Aviation as a test pilot in 1942. He was killed in 1945 when test-flying a Fairey Firefly.

A further 150 Defiants were ordered in December, and another fifty would be added in February, making the total 650 on order. With production considerably behind schedule, it was suggested that Reid & Sigrist at Desford could open a second assembly line. This suggestion fell through, literally, when the hangar designated for Defiant assembly was destroyed when the weight of snow on the roof caused it to collapse. Instead, Reid & Sigrist became the main centre for the overhaul and repair of Defiants.

As the Defiant was an aircraft bolted together from different sub-assemblies, it was very easy to subcontract its various components, and orders were placed for different parts of it with Redwing Aircraft (who bought a factory in Heath Town, Wolverhampton, to make fuselages), Rollasons, Aero Engines Ltd, Daimler Cars, Northern Aircraft and many others. A proposal had been made to bring Boulton

Colin Evans test-flying a production Defiant, N1650. Destined never to serve as a day fighter, this Defiant went to No. 256 Squadron as a night fighter in November 1940.

Paul into a consortium to build thirty of the new Bristol Beaufighters a month, but this was dropped in favour of letting them sort out Defiant production. Eventually all turret production was handed over to Joseph Lucas, and the new turret factory was integrated into airframe production, allowing the company to concentrate on airframe production and gun-turret development.

Further development of the Defiant had been considered even before the war began, and on 31 January 1940 it was agreed that two standard Defiants on the production line – N1550 and N1551 – be fitted with the 1,390hp Merlin XX engine and extra fuel tanks to increase endurance. These would serve as prototypes for a new Mark II Defiant. The initial batch of eighty-seven production aircraft had been fitted with a two-speed propeller, but on 22 April the first constant speed propeller was tested on a Defiant for the first time and,

as it greatly improved climb performance, it was fitted to subsequent aircraft.

Sqn Ldr Hunter had arrived at the factory on 11 April hoping to test this aircraft, but it was not yet ready. He did take the opportunity to complain about the retracting rear wireless mast, which was snapping off at the rate of one a day because it did not retract when the wheels were lowered, and hit the ground on touchdown. When he left Wittering there were only three Defiants with an intact rear mast. An investigation was instituted by the company.

Into Battle

On the 10 May 1940 the balloon went up as the Germans launched their attack on the Low Countries and France. No. 264 Squadron was moved to Duxford, and on the 12th, 'A' Flight took part in the type's

first offensive fighter sweep. They refuelled at Horsham St Faith, near Norwich, and along with a flight of six Spitfires from No. 66 Squadron were then ordered to cross the North Sea and to attack the many German aircraft that were believed to be operating over Holland. Sqn Ldr Hunter was leading the flight, which took off at 13.10hr, with his gunner LAC King in L6973. The other crews in his Red Section were: Plt Off Whitehouse/Sgt Smalley (L6972), and Plt Off Young/LAC Johnson (L7003); Flt Lt Cooke/Cpl Lippett (L6975) led Yellow Section with Plt Off Barwell/Sgt Quinney (L6964), and Plt Off Whitley/LAC Turner (L6970). They patrolled in the area of the Hague, but did not see the hordes of German aircraft they expected, apart from a large number of Junkers Ju 52 transports bogged down on an airfield near Rotterdam.

Eventually they sighted a Junkers Ju 88 attacking three ships. As the Ju 88 dived

Line of five production Defiants at Pendeford. The first two, L6969 and L6965, went to B Flight, No. 264 Squadron, and were both shot down over Holland on 13 May 1940.

for the coast, the Spitfires attacked from the rear, while the Defiants of Red Section instituted a standard cross-over attack in front of the bomber, raking it with fire as they went by. This was just the kind of co-ordinated attack that had been envisaged for the Defiant against single-seaters, and the Ju 88 was set on fire and crashed with a dull explosion in a field full of Dutch cows. A solitary Heinkel He 111 was now seen by Yellow Section, and they, too, made a standard cross-over attack ahead of the bomber, as the other Spitfire section attacked from the rear. After this second co-ordinated attack the Heinkel crashed into a field.

The flight crossed back over the North Sea and landed back at Horsham St Faith at around 15.35hr, all of them very low on fuel. Boulton Paul Aircraft sent a telegram to the squadron, congratulating them on 'drawing first blood'.

The following day B Flight, led by Flt Lt George Skelton, again with six Spitfires from No. 66 Squadron, took off from Horsham at 4.15am, hoping to repeat the success.

Air Battle Over Holland: 13 May 1940

Flt Lt George Skelton, leading B Flight, 264 Squadron, was flying as Blue One in Defiant L6969 with Plt Off Hatfield as his gunner. Blue Two was Plt Off Thomas/LAC Bromley, and Blue Three was Plt Off Chandley/LAC McLeish. Leading Green Section was Plt Off Greenhous with Sgt Greenhalgh as his gunner. Green Two was Plt Off McLeod/LAC Cox, and Green Three was Plt Off Kay/LAC Jones. Flt Lt Gillies was leading 'A' Flight of 66 Squadron.

They were ordered to patrol in the area Ijmuidan and the Hague, and crossed the North Sea in Vics of three, with the Spitfires leading. They crossed the Dutch coast at Ijmuiden at about 6,000ft (1,800m). A Dutch anti-aircraft gun in the harbour opened accurate fire. They flashed the Dutch letter of the day and the fire ceased, but they might just have been out of range. They flew towards Rotterdam, which was blazing, with smoke rising from several separate fires,

At 5.45am they saw seven Junkers Ju 87s dive-bombing a railway, and Gillies led the Spitfires into the attack. Skelton formed the Defiants into line astern, and followed the Spitfires down. As they joined in the fray they saw one of the Ju 87s fire red parachute flares, which they took to be a signal they were under attack. Skelton's gunner, Plt Off Hatfield, saw a Ju 87 on their tail firing with its two front guns from a distance of only 50yd. He called for Skelton to bank, but got no

response. Another Ju 87 appeared on their tail, this time accompanied by a Bf 109 that riddled the Defiant with cannon and machine-gun fire.

Around twenty-seven Bf 109s had come to the assistance of the dive bombers. Hatfield shot down the first Ju 87, and as the Defiant went into a spiral dive, the other Ju 87 followed them. The dive became a spin, and Hatfield assumed that Skelton had been killed. He struggled out through the back of the turret, even though only one of the doors was open, a feat of agility that owed much to the amount of adrenalin in his system. He parachuted down into some water in an area covered with dykes and river channels.

Skelton was not dead, however. He had been hit in the arm and legs, and had in fact ordered Hatfield to bale out, though his gunner had not heard him. He then pulled off a successful crash-landing. He was hauled from the aircraft by the Germans, and taken to hospital with severe injuries.

Plt Off Thomas had followed Skelton down, and flew his Defiant into position for his gunner to shoot down a Ju 87: it fell away out of control. He then manoeuvred onto the front quarter of another Ju 87, which his gunner hit, and it, too, fell away. Straightaway after, Thomas saw a flock of Bf 109s coming in to the attack; he heard LAC Bromley give a cheer, and assumed he had hit one of them – but then their Defiant was hit by cannon and machine-gun fire, and there was silence from the turret. The starboard wing was on fire, the instrument panel had been hit, and part of the control column shot away. Thomas lost control for a while, but then managed to turn the Defiant upside down, which was a signal to bale out. He slid back the hood and parachuted down; but there was no further sign of Bromley. He landed in some tall reeds on an island, and while he was still lying on his back he saw a Defiant explode in mid-air. Afterwards he assumed this must have been Blue Three, Chandler and McLeish's aircraft, shot down by the Bf 109s.

Leading Green Section, Plt Off Greenhous was attacked by Bf 109s flying in line astern before he could get near the Ju 87s. His gunner hit one and it burst into flames, going down on fire. Greenhalgh then fired at the next Bf 109, and it, too, went down, apparently out of control. At that moment the Defiant was hit by cannon fire, one shell exploding in the cockpit, injuring

Pilot Officer Greenhous/Sgt Greenhalgh's Defiant L6977 crash-landed in the midst of a German Army unit in Holland on 13 May 1940.

Pilot Officer Chandler/LAC McLeish's Defiant, L6960, shot down over Holland on 13 May 1940.

followed Greenhous down, and attacked a Ju 87. His gunner managed to deliver several bursts, mostly from above, and the dive bomber went down in flames. They were then attacked from behind by a Bf 109, and MacLeod pulled the Defiant in a steep turn to starboard. After bursts of fire from both sides, LAC Cox reported that all four of his guns were jammed. MacLeod evaded attack for a few moments while Cox got two of the guns working.

MacLeod then noticed a Defiant with two fighters on its tail, probably that of Greenhous and Greenhalgh, and turned to their assistance, but they were then attacked themselves. MacLeod once more pulled into a tight turn, but this time he let his speed drop too much and he went into a high-speed stall, falling away into a spin. As he recovered from the spin he noticed that both wings of the Defiant were ablaze. Cox also reported that all his guns were out of action again, so MacLeod pulled off a forced landing, luckily in Dutch-held territory.

Green Three was Plt Off Kay, and in the initial attack on the Ju 87s he found himself a little left behind, possibly because he did not hear a radio instruction from Skelton. He was flying in the flight's reserve aircraft, L6934, which had to be brought out at 4am because his own was unserviceable: there had not been time to undertake a circuit to tune the radio, something necessary on the Defiant because the aerial had different characteristics when the rear mast was retracted. He quickly lost sight of the other Defiants, but did follow one of 66 Squadron's Spitfires for a while. He saw one of the Ju 87s and pulled into a suitable firing position for his gunner LAC Jones, with it on his port rear quarter. Jones opened fire, but all his guns soon jammed.

Kay climbed to 4,000ft (960m) and watched the action below as Jones cleared the guns. Kay noticed around twelve Ju 87s bombing the village of Gravendeel. He dived down and attempted once more to get one of the dive bombers on his rear port quarter, but he had to slow down so much that the other Ju 87s were able to drive him away, and Jones reported that he was having trouble revolving the turret because the hydraulic motor was damaged. He climbed away, and having only thirty gallons of fuel left, set course for Knocke in Belgium. Somewhere over Flushing he was overtaken by Flt Off Brown in one of the 66 Squadron Spitfires: he watched him land on the bombed airfield, but Brown

Greenhous in the hand, another putting the turret out of action. The starboard wing was also on fire, and so Greenhous rocked the aircraft from side to side, their pre-arranged signal to bale out. There was no sign of his gunner, and in case he was wounded and unable to get out, Greenhous decided to attempt a crash-landing.

Flying as Green Two, Plt Off MacLeod

Unfortunately they came down in the middle of a German infantry unit. Neither Greenhous nor Greenhalgh was injured, and the two scrambled from the aircraft and ran for it; but they were soon caught by an officer on a motorbike, and taken prisoner.

then turned over when a main tyre burst. Kay followed him down, refuelled, and flew back to England.

Plt Off MacLeod and his gunner LAC Cox, and Plt Off Thomas, were all able to evade capture with the help of the Dutch, and returned to England in a destroyer from the Belgian port of Ghent. Flt Off Skelton and his gunner were captured, as were Greenhous and Greenhalgh. Skelton's injuries were so severe that he was repatriated to England in 1943, via Sweden. He returned to the Royal Air Force, and retired in 1959 with the rank of Air Commodore.

Defiants in Action 13 May 1940

L6969	Flt Lt G. Skelton	Captured
	Plt Off Hatfield	Captured
L6958	Plt Off Thomas	Evaded
	LAC Bromley	Died
L6960	Plt Off Chandler	Died
	LAC MacLeish	Died
L6977	Plt Off Greenhous	Captured
	Sgt Greenhalgh	Captured
L6965	Plt Off MacLeod	Evaded
	LAC Cox	Evaded
L6974	Plt Off Kay	Returned
	LAC Jones	Returned

The air battle over Holland on 13 May against the Ju 87s and their escorting Bf 109s, cost five Defiants shot down, three aircrew killed and four captured. No. 264 squadron claimed four Ju 87s and a Bf 109 shot down. No. 66 squadron claimed one Ju 87 shot down. In fact the Luftwaffe lost just four Ju 87s in the engagement. In an uncontrolled melée the Defiants had come off worse; they had shown their ability to shoot down the dive bombers, perhaps with even greater effectiveness that the Spitfires, but when the Bf 109s intervened the Defiants had not been able to defend themselves without mutual support. They had already split up to attack the Stukas, and had no time to reform.

The Luftwaffe was able to examine the two Defiants that had pulled off forced landings and stayed reasonably intact, but in fact the layout of the turret fighter held no surprises for them. Both the Defiant and the Roc had appeared at the Royal Aeronautical Society's Garden Party on the 14 May 1939, at Fairey Aviation's Great West Aerodrome. Cecil Feather had demonstrated the Defiant in poor weather, and photographs of the aircraft, together with technical descriptions, appeared in German aeronautical magazines. The Luftwaffe already knew all about the Defiant and what to expect from its four-gun turret.

The following day it was the turn of A Flight once more, who took off from Martlesham Heath for a further patrol over Holland. But A Flight were recalled as they crossed the Suffolk coast because the Dutch had capitulated.

The Squadron Moves to Manston

No. 264's B Flight had been decimated, and over the next eleven days replacement aircraft and aircrew were drafted in. With the British Army in France retreating into the Dunkirk pocket, the squadron moved from Duxford to Manston on the Kent coast on the 23 May, and flew their first patrol over Dunkirk, Calais and Boulogne that afternoon. During the patrol seven Bf 110s were seen, and one dived as if to attack the Defiants; but before it came within range it broke away, as if the pilot had thought better of it. The squadron flew another patrol in the evening, along with two Hurricane squadrons, but again no contact with the enemy was made.

Patrols Over Dunkirk

During the following afternoon No. 264 flew another patrol over Dunkirk, and on this occasion got into action. Flt Lt E. H.

Whitehouse/Plt Off H. Scott flying Defiant L6972 shot down a Bf 110. In a second patrol they saw a Ju 88 and took up the chase, but Sqn Ldr Hunter called it off when he thought the bomber was leading them towards a concentration of anti-aircraft fire.

On the 25 May, morning and afternoon patrols were flown over the Dunkirk to Boulogne area, but although enemy aircraft were seen, there was no action. On the 26th, the squadron patrolled over a French ammunition convoy near Calais, but no enemy aircraft appeared. Red Section saw a concentration of German tanks and vehicles and dived to investigate; there was intense anti-aircraft fire, but no hits. In the afternoon there was another patrol, but the weather was grey and overcast and there were no enemy aircraft in action.

On 27 May, another patrol made a sortie directly over the Dunkirk beaches, taking off at 08.30hr. Early on they were attacked by some Bf 109s and shot down two, without loss to themselves; they then sighted a formation of twelve Heinkel He 111s. In a co-ordinated squadron attack, the Defiants shot down three of the bombers and claimed two more damaged; the rest then scattered.

And so the Defiant proved itself in the exact role for which it had been designed, as a bomber destroyer. Taking an hour to refuel and re-arm, they took off for a second patrol. They saw a solitary Junkers Ju

No. 264 Squadron air gunners (apart from Sgt Thorn) around 29 May 1940. Left to right, back row: Cpl Lippert, LAC Turner, LAC Barker, LAC Johnson, LAC Hayden, ?, LAC Lillie; front row: Sgt Thorn, LAC King, ?, Plt Off Williams, ?, LAC Cox.

88 and attacked, without noticeable success, as it made its escape.

The following day the squadron set out for Dunkirk, once more from its forward base at Manston; this time only ten aircraft were able to take off. About halfway over the Channel they were attacked by thirty or so Bf 109s, and Sqn Ldr Hunter called his aircraft into the defensive circle they had practised so often: like this, from whichever direction the Messerschmitts attacked, they were faced with defensive fire from several turrets. Six of the Bf 109s were claimed as being destroyed, but in all, they picked off three of the Defiants. One of the missing crews was Plt Off MacLeod and Plt Off Hatfield, who had been shot down on 13 May, but evaded capture. This time there was to be no return, and they and Sgt Daisley/LAC Revill, and Flt Lt Whitehouse/Plt Off Scott were lost.

If 13 May had shown that the Defiant would struggle in a general melée with Bf 109s, the squadron now showed that if they adopted co-ordinated defensive tactics, they could defend themselves against a large force of single-seaters. They were also confident that they could inflict severe losses on unescorted bombers. On the following day, 29 May, they were to emphasize both these things, in what was to become the most famous day in the story of the turret fighter.

An Historic Day: 29 May 1940

At 14.45hr on 29 May 1940 Sqn Ldr Hunter took off with eleven other Defiants and headed for the Dunkirk pocket. They were flying at about 6,000ft (1,800m) with three Hurricane squadrons – 56, 151 and 213 – flying above them. As they approached Dunkirk they were most aware of the great column of smoke rising from the harbour, and the many ships in the Channel below them. The Hurricanes began to engage some Bf 110s escorting some Ju 87s.

Six Bf 109s dived on the Defiants, coming out of the sun in the classic fighter tactic. Hunter saw them coming, but for the time being kept his four Vics of three flying in line astern. As the first Bf 109 came within 300yd, Hunter's gunner, LAC King, opened fire, and it soon burst into flames. As the other Bf 109s shot overhead, Plt Off Welch's gunner, LAC Hayden, hit one and it fell away out of control. The crews of Plt Off Young/LAC Johnson

No. 264 Squadron aircrew in the summer of 1940.

and Flt Lt Cooke/Cpl Lippett each also sent Bf 109s down in flames, the latter shot down right off the tail of another Defiant – probably that of Plt Off Kay/LAC Jones. His Defiant (L6957) was badly hit in the attack, the hydraulics being damaged and the starboard aileron and turret hit; and LAC Jones must have been under the impression that the aircraft was lost, because he baled out. Kay, however, was in fact able to return to Manston and land successfully. Jones' body was later washed up on a French beach.

Eric Barwell's gunner Plt Off Williams also fired on a Bf 109 attacking Kay's Defiant, and saw it going down in flames; this was probably the same aircraft claimed by Young's gunner. Although the squadron believed it had shot down five of the six attacking Bf109s, it seems likely that the true score was four or even fewer. It was an inherent problem with the Defiant that different gunners could be firing at the same target from different directions, and all claimed it destroyed when it fell.

Hunter now saw a Heinkel He 111 approaching Dunkirk and turned to attack

it – but then he saw an even juicier target, a formation of Ju 87s. Sergeant Thorn/LAC Barker saw an isolated Ju 87 and broke away to attack: the Stuka did not see them coming, and was shot down with a burst of fire. Thorn rejoined the squadron as they turned to attack the main force of Ju 87s, but the dive bombers' escort of Bf 110s dived on the Defiants. Hunter ordered the squadron into a line astern spiral dive, and as the German twin-engined fighters attacked, they were always faced with accurate fire from the Defiants' turrets. Six of the Defiant crews claimed the destruction of a Bf 110, Plt Off Stokes and his gunner claiming two. More Bf 109s joined in the frantic battle, and three more of these were also claimed.

Hunter led his men back to Manston, where they landed cock-a-hoop, though their elation was inevitably modified by the news that the thirty-one-year-old Canadian gunner, LAC Jones, was missing. They claimed a total of seventeen fighters shot down, plus the odd Stuka. Refuelled and re-armed, they took off for a second patrol at 18.55hr, Plt Off Kay in a replacement aircraft, L6961, and with a new gunner, LAC Cox.

Once more they had Hurricane squadrons flying above them, and this time the Hurricanes kept the Bf 109s off their backs. Hunter saw large numbers of Ju 87s approaching the beaches from all directions, and wisely did not try to follow them down in their bombing dives, but went to low level to wait for them to pull out. The Defiants then eagerly closed in on the slower Stukas, pouring accurate fire into one aircraft after another, and sending them crashing into the sea. Ten of the crews were able to claim Ju 87s destroyed, four of them two Ju 87s, and Flt Lt Cooke and his gunner an incredible five. It was a massacre, the slow Ju 87s almost sitting ducks at low level, and the Defiants able to take up position on each in turn, slightly below so that their gunners could shoot them down at will.

With the Stukas shot from the skies, the Defiants closed on some Ju 88s, sending one down in flames with their combined fire, and damaging another. They turned for home nearly out of ammunition, and landed having experienced an incredible day's fighting. They claimed thirty-seven German aircraft shot down, and three more probables, the only loss being of one gunner, and Sgt Thorn's Defiant that overshot while landing at Manston with leaking fuel tanks and only one wheel. Flt Lt Nicholas Cooke/Cpl Albert Lippett had claimed an incredible eight victories in one afternoon: three Bf 109s and five Ju 87s.

It was the best day a British fighter squadron has ever had, and many myths have grown around it. Wg Cdr Harry Broadhurst, the station commander at Wittering, but who happened to be at Manston when they landed, was the first to suggest that the Germans had mistaken them for Hurricanes, and therefore attacked from the rear. This ignores the fact that more than half the victories claimed that day were bombers, and it was the Defiants doing the attacking. It also ignores the fact that when they were attacked by fighters in the first sortie, the squadron adopted its proven defensive tactic, a spiral dive, and it did not matter which direction the Germans came from, they faced accurate, defensive fire.

Of course, as already seen, there is little doubt that No. 264 Squadron unintentionally over-claimed. More than one gunner claimed the same aircraft destroyed, though without realizing it, and many of the German aircraft were not actually destroyed. Over-claiming is a feature of all air fighting. Nevertheless, it was clear that the Defiant had had a good day, and back at the Boulton Paul factory, newspaper accounts of the day were soon pinned on notice boards with the words 'Our work' scrawled across them. Nicholas Cooke, who had claimed eight aircraft and a share in the Ju 88, that day told one newspaper reporter: 'It was like knocking apples off a tree.'

By 20.22hr on 29 May 1940, No. 264 squadron had claimed eight Bf 109s, seven Bf 110s, one Ju 88 and twenty-one Ju 87s shot down, for the loss of one gunner killed, and one aircraft crash-landed back at Manston. Their reward was a host of publicity photographs, and by the end of May a clutch of medals. Sqn Ldr Hunter received the DSO, and there was also a DFC for Flt Lt Nicholas Cooke, who, with his gunner Cpl Lippett, had shot down eight aircraft in one day; there were also four DFMs for non-commissioned members of the squadron, Corporal Lippett, Sgt E.R. Thorn, LAC F.J. Barker, and LAC F.H. King.

Final Sorties

On 31 May the Defiants were back in action, taking off at 14.00hr and crossing the French coast at 10,000ft (3,000m) around 14.20hr. With the Hurricanes of 213 Squadron at 15,000ft, and the Spitfires of 609 Squadron above them at 20,000ft (6,000m), Hunter saw a large formation of around seventy Bf 109s at altitude, and about twenty Heinkel He 111s approaching from the south-east. He turned towards the bombers, but they jettisoned their bombs and scattered.

Hunter saw the Bf 109s coming down out of the sun, and called the squadron into a defensive circle. His gunner, LAC King, gave one Bf 109 a burst, and it spun

Defiants in Action, 29 May 1940		
L6956	Sgt R. A. Thorn LAC F. Barker	2 x Ju 87, Bf 110, share Ju 88
L6957	Plt Off D. H. S. Kay LAC E. J. Jones	
L6961	Plt Off D. H. S. Kay LAC Cox	Ju 87 probable
L6964	Plt Off T .D. Welsh Sgt L. H. Hayden	Bf 109, Bf 110, 2 x Ju 87
L6967	Plt Off M. H. Young LAC S. B. Johnson	Bf 109, Bf 110, Bf 110 shared 2 x Ju 87 shared, Ju 88 shared
L6968	Plt Off G. L. Hickman LAC A. Fidler	
L6970	Plt Off G. H. Hackwood LAC P. Lillie	Bf 109, Bf 110, Bf 110 shared Ju 87, 2 x Ju 87 shared
L6972	Sgt A. J. Lauder Sgt.Wise	Ju 87 probable
L6973	Sqn Ldr P.A. Hunter LAC F. King	Bf 109, Bf 110, Ju 87
L6975	Fg Off R. W. Stokes Sgt Fairbrother	2 x Bf 110, Ju 87
L7004	Plt Off D. Whitley Sgt R. C. Turner	Ju 87
L7005	Flt Lt N. Cooke Cpl A. Lippett	3 x Bf 109, 5 x Ju 87, share Ju 88
L7006	Plt Off E. Barwell Plt Off C. E. Williams	Bf 109, Bf 110, 2 x Ju 87

away towards the sea; soon after, Plt Off Young's gunner, LAC Johnson, opened fire on one of the attackers, and it, too, fell away – Young saw just one parachute emerge from the stricken aircraft. But then disaster struck: Johnson yelled that there was another Defiant almost on top of them, and with that, Plt Off Whitley's aircraft crashed into them, and Young's Defiant disintegrated. The other crews watched in horror as pieces of the aircraft fluttered down towards the sea – and again, only one parachute opened. Whitley's aircraft was badly damaged, but he was able to nurse it down and crash-land near Dunkirk. Whitley and Turner salvaged their four guns and then set the Defiant on fire before making their escape; they found their own way back across the Channel.

The attacking Messerschmitts had also shot down Plt Off Hickman's Defiant, but he and his gunner, LAC Fidler, were able to parachute to safety. As Hunter maintained the defensive circle with the nine surviving aircraft, he counted eight parachutes in the air below them, as well as the plummetting remains of Young's Defiant.

Plt Off Barwell, who was leading Green Section, had watched as LAC Fidler had shot down one of their attackers, and had then seen their Defiant fall with smoke and fuel pouring from it. Suddenly Barwell's own gunner, Plt Off Williams, shouted a warning that a fighter was right on them, and tracers flashed around their aircraft. Barwell pulled the Defiant in a tight turn to the right as Williams hit the Bf 109, which fell away in flames.

No. 264 squadron claimed four Bf 109s shot down and another damaged for the loss of three Defiants, two of them in the collision. Only LAC Johnson did not return. Yet again they had proved they were capable of defending themselves against superior numbers of single-seat fighters.

At 18.40hr they took off for a second patrol, this time at 27,000ft (8,230m), with the Hurricanes of No. 111 Squadron behind them and the Spitfires of 609 Squadron at 30,000ft (9,144m). Over Dunkirk they saw a formation of Heinkel He 111s 2,000ft (610m) below them, and the Defiants and Spitfires dived to the attack.

In a classic turret-fighter formation attack, four Defiant gunners all opened fire in a devastating assault on one of the bombers, which fell away into the sea. The Defiants then began individual attacks on the Heinkels, and both Sqn Ldr Hunter's and Plt Off Hackwood's gunners sent their targets down in flames. Another Heinkel flew right above Eric Barwell's Defiant, and his gunner fired straight up into its cockpit and centre fuselage: the enemy bomber fell to the sea, just two of its crew escaping to parachute down.

Barwell and Williams then attacked another bomber, but return fire hit the Defiant's glycol tank, and Barwell had to turn for home, nursing his rapidly overheating engine. As he slowly lost height it became clear he would not reach the English coast, and so he asked his gunner, Plt Off Williams, if he preferred to bale out or ditch. Despite the fact that 'Bruce' Williams had been a stunt man before the war and had made several hundred parachute jumps at air shows, he would not state his preference. Barwell chose to ditch between two destroyers, going in opposite directions. Against standard procedure, Barwell undid his straps and sat on the seat back, operating the aircraft with only the control column. Williams sat on the fuselage with only his legs inside the turret. As the engine stopped completely Barwell stalled the aircraft onto the water. Both he and Williams were thrown clear, but his gunner was knocked unconscious; however, Barwell supported him until they were picked up by a boat from one of the destroyers. Imagine their delight to meet Plt Off Young on this vessel: he had managed to get clear of his aircraft when it broke up during the earlier sortie.

Pilot Officer Stokes' Defiant had also been hit by the Heinkel's defensive fire, and his gunner LAC Fairbrother was wounded. Stokes ordered him to bale out, but then managed to nurse the crippled Defiant back to Manston, and made a successful crash-landing. A crew who did not return were the squadron's top scorers, Flt Lt Nicholas Cooke and Cpl Albert Lippet, who had claimed ten German aircraft destroyed up to that point.

Back to Duxford

No.264 had claimed four Heinkels destroyed and another damaged for the loss of two Defiants, bringing their total score to sixty-four German aircraft claimed during the month of May, for the loss of fourteen Defiants. They had flown 175 sorties during the month, and were in need of a rest. They were moved to Duxford, and replacement aircraft and crews were drafted in, including thirteen New Zealand air gunners. They returned to flying convoy patrols over the North Sea, usually operating out of Martlesham Heath. As we have seen, though, the Dunkirk area had not seen the last of the turret fighter, as No. 806 Squadron of the Fleet Air Arm began operating its Skuas and Rocs from Detling in June. It lost one Roc over Calais.

The Battle of Britain

In April 1940 a second fighter squadron began to receive Defiants. No. 141, the 'Fighting Cocks', had re-formed in October 1939 with Gladiators, but these gave way to Blenheim IFs in November. The squadron was based in Scotland, from February 1940 at Grangemouth, where the first Defiants arrived in April. The aircraft were coded 'TW' and they all received squadron themed names, including 'Cock o' the North', 'Cocksure', 'Cock a'Hoop', 'Cocked for Firing', and so on.

On 16 June, Sqn Ldr Hunter and Plt Off Kay of No. 264 Squadron went to Farnborough to fly a Defiant fitted with a De Havilland constant speed propeller. They also undertook an exercise flying a Defiant in mock combat with a captured Bf 109 flown by Sqn Ldr Wilson.

Evaluating the Defiant's Performance

On the 21 June there was a conference at the office of war tactics at the Air Ministry to evaluate the performance of the Defiant in combat, following its operation over Holland and Dunkirk, and to recommend future practice. Attending were Sqn Ldr Hunter, Wg Cdr Woodhall, his Station CO, and the CO of No. 141 Squadron, Sqn Ldr W.L. Richardson and his flight commanders. Hunter was able to explain the defensive tactic used on the first patrol on 29 May, when the Defiants were put into a spiral dive and the Bf 109s and Bf 110s were forced to attack on the outside of the spiral, sixteen being shot down. He also emphasized the ease with which Plt Off Cooke had flown along a line of Ju 87s on the second patrol, and shot down five, one after the other.

When they were again bounced by Bf 109s on 31 May, there was a very bright sun, and they had not been able to scan that section of sky. They were attacked by fighters diving almost vertically out of the sun, and the first warning was when the first Bf 109 flashed by. There was then a continuous stream of fighters diving on them, and three Defiants were lost, though two were because of a collision. Hunter pointed out that the squadron had maintained its defensive cohesion, and that four of the Bf 109s had been claimed.

Hunter said he was not impressed by the Bf 110, but even so, there were several ways their own tactics against these aircraft could be improved. Continual R.T. problems with the Defiant needed to be rectified, and when they were co-operating with other squadrons, they all needed to be on the Defiant's wavelength. When three-squadron operations were flown, as they had been over Dunkirk, the COs of the squadrons concerned needed to meet beforehand to co-ordinate their tactics. Over Dunkirk, they may have started out together, but they had fought as separate units.

Sqn Ldr Richardson expressed the view that the Defiant needed a bullet-proof windscreen and two front guns to improve it as a fighter. They all agreed that the proper role of the Defiant was against bombers on home defence.

Further Action

On 28 June, No. 264 squadron's Red Section, led by Fg Off Banham, was scrambled at 13.00hr to intercept enemy aircraft approaching over the sea; no contact was made, however. On the 6th they flew their first night operations with three patrols, and then flew one on each of the following two nights. Through the months of June and July they continued to fly a mixture of convoy patrols and night operations.

No. 141 Squadron was moved south to West Malling on 10 July, with their forward base, Hawkinge. The CO, Sqn Ldr W. Richardson, visited No. 264 Squadron who were then at Fowlmere. Sqn Ldr Hunter once more explained to him the tactics they had successfully used many times, but Richardson let it be known that he had a very low opinion of the Defiant, and he was not to be swayed by the enthusiasm of No. 264 Squadron aircrew for the aircraft. In the early hours of 19 July 1940, twelve Defiants of No. 141 Squadron slipped into Hawkinge airfield and refu-

No. 141 Squadron Defiant coded 'TW-O', airfield unknown, with gunners Len Bowman, Ernie Salway, Alf Cumbers, Gerry Holton, Wally Mott, Sandy Powell, Dave Ashcroft and John Townsend.

elled, ready for their first call to arms.

Swansong for No. 141 Squadron

At 12.10pm on 19 July 1940, the sirens in the Folkstone area warned of approaching raiders, and shortly afterwards anti-aircraft guns opened up on a formation of Bf 110s dive-bombing a ship in the Channel. No. 141 Squadron was ordered to scramble, but engine problems prevented three of the twelve Defiants taking off. The remaining nine formed into three 'vics' of three aircraft in line astern, and clawed for altitude as they crossed the coast.

But unknown to them, the Bf 110s had already been escorted back to the French coast by the Bf 109s of III/JG51. The commander of III/JG51, however, Hauptmann Trautloft, finding he still had ample fuel supplies, decided on a sweep along the English coastline. Trautloft flew with his Schwarm at 10,000ft (3,000m), with the rest of the fighters 3,000ft (1,000m) higher. It was a crystal-clear day and he could see right across Kent – and could also see aircraft taking off from airfields near the coast. He spotted the nine fighters as they crossed the coast, apparently heading right for him. With the sun at his back he dived into the attack, and when he was about

2,600ft (800m) above them, recognized them as Defiants.

The Defiants altered course, hoping to intercept the German bombers, and this took them away from the diving Bf 109s, which were then seen by Flt Lt Loudon, leading the squadron, who called out a warning. Trautloft aimed for the right-hand Defiant in the rear vic: and suddenly the Defiant gunners opened up. There were tracers flying past Trautloft's aircraft and he felt several hits, but he closed in to 100m and opened fire. His first burst was too high, but the second caught the Defiant in the centre of the fuselage, and parts of the aircraft came flying off. Trautloft saw a trail of smoke from beneath the Defiant, which suddenly exploded in a huge red ball of flame.

A second Defiant fell in flames to the first Schwarm's attack, and the other Bf 109s followed them down. The Defiants continued to fly straight and level, as Schwarm after Schwarm dived through them, and then used the speed of their dives to curve in for further attacks. Plt Off J.N. MacDougall's Defiant was hit and went into a spin, and with a failing engine he ordered his gunner, Sgt Wise, to bale out; but after Wise had succeeded in this difficult task, MacDougall managed to

No. 141 Squadron Defiant, N1564, at Gravesend, having suffered an undercarriage collapse on 29 November 1940, flown by Flt Lt T.B. Fitzgerald, B Flight commander, with Sgt L.H. Allen in the turret. Standing on the aircraft are Sgt Meredith and Sgt Townsend.

Ernie Ferguson, a parachute packer, in the turret of No. 141 Squadron Defiant coded 'TW-P'.

A No. 141 Squadron Defiant, N1752, coded TW-L, probably flying from Gravesend late in 1940.

level out, and his engine picked up. He nursed the aircraft back to Hawkinge and managed to land; but unfortunately Wise was not seen again.

Flt Lt Loudon had not been a target of the first attack, but then found himself beset by several Bf 109s coming in from both sides. With his engine ablaze, he put the aircraft into a dive, and ordered his gunner, Plt Off Farnes, to bale out; Loudon himself nursed his stricken aircraft almost back to Hawkinge, but crash-landed just short of his destination. Luckily Farnes was rescued by the Ramsgate lifeboat.

Flt Lt I. D. G. Donald's Defiant was another one that burst into flames as a result of the murderous cannon and machine-gun fire. He dived to wave-top height, and headed for the coast. Unable to gain height, he shot low across the rooftops of Dover, and then along the valley behind, until he hit a hill 4 miles from Hawkinge; both he and his gunner, Plt Off A.C. Hamilton, were killed.

No. 111 Squadron's Hurricanes, which tried desperately to reach the battle, reported that four of the Bf 109s had fallen in flames. Trautloft had been hit in the radiator during his attack, and had to nurse his aircraft back to France, with Oblt Kath, his adjutant, who had also been hit. Both men successfully force-landed on French territory.

No. 141 Squadron had been decimated in what would be its sole daylight action of the Battle of Britain. Six out of nine Defiants had been lost, and the others heavily damaged, one of these being written off. Four pilots and six gunners were killed, and although they claimed four Bf 109s shot down, it was clear that No. 141 Squadron had suffered a devastating defeat. By chance, the four men of the leading Schwarm of III/JG51 – Trautloft, Kath, Pichon and Wehelt – all survived the war, almost certainly the only Battle of Britain Schwarm to do so.

Defiants in Action, 19 July 1940		
L6974	Plt Off J. R. Kemp	Died
	Sgt R. Crombie	Died
L6983	Plt Off MacDougall	Forced landing
	Sgt J. F. Wise	Baled out, missing
L6995	Plt Off R. A. Howley	Died
	Sgt A. G. Curley	Died
L6999	Plt Off A. B. Halliwell	Returned
L7001	Flt Lt M. J. Louden	Forced landing
	Plt Off E. Farnes	Forced landing
L7009	Flt Lt I. D.G. Donald	Died
	Plt Off A. C. Hamilton	Died
L7014	Sgt H.N. Tamblyn	Returned
	Sgt S. W. N. Powell	
L7015	Plt Off R. Kidson	Died
	Sgt F. P. J. Atkins	Died
L7016	Plt Off J.F. Gardner	Baled out, rescued
	Plt Off P. M. Slatter	Baled out, died

The loss of six out of nine Defiants and ten aircrew virtually knocked out No. 141 Squadron in one battle. The panic bells went off in Fighter Command headquarters, and No. 264 Squadron, that had already flown three patrols over a North Sea convoy that day, and were taking off at 15.00hr to continue the cover, were ordered to land immediately. The remnants of No. 141 Squadron were ordered back north to Scotland on the 21st. No. 264 was also ordered north, but with the Battle of Britain raging it was decided that such an experienced and proven squadron could not be spared.

No. 141 Squadron moved to Prestwick with a detachment to Grangemouth, and a month later moved A Flight to Montrose and B Flight to Dyce, flying convoy patrols and its first night patrols. No. 264 Squadron was moved to Kirton-in-Lindsey, mainly flying convoy patrols, interspersed with some night-time patrols, but with flights often detached to Coleby Grange and Ringway for the defence of the north-west. Stephen Hardy, the squadron's first CO, was station commander at Kirton, and he encouraged them to give his anti-aircraft defences some practice by simulating low-level attacks. As usual, official permission to 'beat-up' an airfield was seized on with enthusiasm.

The Defiant must Restore its Reputation

On 15 August, eleven Defiants were patrolling over a North Sea convoy when a large force of Ju 88s and He 111s were detected approaching Hull. It would have been an ideal opportunity for the Defiant once more to prove itself as a bomber-destroyer, but No. 264 was ordered to stay with the convoy, while other fighters were vectored onto the raiders.

That same evening on the 15/16 August the squadron had its first night engagement. Plt Off Whitley and his gunner Sgt Turner were on patrol, showing the coloured downward light then required for easy recognition by the Observer Corps though obviously, this also made them visible to bomber crews. Suddenly, tracer started flashing past them: they followed it to its source, and found a Heinkel He 111. Turner opened fire, but the flash of his guns and the tracer immediately blinded him, and the results were inconclusive. When his eyes regained their night vision he found Whitley had managed to stay with the bomber, and so fired another burst – and this time both of them were blinded and lost sight of the bomber; however, it was later confirmed as having crashed.

A New Engine for the Defiant

The apparent success of the Defiant over Holland and Dunkirk may well have influenced the placing of a further order for the aircraft in July. Some 280 Defiants with serials in the AA range were ordered, bringing the total order to 930. As early as August 1939, Boulton Paul had been asked to investigate the installation of more powerful Merlin engines, and in January 1940 the choice fell on the Merlin XX which had a two-stage supercharger and

gave up to 1,390hp with 12lb of boost. Two of the Defiants on order, N1550 and N1551, were authorized to be fitted with this engine.

The installation made the aircraft 6.4in (16.3cm) longer, at 35ft 10in (10.9m); other changes included a pressurized fuel sytem and extra fuel, with a new 27gal (122.7ltr) tank in the port outer wing; and a 28gallon (127ltr) tank in the starboard outer wing. The prototype of what was to become the Defiant Mk.II, N1550, first flew on 20 July 1940, and Cecil Feather quickly determined that increased vertical tail area was required. This was quickly accomplished by bolting an extra section on the front of the fin.

Trials of the new fin were held up when Feather, while taxiing N1550 to the airfield, collided head-on with a production Defiant, N1639, that Lindsay Neale was taxiing back to the factory after a test flight. Repairs to N1550 took three weeks. Flight tests revealed a disappointing increase in top speed to only 313mph (504kph) at 19,000ft (5,791m), rather than the 345mph (555kph) that had been anticipated. Despite this, the order for 280 Defiants was revised, to make the last 210 Mark II aircraft. In addition, the last seven Mark I aircraft on the production line were converted to Mark II status, though it is likely that these were not standard, as they were to remain in store until 1943, never issued to a fighter squadron before they were converted to target tugs. Thus a total of 713 Mark I Defiants were built, plus the two prototypes.

Boulton Paul's Single-Seater

With the Battle of Britain raging, and the Luftwaffe attacking known fighter factories, Boulton Paul began to consider a single-seat version of the Defiant as a stop-gap fighter should Spitfire and Hurricane supplies be interrupted. The prototype, K8310, was converted back to a single-seater, and first flew in this form on 16 August. Boulton Paul also designed a more advanced single-seat version of the Defiant, the P.94, with twelve fixed forward-firing machine guns, or six 20mm cannon, and the Merlin XX engine. Estimated top speed was 364mph (586kph) at 23,500ft (7,160m). Another version with four machine guns and four 20mm cannon was also envisaged, with the cannon able to swivel downwards to an angle of 17 degrees, for strafing ground troops.

The prototype Mark II Defiant, N1550, with the more powerful Merlin XX engine, at Pendeford in August 1940.

The Defiant prototype, K8310, on the taxiway at Pendeford, converted back to a single-seater as part of a proposal to produce a conventional single-seat Defiant with fixed forward-firing guns.

A crew truck taking No. 264 Squadron aircrew to their aircraft.

In the event, a stop-gap Defiant single-seater in either form was never needed, a shortage of pilots, rather than of aircraft, being the critical factor in the battle. A conference on the proposal in September expressed the opinion that it would be wrong to disrupt the production of standard Defiants, which were needed to create new turret-fighter squadrons. For six months after this, K8310 was operated as a high-speed communications aircraft with a rear seat under a simple sliding hood, in the area where the turret had been.

On 22 August, with the Battle of Britain raging in earnest, No. 264 squadron was moved south again, to Hornchurch in Essex, just out of range of Bf 109s – though this was obviously not the reason that Hornchurch was chosen. It was because Manston was to be their forward operating base, and that same afternoon Red Section undertook a patrol over Manston, followed by a full squadron patrol in the evening.

At 5.10am on 24 August they were moved to their forward base of RAF Manston, and thus as near to the German fighter airfields as they could possibly get. And so the scene was set for No. 264's first engagement in the Battle of Britain.

An Eventful Day: 24 August 1940

No. 264's Blue Section arrived over Manston first, and remained aloft as the other three sections landed to refuel. At 08.00hr Red, Yellow and Green Sections were ordered to take off and patrol over Manston. Flt Lt Campbell-Colquohoun, who was a new pilot to the squadron and had not had time to familiarize himself with the Defiant, had trouble starting his engine and took off late. In the misty early morning conditions he saw two fighters that he thought were Defiants and formatted on them. Suddenly, to his horror, he realized that they were Germans – and his aircraft recognition skills were doubly suspect because he later reported that they were Heinkel He 113s, a type that only ever operated at Heinkel's home airfield. The Germans attacked him, and some shells struck the Defiant just behind his gunner, Plt Off G. Robinson, igniting Very cartridges.

Campbell-Colquohoun put the Defiant into a steep dive, and in the mist he was able to avoid the German fighters. Robinson, however, thought that his pilot had been hit and started to bale out – though as soon as he put his head through the tur-

ret doors into the slipstream, his helmet was ripped off, complete with the intercom lead. Struggling to squeeze out through the doors, he realized the aircraft was levelling out, so he squeezed back inside again. They landed back at Manston in the middle of a bombing raid, somehow avoiding the bomb craters. As soon as the aircraft came to a halt they made a dash for the air-raid shelters, each expressing surprise that the other was alive. The heavily damaged Defiant was pushed into a hangar.

The other airborne Defiants had also seen the Bf 109s, and there was inconclusive firing before disengagement; after thirty minutes in the air they returned. At 11.30hr they were sent back to Hornchurch, but after a short while twelve aircraft were ordered to orbit Manston, which they did so for an hour; but with no sign of a German attack, nine landed to refuel, leaving Yellow section in the air as cover.

But then at lunchtime, as the Defiants were re-fuelling, the air-raid warning was sounded, and almost immediately twenty Ju 88s appeared overhead, diving from 13,000ft (4,000m), and bombs were already falling when the squadron was scrambled. Two of the nine Defiants had trouble starting their engines and took off late, and the other seven had no time to form up as they clawed for altitude underneath the bombers: they all picked out their targets individually, as the bombers flattened out after their dive attacks.

Flt Lt Banham/Sgt Baker and Plt Off Whitley/Sgt Turner both destroyed Ju 88s. One of the flight commanders, Flt Lt Garvin, with Flt Lt Ash as his gunner, also claimed a Ju 88, as did the veteran team of Thorn and Barker, now both sergeants after a recent directive that all air gunners were to be sergeants. Plt Off Knocker claimed a Ju 88 damaged, and Sqn Ldr Hunter with his gunner Sgt King were last seen chasing another Ju 88 towards France, and it is likely that he shot it down, as KG76 reported the loss of five Ju 88s in the engagement.

As the Bf 109s came to the assistance of the bombers, two of the Defiants were shot down, including that of Fg Off Shaw/Sgt Berry. The other was flown by a new crew, Plt Off Jones/Plt Off Ponting, who were flying with Eric Barwell's section. Barwell saw five Bf 109s attacking and called a tight turn, but Jones did not respond quickly enough and was shot down. As each of the German fighters attacked Barwell's Defiant, he pulled into a tight turn to give his gunner, Plt Off Martin, a simple no-deflection shot. They saw hits on two or three of the Bf 109s, and one from JG51 was in fact so damaged that it crashed into another Bf 109, unbeknown to the Defiant crew; both of these German fighters crashed. The attacks continued unabated, though during one of Barwell's tight turns Martin did not fire; when Barwell swore at him, Martin's indignant excuse was 'You blacked me out!' Barwell was beginning to worry about how he was going to break off the action, but suddenly the surviving Bf 109s disappeared, possibly low on fuel, and he was able to fly home to Hornchurch.

The rest of the squadron also landed back at Hornchurch, where four Junkers Ju 88s and a Bf 109 were claimed for the loss of three Defiants: one of these was that of their well-liked commander Phillip Hunter, and this was a devastating blow. In a reversal of the usual situation it is possible that the Defiants actually accounted for more enemy aircraft than they claimed that day, if Hunter did bag his Ju 88 and Barwell/Williams caused the collison of two Bf 109s.

Flt Lt George Garvin, who had been a supernumerary acting squadron leader temporarily attached to No. 264, became acting CO, despite the fact that he had not previously flown fighters. But he did not have long to wait to lead the squadron into action, because at 15.40hr they were scrambled to meet a heavy raid approaching London. Nine Defiants were ready for take-off, but those of Flt Lt D.K.C. O'Malley and Plt Off A. O'Connell collided with one another on the ground, so that only seven took off to be vectored on to a mixed force of Ju 88s and He 111s.

Afternoon Sortie: Defending the Thames Estuary

The afternoon was a beautiful summer's day, with a radiant blue sky and only a few scattered clouds. As the German formation approached the Thames estuary they were attacked from above and to the right by other squadrons, drawing off the Bf 109s of JG3 that were escorting them. The Defiants climbed underneath the bombers, their gunners picking their targets and firing up into their bellies. Garvin's gunner shot down two Ju 88s in quick succession, while Flt Lt Banham and Plt Off Goodall attacked the same Ju 88, claiming it damaged.

Plt Off Young climbed under a Heinkel formation and his gunner shot down one He 111; and Plt Off Welsh spotted a straggling Ju 88 and shot that down. The German fighter pilots began to notice the bombers falling in flames below them, and dived down to pick off the attacking fighters. Plt Off Walsh was attacked by three of them, but managed to fight them off. The commander of JG3, Hauptmann Gunther Lutzow, had already shot down a Spitfire and engaged in a head-on attack with another; when he pulled out of this, after a near collision, he saw one of the smoking bombers and dived to investigate.

He saw the Defiants and closed in for

Sqn Ldr Phillip Hunter's Defiant, N1535, last seen chasing a Junkers Ju 88 across the Channel on 24 August 1940.

the attack. He got within 30m of one, and saw pieces flying off the aircraft, before it burst into flames. He circled on to the tail of another Defiant and opened fire: a large piece came off the port wing, and Lutzow left that one, to attack a third. After a few rounds his guns stopped firing, out of ammunition, but the Defiant's guns were pointing straight up, as if the gunner had been hit. Lutzow turned for home.

One of the Defiants he had attacked was that of Plt Off R.S. Gaskell/Sgt W.H. Machin; the latter was in fact firing at another Bf 109 when Lutzow's cannon shells struck home: they destroyed the port side of his cockpit, smashing the throttle quadrant, and injuring Gaskell's hand. Machin himself was very severely injured in his turret, so there was no thought of baling out. Gaskell managed to bring the shattered Defiant down for a belly-landing in a potato field near Boreham Hall, Essex. Both men were taken to Chelmsford Hospital, but sadly Machin died of his wounds shortly afterwards.

One of the people who had rushed to the crash site of the Defiant was Ron Cheeseman, an air gunner on leave from No. 149 squadron, a Wellington squadron at Mildenhall. When he arrived at the site, to his horror he found an army captain sitting in the turret playing around with the guns, which were all cocked. He politely pointed out to the captain what might happen to the gathered throng if he should touch the firing button. The captain quickly but carefully left the turret, and Ron de-activated the guns.

When the seven Defiants had climbed to the attack it was in two vics of three, with Fg Off Barwell/Plt Off Martin as tail-end Charlie. In this exposed position they were afraid of being bounced out of the sun – which is in fact just what happened, their Defiant being hit in the starboard wing by a Bf 109 that plummetted past them. Barwell had instinctively turned when the aircraft was hit, and in doing so lost sight of the other Defiants that were still climbing towards the bombers. He called Control and explained that he was detached and his aircraft damaged – and was surprised to be ordered to patrol over Dover at 10,000ft (3,000m). He was not flying his usual Defiant, and so did not know if it had the self-sealing fuel tanks that were in the process of being fitted. Barwell repeated his situation to Control, who verified the order to patrol by himself over Dover. So off he went on this solitary

mission, keeping a very wary watch on the surrounding skies, until his fuel ran low (at the expected time, so the self-sealing tanks had obviously been fitted), when he returned to Hornchurch.

After two actions during the same day, with four Defiants lost for nine German aircraft claimed, No. 264 Squadron was able to recuperate a little the following day as the Luftwaffe launched attacks on the West Country. A ten-aircraft patrol was sent over Dover, and the groundcrew accepted seven replacement aircraft – and found there was much work to be done to bring them up to operational standard. Indeed, there was usually two days' work to be done to an aircraft just arrived from a maintenance unit before it was ready for action.

Further Action Over London

On the morning of 26 May a five-aircraft patrol was sent up over Thameshaven, but no enemy aircraft approached. Later in the morning a large force approached London once again, consisting of around forty He 111s and a dozen Do 17s escorted by about eighty Bf 109s. The squadron was scrambled at 11.45hr, led by Flt Lt Banham, and was vectored onto the Dorniers, intercepting them in the area of Herne Bay.

As the Defiants opened fire on the Dorniers, the escorting Messerschmitts had already seen them and were diving to the attack. Banham's gunner Sgt Baker

shot down a Do 17, but their aircraft was immediately hit by raking cannon fire from a Bf 109. The Defiant burst into flames, and Banham rolled it onto his back and ordered Baker to bale out. Banham parachuted into the sea, where he spent an uncomfortable hour before being rescued, but Baker was never seen again.

Plt Off Desmond Hughes/Sgt Fred Gash shot down two of the Dorniers in their first engagement. Plt Off Goodall was attacked by a Bf 109 before he could 'get at' the bombers, but survived to open fire on a Dornier, from which he saw at least two parachutes descending. Sgt Thorn/Sgt Barker also shot down two of the Dorniers, and were just attacking a third when they were hit in the engine compartment by a Bf 109. Glycol and oil began streaming from the Merlin as Thorn threw the Defiant about the sky to try and evade the attacking fighter, and Barker kept firing bursts at their assailant. The Merlin was on its last legs, but Thorn put it down in a skilful forced landing; but as he did so, the German came diving in for another attack. Unlike most fighters that were 'sitting ducks' when attacked during an engine-off forced landing, the Defiant was still a dangerous adversary as long as the turret was still working. Barker gave the attacking Bf 109E one more burst, and he must have hit something vital, because it force-landed only a couple of fields away. The two sergeants scrambled unhurt from the smoking Defiant. For this action the two

No. 264 squadron aircrew at Duxford.

71

men were awarded bars to their DFMs.

Flt Lt Campbell-Colquoquoun's gunner Sgt Maxwell opened fire on another of the Dorniers and certainly damaged it, but they were forced to break off the action when a Bf 109 came in to the attack. The squadron then returned to Hornchurch, having shot down six of the Dorniers and successfully fought off the Bf 109s, shooting one down in the process for the loss of three of their own number. The Hurricanes of No. 1 (Canadian) Squadron had been attacking the Heinkel formation unmolested by fighters, and had also lost three of their number, but without scoring themselves. Thus it wasn't always the Defiants that put up the poorest performance in the few actions they took part in during the Battle of Britain!

The Defiant's Last Daylight Action

On 27 August, the surviving serviceable Defiants were deployed to their forward airstrip at Rochford, but they saw no action, though a section of three did patrol along the Thames estuary. Then on the morning of 28 August, a large German raid began gathering over France at 08.00hr, and headed for London. Three Hurricane squadrons were sent up, followed by 264 Squadron with its twelve Defiants. The German formation split as it approached Deal, and the Hurricanes were engaged by the escorting Bf 109s.

Sqn Ldr Garvin was leading No. 264 Squadron, and he brought them up underneath the formation of around thirty Heinkel He 111s. He had been having

trouble retracting his undercarriage during the climb, and had to recycle it several times; and as his gunner, Flt Lt Ash – the senior gunner on the squadron – was about to open fire, his turret blew a fuse. As Ash was changing it, a Bf 109 came into the attack, and the Defiant was badly hit and caught fire. The two men baled out, but when they reached the ground, Ash was found to be dead.

Pilot Officers Carnaby and Bailey were both on their first action, but both successfully manoeuvred under the German formation, and their gunners each succeeded in shooting down Heinkels. As Bailey's gunner, Sgt Hardie, was switching his aim to another bomber, they were hit by return fire, and he called out that they were being attacked by a Bf 109 from astern. Bailey thought he said he was wounded, and dived away, spiralling down to ground level. But as he levelled off the engine refused to pick up, and he had to make a forced landing – on top of a hedge, to avoid the anti-glider poles in all the fields.

The fighters of Adolf Galland's JG26 had seen the Defiants attacking the Heinkel formation, and swung into the attack. As well as Garvin and Bailey, they also shot down the veteran team of Plt Off 'Bull' Whitley and Sgt Robert Turner, whose aircraft crashed in Challock Forest, and also Plt Off Kenner/Plt Off Johnson, their Defiant crashing at Hinshill. They had destroyed four Heinkels, but four Defiants were shot down (though Bailey's was later repaired), and five aircrew were killed.

The eight surviving Defiants landed back at Hornchurch, but five of them were too badly damaged for another sortie that day. Despite the pleas of the crews they were not allowed to take off as Hornchurch itself was bombed; only three Defiants left the ground, at 12.45hr, landing back after the raid at 13.10hr.

In the afternoon, No. 264 was scrambled yet again at 16.05hr, against a force of around thirty German aircraft approaching across Kent. Only the Defiants of pilot officers Desmond Hughes and Richard Stokes were in a fit state to take off, finding a clear path through the bomb craters from the recent raid. As the two of them climbed through 12,000ft the Controller came on the radio with the message: 'Terribly sorry, old boy, but they've turned away!'

Neither Hughes, nor Stokes, nor their gunners were 'terribly sorry', and their two-Defiant formation turned back to base with four very relieved men on board. While they were up, three more Defiants had managed to take off, but they were recalled and landed at 17.15hr, fifteen minutes before Hughes and Stokes.

During four daylight actions in the Battle of Britain, No. 264 Squadron had claimed nineteen German aircraft shot down (plus one at night), but had lost eleven Defiants. This was not the worst performance of any fighter squadron in the Battle of Britain, but they were obviously in need of a move to a quieter sector to rest and receive replacements. Dowding moved them to Kirton-in-Lindsey in Lincolnshire – and the Defiant had fought its last daylight action.

A No. 264 Squadron Defiant slung inside a hangar, location unknown but probably Kirton-in-Lindsey, on 31 October 1940.

CHAPTER FIVE

Night Fighting

One more Defiant fighter squadron was to see daylight operations. On 5 September, No. 307 (Lwow) Squadron, a Polish unit, was formed at Kirton-in-Lindsey, which became a Defiant base for a considerable time. The squadron had an inauspicious start, in that when the first Poles arrived they found the station commander was flying the Prussian flag, a black eagle on a white background, instead of the Polish flag, a white eagle on a red background. Their first eight aircraft arrived on the

14th, and on 17th the aircraft N1671 – now preserved in the RAF Museum – was delivered to them.

Although No. 307 was seen as a night-fighter unit from the outset, while they were working up they did operate daylight convoy patrols over the Irish Sea, after they moved to Jurby on the Isle of Man on 7 November; but there were no contacts with the enemy during this period.

With the Luftwaffe beginning to switch to night-time operations, the British

night-fighter force was seriously inade-quate, just a handful of Blenheim IF squadrons, admittedly equipped with early AI radar, but often too slow to catch the bombers they were vectored towards. More and more Hurricane squadrons would be switched to night operations, but since the Defiant had been envisaged as a day or night fighter from the outset, it was logical to switch the Defiant force to nights. No. 264 undertook convoy patrols, but also began practising more night

Bristol Blenheims in formation. Though the Blenheim served as a night fighter and was armed with a turret, it was hardly a turret fighter as the turret was only for defensive purposes.

flying, usually from their satellite at Caistor, to avoid lighting up Kirton-in-Lindsey, as well as helping No. 307 become operational.

The 264 Squadron aircrew felt they were being 'condemned' to night-time operations. Few of them welcomed the decision, being completely confident in the Defiant and their ability to hold their own in any tactical situation, even being bounced by Bf 109s. It was explained to them that the Defiant had always been intended as a night fighter, and the move to nights should not be thought of as a relegation; but few of them believed it, preferring to blame No. 141 Squadron after the debacle of their solitary daylight action.

First Night Patrols

One flight of No. 264 was moved to Northolt on 12 September and flew its first night patrols the following evening – though Northolt was not an ideal night-

A No. 264 Squadron Defiant night fighter, N1773, with the gunner giving a 'thumbs up'.

fighter base, being ringed by barrage balloons. Control of the aircraft was then from the Sector Operations Rooms, with the controller following the progress of 'bandits' and the night fighter he was directing on a large operations table. When the two arrows on the table coincided he became quite excited, but the Defiant crews found that the heights given them were often inaccurate, and they were rarely placed within a mile of the 'bandit', and usually too far away to see the bomber.

Some of the crews were still being trained in night-time operations, and the crew of Smith/Robinson on such a practice flight were followed into Caistor by a Heinkel He 111. The bomber opened fire with its machine guns, but there were no hits on the aircraft, and the only damage was twelve hits on the chance light. However, it did serve to show that at night the hunted could turn on the hunter.

After a week at Northolt, 'A' Flight was moved to Luton, which did not have the barrage balloons, but had other problems. First of all, it was quite a small airfield for night landings, with a maximum length of flare path into the prevailing wind of only 600yd (550m). Also there was no homing assistance in place, and below 2,000ft (600m) they could not contact Northolt for help, either; so the squadron rigged up its own system, with a radio in the dispersal hut. When a crew was returning, one man posted outside would listen for the aircraft, and then tell the man on the radio, so he could advise the crew their direction from base.

They had not been at Luton long when, on 21 September, they were visited by ACM Sir Hugh Dowding. His opening words when he visited them in their dispersal hut were 'Well, lads, you have a fine airfield here!' The flight commander, Flt Lt S.R. Thomas, thought it was just the moment to explain some of the difficulties they were having – but Dowding cut short his catalogue of woes with a stern reprimand, and stormed out. Thomas may well have paid for his temerity later, as it took

an inordinately long time before he was promoted to a squadron leader.

The Defiants of No. 141 Squadron had moved to Turnhouse on 30 August, but on 13 September the squadron was brought back south, to Biggin Hill and then Gatwick, for the night defence of London.

Adapting the Defiant to Night-Time Operations

The only changes made to the Defiant for night-time operations, apart from painting them all black, were the fitting of flame-damper ejection manifold exhausts, the removal of the pilot's armour plate, and dimming the gunner's call-lights, which sat on top of the pilot's instrument panel. A conference that took place on 5 September between the deputy chief of the Air Staff and the Director General of Research and Development had discussed the possibility of removing the Defiant's turret and replacing it with an AI operator's position, with twelve fixed forward-firing machine guns fitted to the wings. But with the Bristol Beaufighter already in production, and other new night fighters being considered, it was decided not to interfere with the Defiant, so as to speed its switch to nights; although the installation of AI radar as it became available was not ruled out, or the introduction of the Mark II version.

The Difficulties of Night Fighting

The first night-time claims by a Defiant squadron after Bull Whitley's early effort in August were on 16 September, when Plt Off Waddingham/Sgt Cumbers of No. 141 Squadron claimed two Heinkel He 111s shot down; however, these were never confirmed as being destroyed. The first confirmed claim was the following night, when Sgt W. Laurence/Sgt G.T. Chard, also of No. 141, shot down a Junkers Ju 88A-1 of I/KG.54, which crashed on a Maidstone housing estate.

The Defiant squadrons quickly discovered the difficulty of finding the German raiders in the blackness of the night. For instance, Eric Barwell with Plt Off Goodall as his gunner spotted a bomber on the 13 September, their very first night patrol, but they lost it before they were

Fg Off D.C. Williams and Plt Off G.F. Pledger in front of No. 141 Squadron Defiant T3913 at Gravesend early in 1941. They were killed in this aircraft when they crashed just over 2 miles (3km) from the airfield, returning from a night patrol.

able to open fire. If they had thought finding targets was going to be easy, they were quickly disillusioned as they flew patrol after patrol without a hint of a target. They tried flying high to spot the bombers silhouetted against the flames of London, and flying low to spot them silhouetted against the stars, but all to no avail. 'B' Flight moved from Luton to Rochford, Southend, in November, and were joined by 'A' Flight which had been operating aircraft from Ringway, in the defence of Manchester; but still there were no successes.

Up until now the squadron's morale had always been high, but by this time it was beginning to flag. Basil Embry, the CO at Rochford, arranged to replace Sqn Ldr Garvin with Sqn Ldr A.T.D. Sanders, who had been in one of his previous squadrons. 'Scruffy' Sanders became an excellent CO and morale improved, helped also by new night-time successes.

It fell to Plt Off Desmond Hughes/Sgt Fred Gash to score No. 264 Squadron's next night-time victory, on 16 October.

Robin Lindsay Neale talking to Boulton Paul flight shed personnel before test-flying a Defiant night fighter.

They had flown 200 sorties without even seeing a German bomber, and when at last they did, it caught them by surprise. They were suddenly aware that they were flying alongside a Heinkel He 111 that must have been only 25yd off their port wing-tip: Hughes spotted it out of the corner of his eye, peripheral vision being very important in 'cat's eyes' fighters. Hughes moved slightly below the bomber, and Gash aimed at its starboard engine, immediately blowing a hole in it with his de Wilde explosive ammunition. He fired two more bursts, and there was no return fire from the Heinkel, perhaps because they were unable to train their guns at the position the Defiant was flying in. The Heinkel, of II/KG126, rolled on its back, one engine ablaze, and came down at 01.30hr in the Brentwood area. As the Defiant came in to land in awful weather conditions, Hughes and Gash overshot, though fortunately the aircraft suffered only minor damage.

On another evening they came across a condensation trail at 18,000ft (5,500m), and reasoned that if they followed it at full throttle they would eventually catch up with a raider. After a while Hughes realized the trail was turning, and thought the bomber must be taking evading action. They flew three complete circles before they tumbled to the fact that they were following their own condensation trail in ever-decreasing circles.

On 23 November the same crew intercepted another Heinkel He 111 over Braintree, but after Gash had fired a 2sec burst into one of the bomber's engines, his turret drive jammed. He could still fire his guns, however, and so Hughes attempted to manoeuvre the Defiant so that the tracer from the guns hit the bomber. This was extremely difficult, and continued from 17,000ft (5,000m) down to 8,000ft (2,400m) as they crossed the coast. Eventually they broke off the action and returned to base, only able to claim the Heinkel as a probable.

Like Northolt and Luton, Rochford was not an ideal night-fighter base, largely because when convoys gathered just off Southend pier, only a mile away, naturally they had barrage balloons flying. On New Year's Day 1941, No. 264 moved again, across the estuary to Gravesend, where No. 141 Squadron were already in residence. The two Defiant squadrons only stayed on the same airfield for ten days, before No. 264 was moved on to Biggin Hill. The No. 264 Squadron airmen still blamed No. 141 Squadron for the Defiant being taken off day fighting, and were not slow to tell them. Inevitably fights broke out in local pubs and elsewhere, and it was considered prudent to separate the two units.

New Defiant Night-Fighter Units

With production at Boulton Paul finally achieving the target of fifty per month, and a growing number of aircraft held in reserve, it became possible to form new Defiant night-fighter units. No. 307 had been the first at the beginning of September, and then on 23 November two more were created, No. 255 at Kirton-in-Lindsey, and No. 256 at Catterick, though they would not be declared operational until January 1941.

On 9 January 1941, five Defiants of No. 307 Squadron, and a Handley Page Harrow filled with groundcrew, left Jurby for Squires Gate near Blackpool. One of them, N3401, flown by Sgt A. Joda/Sgt W.G. Andurski, took off for a patrol that night, but did not return. The following day the Defiant was discovered upside down in Barmouth Bay: both crewmen were killed, having apparently attempted to ditch while lost.

News came through later in the month that the rest of the squadron was to move to Squires Gate, and on 23rd a section was ordered to fly over from Jurby. The weather conditions were poor, and only one of the three reached the new airfield. One, N3439, force-landed in a field but was later flown on, and the other, N3320, force-landed near Ormskirk, causing damage to the aircraft. On 26th, seven Harrows arrived at Jurby from Doncaster to transport the rest of the squadron, but because of the continuing bad weather this was not achieved until the 27th, the last aircraft not arriving until 1 February.

When No. 307 Squadron was formed, the cream of the available Polish fighter pilots were posted to it, but when they discovered that they would just be drivers for back-seat gunners, their pride was touched, and they objected strongly, demanding transfers to single-seaters. These requests were largely granted, and they were replaced by pilots of lesser quality – which may explain the high accident rate suffered by the squadron in the early months of its existence.

It had been decided to start equipping some of the Hurricane squadrons that had been switched to night fighting with some Defiants, enabling them to fly single- and two-seat 'cat's-eyes' fighters. The first of these was No. 151 Squadron at Bramcote and then Wittering, which began equipping two flights with Defiants in Decem-

The sticky end of a No. 141 Squadron Defiant, most probably N1795, which struck a bank attempting a forced landing on Watling Street near Gravesend on 23 March 1941.

Polish air gunner, Sgt W. G. Anurski of No. 307 Squadron, killed in Defiant N3401 on 10 January 1941, aged twenty-five. His pilot attempted a ditching off Barmouth after becoming lost while on patrol from Jurby. They were casualties of No. 307's early high accident rate.

An armourer in a No. 307 Squadron Defiant turret, location unknown.

ber, retaining Hurricanes for the third flight. They were not best pleased with the arrival of the Defiant, and it was the squadron's avowed intention at the time to prove the Hurricane a better night fighter.

Being an experienced squadron, No. 151 was quicker into its stride than the new Defiant squadrons, and scored its first success with the Defiant on the night of 4/5 February when at 21.40hr Sgt Bodien/Sgt Jones were vectored onto a Dornier Do 17Z west of Wittering. Bodien closed

No. 151 Squadron, AA435, coded DZ-V, which later went to No. 515 Squadron.

to 50yd, and Jones fired a 5sec burst, and then a second from only 25yd. The Dornier's fuselage began burning, and then there was a small explosion and it went down and crashed near Weedon, Northamptonshire. There was little of the aircraft left, but enough to show that it had been a Do 17 night-fighter conversion, obviously on an intruder mission.

The second Hurricane squadron to begin receiving Defiants was No. 85, in January 1941, while at Debden. They, too, were not anxious to lose their Hurricanes, and considered that the Defiant's only advantage was that it gave their hard-working groundcrew the chance of the occasional flight. They only flew three patrols with the nine Defiants they received, and then relinquished them to another Hurricane squadron, No. 96 at Cranage in Cheshire, mostly on 15 February. But if they had thought that they would be able go back to their beloved Hurricanes, then they were sadly mistaken, as they were immediately re-equipped with the Douglas Havoc.

On 26 February 1941, a No. 256 Squadron Defiant flying a dusk patrol from Middle Wallop in Hampshire sighted three enemy aircraft, which dropped their bombs and fled when they saw the threat. On the same night, N3520, flown by Flt Lt S.F.F. Johnson, was low on fuel, and ordered his gunner, Sgt C.S. Lewis, to bale out. Johnson then attempted a crash-landing, near Upavon in Wiltshire, but was killed.

By March 1941 there were seven Defiant night-fighter squadrons. In No. 11 Group, No. 264 was now at Biggin Hill, No. 141 at Gravesend, and the Fighter Interception Unit had one Defiant amongst its aircraft at Ford. No. 9 Group had No. 307 at Squires Gate near Blackpool, and No. 96 at Cranage in Cheshire. No. 12 Group had two squadrons: No. 255 at Kirton-in-Lindsey, and No. 151, with eighteen Defiants and ten Hurricanes, at Wittering. Finally No. 10 Group in the south-west had just one Defiant squadron, No. 256 at Colerne.

Better Luck for the Poles

Nos 256 and 307 Squadrons would shortly change places. No. 307 had their first confirmed victory when Sgt Jankowiak and Sgt Lipinski shot down an He 111 on 12 April over Dorset. They patrolled at

A No. 256 Squadron Defiant, N3494, location unknown.

No. 307 Squadron Polish aircrew at Church Parade in Bath, after the squadron had moved to Colerne.

15,000ft (4,600m) and were vectored towards a 'bandit' at 180 degrees. They saw a Heinkel He 111 when it was about 3,000ft (900m) away and 2,500ft (750m) below, flying just above the 10/10th cloud cover in the opposite direction towards Bristol. As the bomber passed them by, Lipinski opened fire at a range of only 120ft (36m). There were flashes and explosions all over the Heinkel, with pieces of fuselage flying off, and the bomber then dived away and crashed near the village of Lydlinch.

No. 307 Squadron's only successes through the previous winter had been on 12 March when an He 111 was damaged by a 3sec burst over North Wales delivered by Sgt Jank/Sgt Karais, and on 14 March when Fg Off Lewandowski/Sgt Niewolski

claimed a probable. They had intercepted a raider while patrolling at 20,000ft (6,000m), and Niewolski had fired a 1sec and then a 3sec burst from only 50yd (45m). Hits were seen on the aircraft's nose and starboard engine, and the bomber then turned violently to port and dived straight down.

On 16 April the squadron had a second confirmed victory when Fg Off Lewandowski/Sgt Zakrocki shot down a Heinkel He 111: they had spotted it flying 300yd (275m) ahead of them and about 150ft (45m) above, which meant they were in an ideal position to stalk a night raider, able to creep up undetected to just 50yd (45m) behind before opening fire. Zakrocki let fly, and kept firing until he had used up all his ammunition, and the

Heinkel fell in flames. These two victories seemed to indicate a change of luck for the Poles, after their move to Colerne.

Mixed Fortunes for the Night Fighters

Through the poor weather and the dark winter months of December, January and February there had been little 'trade' for any of the night fighters. No. 264 was only able to claim one Ju 88 damaged by Sgt Endersby/Sgt Chandler in this period.

No. 255 Squadron crews claimed three bombers as probables during February, all over the Humber estuary. On the night of 12/13 March the Luftwaffe launched a large raid against Liverpool, which would last for nearly six hours. Across the country all the night-fighter squadrons were busy. No. 96 at Cranage launched eighteen sorties, and one of their Defiants was first in action: after taking off at 21.55hr, Fg Off Vesely (a Czech)/Sgt Heycock saw an He 111 off their port side – but Heycock's guns would not fire. Vesely continued to line up on the bomber as Heycock tried desperately to get the guns to work. The Heinkel began to dive and Vesely stayed with it,

moving over to the starboard side. Still Heycock could not get the guns to work – and then one of the Heinkel's gunners fired two bursts that hit the Defiant and injured Vesely in the head, chest, left arm and shoulder. The Defiant fell into a spin with the pilot unconscious, but he came to and managed to recover and land the damaged aircraft. It had been first blood to the Luftwaffe.

But No. 96 Squadron had their revenge later that night when Sgt McNair, flying a Hurricane, shot down another Heinkel at Wychbold, and the all-New Zealand Defiant crew of Sgt Taylor/Sgt Broughton claimed a probable. After they had opened fire on a Heinkel, Broughton's guns jammed after six rounds, but they continued to chase the bomber at low level into the Welsh mountains – they were flying below the mountain tops that were obscured by cloud above 1,000ft (300m). When Taylor pulled up into a climb he cleared a hilltop by only 70ft (20m) and considered the Heinkel unlikely to survive. As already recorded, No. 307 claimed another Heinkel damaged over North Wales at about the same time.

A No. 96 Squadron Defiant, T4052, believed to have been photographed at RAF Valley.

The No. 264 Squadron Defiant of Desmond Hughes/Fred Gash with their five victory markings beneath the canopy.

The same night, No. 264 Squadron was busy on the south coast, claiming two He 111s shot down: Plt Off Hughes/Sgt Gash their second night-time success, and Plt Off Walsh/Sgt Heydon their first. Over in the east, Flt Lt Sanders/Sgt Hill of No. 255 Squadron set a Heinkel on fire and saw it diving towards the sea; they claimed it as a probable.

These successes across the country on the night of 12 March 1941 indicated the return of the Luftwaffe in some numbers as the spring brought better weather. It also indicated that there was no substitute for experience in night operations, which were often as dangerous to the fighter crews as the enemy: flying over a blacked-out countryside in filthy weather was in itself more hazardous than return fire from enemy bombers. All the squadrons had their catalogue of accidents, even the most experienced, No. 264.

On 4 September 1940, Fg Off O'Malley/Sgt Rasmusson were killed when their Defiant struck the ground taking off from Kirton-in-Lindsey at 21.30hr. On the 28th of the same month, N1630 undershot at Luton and suffered an undercarriage collapse after a night patrol, and the small airfield at Luton claimed a second victim on 7 October when N1578 crashed on take-off, injuring Fg Off Hackwood and Fg Off O'Connell. The very next night N1627 crashed at Marlow while on a night patrol and Plt Off Goodall/Sgt Young were killed, the cause of this crash being unknown; they may well have been shot down, perhaps by return fire from a bomber, perhaps by a German intruder. Only eight days later, N1621 also overshot after a night patrol and hit a hedge. On 15 November the engine of N1547 failed on a night patrol, and the aircraft crashed on the approach to Rochford, killing Plt Off Knocker/Plt Off Toombs.

The Frustrations of Night Flying

Such a catalogue of accidents was experienced by all the night-fighter crews, whether they were flying Defiants or not. Losing radio communications was often enough to claim the aircraft, as navigation at night in British weather, above cloud and a blacked-out countryside, was often impossible. For instance, on 13 April, Plt Off Paul Rabone and his gunner Sgt Ritchie took off from Cranage in Defiant

N1766 on a routine training flight. They lost radio contact with the ground, and then began suffering engine trouble. Rabone was an experienced pilot, with two victories over Bf 109s and one night victory, all flying Hurricanes, but he was completely lost. They did the sensible thing and took to their parachutes, and the aircraft crashed at Rowlees Pasture in the Peak District. Perhaps a less experienced pilot might have tried to descend blindly through cloud, and would have died. As it was, Rabone went on to build a total score of nine victories, mostly flying Mosquitos. The engine and propeller of this Defiant are now displayed at the Yorkshire Air Museum, in the care of the Night-Fighter Preservation Team.

The frustrations for the crews were immense: they would go out on one patrol after another, night after night, without a hint of the enemy – and yet they risked death at every take-off. But the return of the Luftwaffe was to bring targets in numbers, and they would be able to take their revenge. Beginning with the two successes on 12 March, No. 264 squadron had a series of victories through until mid-July, by which time they were the top-scoring Defiant night squadron, with fourteen victories.

Fortunes Improve

During April 1941 they flew seventy-six experimental sorties in the Kenley sector in conjunction with ground control using a gun-laying radar: these were accurate but of short range, requiring a large number of sets. There were fifty-six attempted intercepts during the seventy-six sorties, seven visual contacts, and four bombers claimed destroyed. It was decided that although the concept had promise, there were still limitations to its use.

Sqn Ldr Sanders/Plt Off Sutton shot down one Heinkel on 8 April, with Hughes/Gash claiming another as probably destroyed. The following night the veteran team of Thorn/Barker shot down a Heinkel He 111 at Godalming, their first – and last – night-time success. This brought to thirteen their victory total, making them the top-scoring Defiant crew. It also probably made Fred Barker the top-scoring air gunner of all time: it is hard to imagine that any gunner on a bomber, or even a fighter with rear defence, such as a Blenheim or Bf 110,

could possibly have shot down more than Barker's total.

Only two days later another veteran of the Dunkirk days, Eric Barwell, scored his first night-time successes. Up until then he had been flying night patrols for seven months and had only seen a German aircraft twice – a brief glimpse on his first-ever night patrol, and an exhaust that he chased all the way to France without ever being near enough to open fire before having to return – and then in the space of just one night he scored two successes.

Flying with Sgt Martin as his gunner, they were patrolling in the Kenley sector at about 15,000ft (4,500m). Vectored onto a 'bandit', they finally spotted it 500ft (150m) above them and about 1,000yd (900m) ahead. Barwell closed in, and they identified it as a Heinkel He 111. Martin opened fire at about 300yd (270m), firing four bursts as they closed to 50yd: they saw strikes all over the underside of the bomber, which pulled up in a steep climb, so steep that as Barwell tried to follow, the Defiant almost stalled. The Heinkel then suddenly fell into a dive, and though they tried to follow it through the cloud, they lost it; they later learned that it had crashed at Seaford, near Beachy Head. They landed at Tangmere at 22.15hr, and the Defiant was re-fuelled and re-armed with 435 rounds of ammunition.

They took off again at 02.35hr, and patrolled the coast at 12,000ft (3,660m). They were vectored towards another raider, flying south towards Beachy Head, and saw it at about 2,000yd (1,800m) range, about 2,000ft (600m) below them. It was a bright moonlit night, almost like daylight, ideal conditions for a 'cat's-eyes' fighter. Barwell set off in pursuit, but they must have been spotted, because the bomber, which they identified as a Heinkel, began climbing towards some cloud cover. Martin again opened fire at about 300yd (270m), and the Heinkel began taking violent evasive action, with its rear gunner firing back. Unusually for a night-time engagement, a real dog-fight ensued, and Martin fired over 600 rounds. Hits were seen all over the bomber, and various pieces of it could be seen falling off; and then suddenly it dived vertically, and Barwell lost it in the clouds. The radar trace disappeared 15 miles (24km) out to sea, but as it was not seen to crash, Barwell/Martin could only claim it as a probable. They landed back at Biggin Hill to find that Desmond Hughes/Fred Gash

The top-scoring Defiant crew of Sgt R. Thorm DFM and bar, and Sgt F. Barker DFM and bar, just after their first night victory, and their thirteenth overall.

The Heinkel He 111 shot down on 9 April 1941, by Thorn/Barker near Godalming.

No. 264 Squadron Successes during the Blitz

Date	Crew	Target	Result
16.10.40	Plt Off Hughes/Sgt Gash	Heinkel He 111	Destroyed
23.11.40	Plt Off Hughes/Sgt Gash	Heinkel He 111	Probable
09.01.41	Sgt Endersby/Sgt Chandler	Junkers Ju 88	Damaged
12.03.41	Plt Off Hughes/Sgt Gash	Heinkel He 111	Destroyed
12.03.41	Plt Off Walsh/Sgt Heydon	Heinkel He 111	Destroyed
13.03.41	Sgt Wilkie/Sgt Crock	'Bomber'	Probable
08.04.41	Sqn Ldr Sanders/Plt Off Sutton	Heinkel He 111	Destroyed
08.04.41	Plt Off Hughes/Sgt Gash	Heinkel He 111	Probable
09.04.41	Fg Sgt Thorn/Fg Sgt Barker	Heinkel He 111	Destroyed
16.04.41	Plt Off Hughes/Sgt Gash	Heinkel He 111	Destroyed
16.04.41	Flt Lt Barwell/Sgt Martin	Junkers Ju 88	Destroyed
		Heinkel He 111	Probable
08.05.41	Plt Off Curtice/Plt Off Martin	'Enemy a/c'	Destroyed
08.05.41	Plt Off Gray/Plt Off Hil	Heinkel He 111	Destroyed
		2 x He 111s	Damaged
09.05.41	Fg Off Young/Sgt Russell	Bf 110	Destroyed
11.05.41	Sqn Ldr Sanders/		
	Plt Off Sutton	Heinkel He 111	Destroyed
11.05.41	Flt Lt Stephenson/		
	Plt Off Maggs	Heinkel He 111	Destroyed
11.05.41	Plt Off Curtice/Plt Off Martin	Dornier Do 17	Destroyed

had downed another Heinkel that night, the aircraft crashing near Dorking.

Replacing No. 307 Squadron at Squires Gate on 26 March, No. 256 Squadron did not have their first confirmed success until 7 April, when Flt Lt D. R. West/Sgt R. T. Adams shot down a Ju 88 over Southport, the bombs exploding on impact. That same night, the radio on Defiant N1694 failed, and when the crew, Flt Sgt J. Stenton/Sgt W. Ross, realized they were lost and running out of fuel, they baled out. The Defiant crashed at Helsall, not very far from the Junkers Ju 88. The following night Sgt J. D. H. Cunningahm/Sgt A. D. Wood were killed on take-off from Squires Gate in Defiant N3424.

Bombers Over Birmingham

After such tragedies, and with the only success being that of West/Adams, many of the No. 256 crews were losing confidence during those long winter months. One such was Flt Lt Christopher Deanes-

A No. 256 Defiant flying near to Squires Gate, Blackpool.

ly, who had answered the call for volunteers for the new Defiant night-fighter squadrons the previous autumn, and at the time commanded 'B' Flight of No. 256 squadron.

The day after the crash of N3424, on the 10 April, nine of the squadron aircraft had moved to Tern Hill in Shropshire in preparation for a 'Fighter Night' over Birmingham. On Fighter Nights, certain areas and altitudes were left free by the anti-aircraft guns so that the night fighters could roam at will. Deanesly was scheduled to take off at 21.55hr, and as he taxied to the runway in Defiant N1771, coded JT-U, his gunner, the New Zealander Sgt Jack Scott, remarked: 'Well, sir, I'd far rather go with you than anyone else!' This helped boost Deanesly's morale enormously.

They were vectored towards Birmingham, and as they climbed through 14,000ft (4,300m), they could see a large fire in the middle of a cloudless area of about 10 miles (16km) in diameter. There was a full moon, and they could see condensation trails above them, so they climbed slowly to 20,000ft (6,000m). Four more fires broke out below them, and they could see that the condensation trails passed from north to south, and lost height quickly beyond the fires as the bombers dived for home after releasing their load.

As they reached 20,000ft (6,000m) the intercom was jammed – by the BBC South African Service, of all things! Just then Scott saw a bomber to starboard, and pressed the green call light warning Deanesly to turn after it; but he lost sight of it as he did so. At around 23.55hr they saw another bomber on the port side about 300yd (275m) away and 300ft (90m) below. A quick turn brought them 600–800yd (550–730m) behind the bomber, which was throwing out a condensation trail and already diving. Deanesly dived after it and closed rapidly, throttling back to drop below it and to port.

When the bomber was on their beam, Scott opened fire and they saw strikes on the engine. A second burst set the bomber on fire, and this lit up the glazed nose, confirming that it was a Heinkel He 111. The bomber turned in towards them, thereby closing the range from 200 to 50yd (180 to 45m), and Scott fired again. The fuselage was now well alight, and they followed the burning bomber down to 10,000ft (3,000m), until Deanesly became increas-

ingly worried about barrage balloons, and climbed away.

The Heinkel hit a balloon cable and crashed between two houses in Hales Lane, Smethwick, the wings demolishing the houses and killing seven inhabitants, who could not go in their Anderson shelters because they were flooded. Two of the crew baled out and were captured, but the others died in the crash. Deanesly landed back at Tern Hill particularly satisfied with his night's work: not only had he broken his duck, but he had done so not far from the place of his birth, Wolverhampton, where his Defiant had also been made. His grandfather was John Marston, who had founded John Marston Ltd, which made Defiant radiators amongst others, and the Sunbeam Motor Car Co., which had made aero engines and aircraft during World War I.

Jack Scott was commended for having fired only 494 rounds to bring down the Heinkel. But yet again their success was followed immediately by another No. 256 Squadron Defiant lost: the next night N3460 crashed at Cheslyn Hay near Cannock, only 20 miles (30km) from the Heinkel in Smethwick, after the crew, Sgt R. Dean/Sgt R. Robinson, experienced radio failure and baled out.

Successful Sorties over Liverpool

On the 5 May the Deansely/Scott team were to score a double. Taking off from Squires Gate at 22.30hr to patrol west of Liverpool at 12,000ft (3,660m), they saw many fires break out in the city. With a half moon and the light from the blazing city illuminating the cloudless sky, they spotted a Ju 88 only 150yd (140m) away at the same height. Deanesly got below and to starboard of the bomber, and Scott fired several short bursts, though his turret was not rotating at maximum speed. There was some return fire, but then the Ju 88 disappeared in a steep dive: it crashed near Wrexham, and only two of the four crew baled out.

With plenty of fuel and ammunition left, Deanesly and Scott decided to continue to patrol. At 23.55hr they saw a Dornier at the same height about 250yd (230m) away, passing right over them. Deanesly turned and chased, closing in below and astern. Once more Scott opened fire, and hits were seen on the fuse-

lage. As the Dornier swerved from side to side they followed it down until they entered haze at 2,000ft (600m). Immediately afterwards there was a terrific flash as the bomber hit the ground.

They returned to Squires Gate, where they landed with only 20gal (90ltr) of fuel left – but found that Scott had expended only 416 rounds in the two combats. They were also shaken to discover bullet holes in the glycol header tank, the port petrol tank, the main spar and through the rear fuselage. And they also discovered corrugations on one propeller blade, which suggested they had come into contact with some sort of wire, perhaps one of the bomber's aerials.

The experience of the three combats had shown Deanesly that there was little hope of seeing bombers if the night fighter flew patrol lines across the raiders' lines of approach. The best chance was to risk the anti-aircraft fire and fly over the target, where the light of the fires started by the bombing would help them see the bombers. All they required would be the heights at which the bombers were operating. They were also quite sure that they would not have scored these three victories in a fixed-gun fighter.

A Run of Success

In No. 151 Squadron however, just such a fixed-gun night-fighter pilot was having conspicuous successes. Plt Off Richard Playne Stevens was finding and shooting down German bombers on a regular basis in his Hurricane, including two in one night during a Fighter Night over Coventry on 8 April. On the same night, two of the Squadron's Defiant crews also shot down Heinkels: Flt Lt McMullen/Sgt Fairweather, and Sgt Wagner/Sgt Siedengart. The latter were flying Defiant N1790, and had taken off from Wittering at 00.48hr. They saw the Heinkel about an hour later, at a distance of around 4 miles (6/7km), showing what good visibility there was that night. After stalking the bomber Siedengart opened fire with controlled bursts which set the engines ablaze. The Heinkel crew baled out, and the aircraft then began a long, uncontrolled glide and eventually crash-landed on a farm near Desford in Leicestershire.

Two crew members had not heard the call to bale out and were still in the rear fuselage when the aircraft landed itself, but miraculously they survived; they were

A No. 151 Squadron Defiant with very unusual shark's mouth markings.

taken prisoner, one of them for a second time, having been shot down over Belgium in May 1940 and then released when that country surrendered.

The following night there was a Fighter Night over Birmingham, and the No. 151 Squadron Defiants shot down three of the raiders: two Ju 88s and another Heinkel. Sgt Bodien/Sgt Jones had claimed one of the Ju 88s, and then Bodien dived after another bomber into the balloon barrage. Sgt Jones in the turret was thoroughly alarmed, and could not raise Bodien on the intercom. Thinking his pilot must have been killed in the first combat, he proceeded to bale out. Both landed unhurt, Bodien in Defiant N3387 and Jones beneath his parachute.

May: Best Month of the Night War

This run of success continued into May: on the 2nd a Ju 88 was shot down by Plt Off Edmiston/Sgt Beale; and Plt Off Stevens flying his Hurricane destroyed one He 111 on the 3rd, and two in one night on 7 May. Sergeant Bodien had parted company with his gunner in more than one way. On 3 May he was flying with Sgt Wrampting, when they claimed a Heinkel He 111 after a running fight that lasted 45min. The following day Bodien was commissioned as a pilot officer.

During the first ten days of May the Luftwaffe returned to Great Britain in force, making one last great effort before moving east. No. 151 had two further success over the Wash, a favourite route for the raiders, bringing them as far west as they could go before crossing the coast. On 3 May a Ju 88 of I/KG30 was fired on by a

Defiant, and though there was little apparent damage it eventually lost engine power and belly-landed in Norfolk.

On the very next night, 4 May, a Heinkel He 111 of KG53 had bombed Liverpool, and its crew must have felt relatively safe when they reached the Wash on the way home. But suddenly the devastating fire from a Defiant turret crashed into their underside, killing the wireless operator instantly. Then the engines began losing oil, and the pilot had no other choice than to belly-land at Brinton Nr Holt. Once again the crew were Sgt Bodien/Sgt Jones, making their third Defiant victory. Later in the war, Bodien would claim two more, flying Mosquitos.

In the North, No. 141 Squadron were also having a series of victories. During May they shot down a total of eight raiders, including two in one night by Fg Off R. L. F. 'Bingo' Day/Plt Off F. C. A. Lanning. Flying from Acklington, they saw a Heinkel He 111 flying below them, creeping over a blanket of white cloud like a fly walking across a white tablecloth. Day sideslipped and gained speed to achieve an attacking position below the bomber. He flew to within 100ft (30m) of the Heinkel's belly, and then Lanning opened fire, sweeping his tracer across the undersides of the bomber from engine to engine. The Heinkel burst into flames and dived away, and Day followed it until it fell into the grounds of Morpeth Hospital.

They landed, refuelled and re-armed, and then went up for a second patrol. As soon as they arrived at their assigned altitude they spotted a Junkers Ju 88 in the distance, heading out to sea. Day opened the throttle wide, and they chased after it. They gained very slowly, and at about 400yd (360m) Lanning opened fire. The

Junkers turned north, away from them, and increased speed. They chased, but were unable to gain on it, though they managed to avoid the odd burst of fire from the German gunners. Nevertheless, Lanning's first burst must have hit something vital, because the Junkers eventually crashed on Holy Island. When they landed back at Acklington the Defiant had only a few gallons of fuel left in the tanks. The two men received DFCs for the night's work.

Frank Lanning had been given his first flight in 1919, when he went up with his parents and brother in the capacious rear cockpit of an Avro 536 during a joy-riding session at Hounslow. The pilot was Frank Courtney, who was also a freelance test pilot, and who did all the early flight-testing for Boulton & Paul Ltd.

Another No. 141 squadron crew, Sgt Meredith/Sgt Mott, also had a meritorious combat in May. They shot down a He 111 on 5 May after the expenditure of only sixty rounds of ammunition.

On 6 May, Fg Off Verity/Sgt Wise of No. 96 Squadron were on patrol trying to intercept raiders that were bombing Liverpool. They decided to dive to 10,000ft (3,000m) and to fly right over the fires burning below. Wise saw a Heinkel illuminated by the glow, and Verity banked and dived after it. Wise opened fire at 150yd (140m), and sent the bomber down in flames. Continuing their patrol they saw a Ju 88, and attacked it; however, they lost sight of it before they could be sure of its destruction, and could only claim it as a probable.

A Run of Successful Nights for Defiants: 7 May

The night of 7 May began a run of very successful nights for the Defiant crews as the Luftwaffe mounted a series of heavy raids in good weather, with little cloud and a half moon – just the conditions 'cat's eyes' fighters needed. On the 7th, Liverpool was the target for the second successive night, and No. 96 Squadron at Cranage and No. 256 Squadron at Squires Gate were heavily engaged. Fg Off Verity of No. 96 took off with good heart after claiming two the night before. He spotted a Ju 88, and his gunner shot it down in flames; but he was then attacked himself by another Ju 88 that he assumed was a fighter version on an intruder mission.

In an engagement that lasted nearly ten

minutes, the two fighters twisted and turned in a night-time dog-fight. When they lost sight of one another Verity believed he must have shot it down and claimed it as a probable. The No. 96 Squadron's Operational Records Book commented that Verity's victims had 'paid the price for getting too close to the four guns of a Defiant'.

The other Defiant crews of No. 96 Squadron claimed two Heinkels destroyed as well as a probable. Sgt Scott/Sgt Streeter shot down an He 111 that crashed east of Wrexham, and Sgt Taylor/Sgt McCormack took out another, which broke up in the air near Malpas, Cheshire. Then they chanced upon another raider, and after a 3sec burst that hit the port engine and cockpit, the bomber dived away and was claimed as a probable.

The other successes were by Plt Off Hibbert/Plt Off Haycock, who hit an He 111 that dived vertically away; and Sgt Nain/Sgt Windman who fired bursts at two different Ju 88s, one of which was hit in the fuselage and one in an engine. Thus the total score for No. 96 Squadron on 7 May was four aircraft destroyed, three probable and one damaged. This was the best score in one night for a Defiant squadron – but it was a record that would not last long.

On the same night No. 256 squadron claimed three Heinkels shot down, and

A No. 141 Squadron Defiant on night patrol.

A No. 256 Squadron night fighter attached to the trolley ack ready for an instant start-up.

A No. 264 Squadron Defiant, location unknown, in front of a Fairey Battle.

three other bombers damaged: two Heinkels and a Ju 88. It may well have been that several Ju 88 intruders were operating with the bomber stream, because one shot down a Defiant, N3500, near Widnes, though the crew, Sqn Ldr Gatheral/Fg Off D. S. Wallen, baled out.

Run of Success: 8 May

On 8 May 1941, No. 264 Squadron returned to the skies over France for the first time since their last battle over Dunkirk nearly a year before; this was to begin intruder operations. No. 141 Squadron had flown the first Defiant intruder operation on the night of 7/8 April, but without success. No. 264 were to have better luck: operating over the German night-fighter airfields in the early hours, Plt Off Curtice/Plt Off Martin shot down one Bf 110 and damaged another, and Plt Off Gray/Plt Off Hill similarly shot down one He 111 and damaged two more.

On this night the Luftwaffe were sending bombers to the north-west for the third night running, and as the Germans approached in the early hours of the 8th, both No. 96 and No. 256 Squadrons once more sent up patrols from Cranage and Squires Gate, hoping for the same level of success. No. 96 Squadron drew a blank, but No. 256 had several more victories.

Sqn Ldr E. C. Deanesley/Sgt Jack Scott took off at 00.30hr and climbed to 14,000ft (8,700m) over Manchester, already burning in several places. Scott spotted one bomber 2,000ft (600m) below, but was unable to direct Deanesly onto it. Then at 01.15hr they both saw an aircraft at the same altitude coming out of the anti-aircraft barrage, 500yd (460m) away off their port bow. Deanesly turned after it and approached slightly below until they recognized it as a Heinkel He 111 – they could even see the black crosses on the wings and fuselage. At a distance of about 100yd (90m) Scott opened fire, but no return fire came their way. The bomber dived steeply away. They moved to dead astern below the tail, and Scott aimed at each engine in turn, setting them both

J.D. North shows Sir Stafford Cripps the component parts of a Boulton Paul Type A turret.

alight. They followed the burning Heinkel down to 8,000ft (2,500m), and only broke away when they were so low that they could see the ground fires highlighting the barrage balloons. The Heinkel crashed at Hazel Grove, near Stockport, at 01.30hr, though the German crew had baled out. Scott had expended 800 rounds in the short action.

The team of Flt Lt West/Sgt Adams achieved their second victory, shooting down a Heinkel He 111, and Plt Off Toone/Plt Off R.L. Lamb got a third He 111, hitting it with a burst from 150yd. The Heinkel turned onto its back and dived vertically, crashing and exploding in Liverpool Docks.

Over on the other side of the country, No. 255 Squadron had the satisfaction of a victory within sight of their base at Kirton-in-Lindsey: Sgt Johnson/Sgt Aitcheson shot down a Heinkel He 111 over the Trent, and it fell in flames from 10,000ft (3,000m). It wasn't very often that the groundcrews actually witnessed such a success, made possible by their labours.

On the same night Flt Lt Trousdale/Sgt Chunn, flying Defiant N3378, saw an enemy raider but could not catch it; but

Plt Off R. L. Lambe (left) and his gunner Plt Off John Toone at No. 256 Squadron dispersal hut, Squires Gate. The cross is from the Heinkel He 111 they shot down on 8 May 1941; it crashed into the River Dee marshes, Bagillt. Lambe survived the war, but Toone was killed in a Beaufighter in 1943.

they were to make up for this on the following night.

Run of Success: 9 May

The following night, 9 May, the seven Defiant squadrons prepared for another Luftwaffe assault, wondering in which sectors it would fall. But No. 264 Squadron did not have to sit and wait, as 'A' Flight again sent intruders over northern France, and once more achieved success. Plt Off Young/Sgt Russell shot down another Bf 110 night-fighter over Merville, the German crew baling out. After two recent bombing attacks on Belfast, 'B' Flight had been despatched to Nutts Corner; but the Germans did not return to Northern Ireland for a while.

Smith now attacked another He 111, but his aircraft was damaged by return fire and he had to land.

The other successes for No. 255 were to be credited to the Defiants. Plt Off Wyrill/Sgt Maul were first, shooting down another He 111 over Hull at 01.25hr. Only three minutes later, Plt Off Wynne-Williams/Sgt Plant shot down another at Patrington, and then Plt Off Wright/Sgt McChesney shot down a Ju 88 into the sea. The final two bombers shot down that night were again credited to N3378, but now flown by its usual crew, Flt Lt Trousdale/Sgt Chunn. They shot down two Heinkels in the space of just ten minutes, the first at 01.40hr, a few miles south-east of Leconfield, and the second at 01.50hr; this one fell into the sea.

during World War I, but rather than leave military service, he had become an SE.5A pilot with No. 74 Squadron, shooting down eleven German aircraft. He was awarded the Military Cross, the DFC and the DFM, and was one of three Defiant gunners entitled to wear Royal Flying Corps pilot's wings. He was known on the squadron as 'Timbertoes', and sadly he was killed by one of the bombs.

In Scotland, No. 141 Squadron took part in a Fighter Night over Glasgow on the 9 May, and Sqn Ldr E. Wolfe/Sgt Ashcroft had their first victory of the war when they shot down a Junkers Ju 88 at 01.09hr.

While all this action had been going on in the north, down in the south-west the skies had been quiet, and No. 307 Squadron had flown four uneventful patrols on both the 7th and the 8th. On the 9th, however, the war came their way once more when their own airfield at Exeter was bombed, and two Polish officers were injured. The squadron once more flew four patrols, but no contact was made.

No. 255 Squadron Defiants at dispersal at Kirton-in-Lindsey.

The German attack was against three cities: 129 bombers crossed the North Sea to bomb Hull, ninety-five headed for Nottingham and thirty-four for Sheffield. Covering that area was 255 Squadron, who sent aloft every Defiant they could, as well as a small number of Hurricanes they had also taken on charge. A Hurricane flown by Sqn Ldr Smith achieved the first success, shooting down an He 111 just offshore. Only five days earlier he had chosen to fly a Defiant, and took as his gunner Plt Off Farnes, who had been Flt Lt Louden's gunner in No. 141 Squadron's sole disastrous daylight action, and had baled out into the sea. In N3378 – the Defiant now on display at the Boulton Paul Aircraft Heritage Project – they had shot down a Ju 88 just off the coast. In his Hurricane,

With six raiders shot down in one night, five of them by the Defiants, it was the best score of any British night-fighter squadron in the war, and brought immediate messages of congratulations from Sir Archibald Sinclair, the Secretary of State for Air.

Just further south, No. 151 Squadron were not so lucky, because a stray Junkers Ju 88 bombed Wittering, and a stick of bombs landed across 'A' Flight dispersal, destroying two Defiants and damaging four others. As the bomber attacked, Plt Off Sidney Carlin ran towards his Defiant hoping to climb into his turret to use it as an anti-aircraft battery. At fifty-two years old he was the oldest Defiant gunner, and was hampered in his run by having a wooden leg. He had lost his leg in the trenches

Run of Success: 10 May

Revenge for No. 151 squadron came the following night when two Defiants, crewed by Flt Lt Mcmullen/Sgt Fairweath and Sgt Copelow/Sgt Sampson, shot down a Ju 88 and an He 111, respectively; and the indefatigable Plt Off Stevens destroyed one He 111 and damaged another in his Hurricane. Plt Off Wagner/Sgt Siedengart shot at three different Ju 88s, but each got away because their Defiant was too slow to catch them. Plt Off Gayzler/Plt Off Pfleger intercepted a Bf 110 on an intruder mission over Peterborough, but again, their Defiant was too slow to catch it.

The night of the 10 May was also notable for an interception that a Defiant did not make. No. 141 Squadron were at Ayr, and at around 22.00hr, Fg Off William Cuddie, a Canadian, was scrambled to intercept a fast-moving 'bandit' coming in over the North Sea at about 5,000ft (1,500m). His squadron commander, Ted Wolfe, ordered him to patrol at around 25,000ft (7,600m), conserving fuel, and waiting until the target arrived. Then he should dive at full throttle, and 'with the assistance of Isaac Newton', he might be able to catch the target. At the right moment ground control ordered

Down in the south-west, Exeter airfield was bombed once again on the 10th, but only slight damage was done, and No. 307's five patrols could not find the culprits.

Run of Success: 11 May

On the 11 May, No. 264 once more staged successful intruder missions over northern France, Sqn Ldr Sanders/Plt Off Sutton shooting down one Heinkel He 111 and Flt Lt Stephenson/Fg Off Maggs another. Plt Off Curtice/Plt Off Martin had their second intruder victory when they shot down a Dornier Do 17. With three bombers shot down in one night, No. 264 had achieved an echo of the successes they recorded a year earlier, also across the Channel.

Run of Success: 12 May

The following night, bombers returned to the Exeter area once more, and Sgt Malinowski/Sgt Jorzembowski sighted a Heinkel He 111 flying at only 1,000ft (300m). They crept up on it and opened fire, whereupon the Heinkel went into a half roll and dived out of sight. The Defiant crew then spotted another Heinkel, and they turned on that and exchanged fire; but the bomber dived to sea level and was lost. They then came across a third Heinkel, and this one they definitely destroyed. When they landed back at Exeter they found the airfield had suffered heavy damge from three waves of attacking bombers, and two Defiants and one Fairey Battle had been damaged by strafing.

No. 141 Squadron aircrew in the crew room late in 1940; one pilot is wearing dark goggles to preserve his night vision. Frank Lanning is third from the left, and another air gunner, Sgt L.H. Allen, is fifth from the left.

Cuddie to dive, which he did, reaching an incredible speed of 430mph (690kph). For a short while the two blips on the radar screen were on top of one another, but the Defiant crew could not see anything. Cuddie began to pull out of the dive, but only managed to at around 1,000ft (300m). Sqn Ldr Wolfe was so concerned at the effect of this on the Defiant that he got the groundcrew to check the airframe for damage after Cuddie landed; but such was the strength of the Defiant that all was well.

The 'bandit' had continued on its way, but was soon to disappear from the radar screens. It was the Bf 110 flown by Rudolf Hess, undertaking his crazy plan to arrange peace terms through Lord Lovatt. As an aftermath of the Hess Affair, Sqn Ldr Wolfe was asked on 16 May to provide an aircraft to take Lord Lovatt from Ayr up to Aberdeen. He thought it appropriate to make Bill Cuddie the pilot, and arranged for a Defiant turret to be locked in the forward position so that Cuddie could fire the guns if the need arose; Lord Lovatt made the journey with his long frame squeezed in the turret. The reason for the journey had nothing to do with Hess, but was because Lord Lovatt's son had just been born, though it was recorded as 'cross-country practice' in the Squadron's ORB.

Wolfe knew Lovatt well, because Lovatt's Commando unit had 'captured' No. 141 Squadron's dispersal during an exercise; but the RAF boys got their own back two weeks later when they were waiting with torches attached to the Defiant turret guns, operated manually, and able to claim all the attacking Commandos well and truly torched.

The Night-Fighter Force is Reshuffled

The month of May was also the best month of the night war for No. 141 Squadron, way north at Ayr, with detachments at Drem and Acklington: they claimed eight bombers shot down, their Defiants finally moving into credit in their fight with the Luftwaffe. The following month, however, they began converting to Beaufighters, and this was to signal a reshuffle of the night-fighter force over the coming summer, the German raiders becoming scarce as the Luftwaffe turned its attention to Russia.

Night-Fighter Successes by Type, 1940–41

Up to and including 2 April 1941:

Type	Destroyed	Probable	Damaged
Beaufighter	16	3	11
Blenheim	21	18	11
Defiant	6	3	6
Hurricane	12	8	11
Spitfire	15	8	4
Unknown	1	-	1

3 April to 28 May 1941:

Type	Destroyed	Probable	Damaged
Beaufighter	54	10	24
Blenheim	1	-	-
Defiant	43.5	9	17
Havoc	10	9	12
Hurricane	31	8	14
Spitfire	9	1	5

CHAPTER SIX

New Turret Fighters

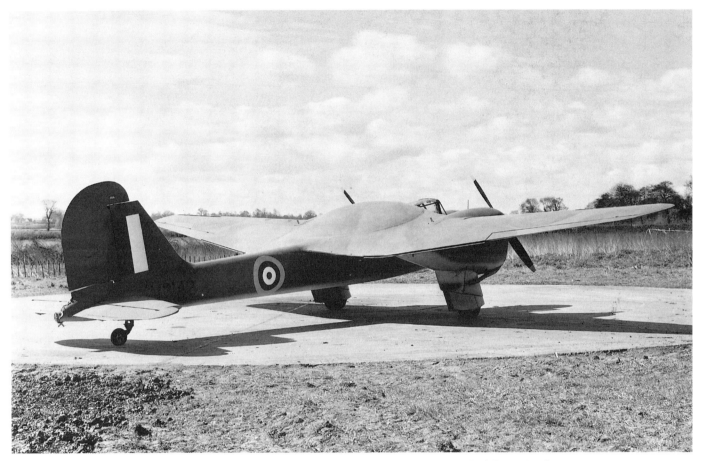

The P.92/2 on the compass-swinging circle at Pendeford, showing the low dome simulating the gun turret on the full-size aircraft.

As the war progressed, Boulton Paul had continued to work on the P.92, the potential Defiant replacement. The order for a half-scale flying model of the aircraft, the P.92/2, had gone to Heston Aircraft, and construction of the first prototype was under way, as well as testing of the large turret ring and the surrounding structure. Then Lord Beaverbrook was appointed Minister of Aircraft Production by Churchill, and set about rationalizing the aircraft on order.

The Bristol Beaufighter had already flown in prototype form, a heavy fighter that had come about almost by accident. It was seen as the obvious replacement for the Blenheim night fighters then in ser-

vice, and was ordered in large numbers. Boulton Paul were actually given an order for 280 Beaufighters as part of a consortium to build the aircraft, but with Defiant production still not achieving the desired fifty aircraft a month, wiser councils prevailed and the Beaufighter order was cancelled.

Also cancelled, on 26 May 1940, was the P.92. The first prototype was about 5 per cent complete, but the type's introduction into service was unlikely to be within twelve months, possibly twice that. In view of the difficulties with the P.92's specified engines, the Rolls-Royce Vulture and the Napier Sabre, when they went into service on other aircraft, it is clear that the

P.92 might well have been delayed even more than that. The Type L four-cannon turret was not needed for the new RAF heavy bombers, as another of Beaverbrook's decisions was to concentrate on the rifle-calibre machine-gun turrets already in production. Whether the difficulties the company was experiencing with the turret's 13ft (4m) diameter ring had any bearing on the decision to cancel the aircraft is not known.

The P.92/2 and its Short-comings

Despite the cancellation of the P.92, it was

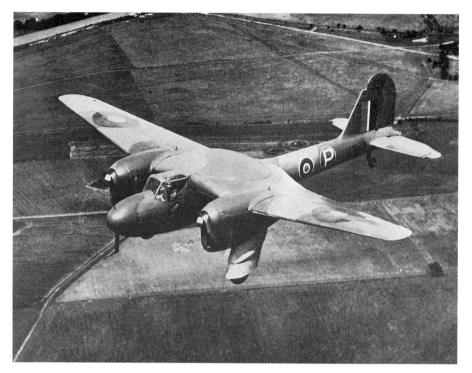

An air-to-air shot of the P.92/2, which spent most of its short life at Pendeford.

decided to complete the half-scale P.92/2 that was already under construction at Heston Aircraft. This all-wooden aircraft made its first flight in the spring of 1941 at the hands of Boulton Paul's chief test pilot, Cecil Feather. After a small number of familiarization flights at Heston, it was flown to Pendeford, and the centre section was fitted with pressure pick-up points and was tufted for aerodynamic trials. Robin Lindsay Neale had his first flight in V3142 on 4 September 1941, and the P.92/2 finally went to Boscombe Down for handling trials in June 1943.

The P.92/2 was not exactly a practical aircraft, as it was limited by its role. The pilot could only enter the cockpit via temporary steps when the engines were not running, because of the proximity of the propeller arc, and the canopy was a one-piece removable item that could only be fixed with the help of someone on the outside. The A & AEE pilots were alarmed to find they could not reach the handle that collapsed the seat prior to making an emergency exit through the fuselage hatch provided for the purpose. A piece of string attached to this handle eased their minds, though happily it was never needed.

Because of a lack of room in the narrow, cramped cockpit, the engine instruments had to be placed on the inside of the engine nacelles. The fact that they could still be read quite easily demonstrated just how near the pilot was to them, and explained why complaints were made about the noisiness of the cockpit. The full-size P.92 would have had extensive sound-proofing to alleviate the noise problem, and the pilot would have sat slightly further forward in relation to the engine nacelles, which would have improved the view sideways – another cause for complaint.

The trials proved that the P.92/2 was very pleasant to handle, but that its drag was higher than the figures suggested by the RAE wind-tunnel model. However, the stability was better than that suggested by the 2/7th scale model, probably because of the lower power of the Gipsy Major engines. It was thought that the full-size aircraft, if it had been built, would have had stability figures nearer to those of the model. Obviously those in the RAE preparing the report were unaware of the intermediate 1/7th scale model with a new wing plan. In October 1944 the company submitted a report pointing out that the P.92/2 had the same wing plan as this model, which had satisfactory stability, and that therefore the P.92 would be more likely to conform to this, and not to the 1/7th scale model, which was no longer

relevant.

After the P.92/2 had flown, a half-scale dummy turret was ordered, to be powered by an electric or an electro-hydraulic motor, with half-scale cannon barrels that would range in length from 18in (45cm) to 5ft (1.5m). It was then estimated that this would take five to six months to build, and there would be another five to six months to iron out the bugs in its operation. It was decided that this was not worth the many thousands of pounds that would be expended on a purely academic exercise, and the half-scale turret was cancelled.

The P.92/2 was returned to the company on completion of the handling tests, which had been of only academic interest after the cancellation of the P.92. The little aircraft was stored for some time in a shed half-way between the factory and Pendeford airfield, alongside the connecting taxiway, but before the end of the war it was chopped up for firewood.

A Replacement for the Defiant

The Type A gun turret fitted with a single 20mm cannon, which had been tested on the Defiant prototype, K8310, before the war, was in November 1941 fitted to Defiant N1622 to test a new fairing to be fitted to the cannon barrel, designed to alleviate drag. As related previously, the first fairings designed by the RAE had broken up in the air, and they were redesigned by Boulton Paul. They were fitted to the greater part of the barrel protruding from the turret, and had a cross-section like an elongated teardrop, with a fish-tail. There was 54oz of lead in the leading edge, and the fish-tail was tested at different diameters. Both Cecil Feather and Lindsay Neale test-flew the aircraft, with RAE observers, Mr Cameron or Mr Tomkins, in the turret. In its best form the fairing decreased torque considerably and was satisfactorily stable in all conditions. With the P.92 cancelled, its most likely use would have been on the cannon turrets planned for heavy bombers, but in fact no such fairing was ever fitted to an operational turret.

Even after the cancellation of the P.92, the need for an eventual replacement for the Defiant and Beaufighter was, however, still seen. The Luftwaffe had launched its first night-time attack on 18 June, when

The P.92/2 a few yards from where it was eventually broken up. The fixed undercarriage and the slight widening of the nose to accommodate the pilot were the main changes to an exact half-scale model.

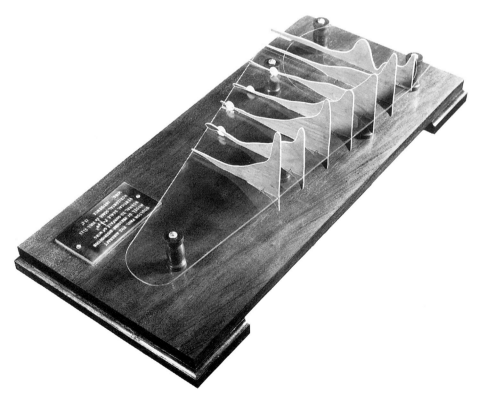

An unusual model produced by Boulton Paul, showing the pressure distribution along the surface of the P.92's wing.

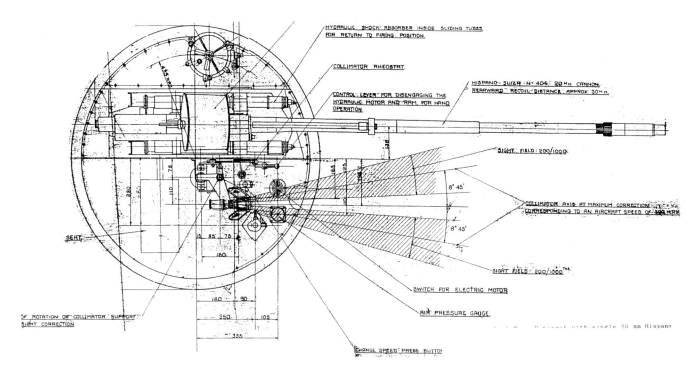

The Type N cannon turret, a Type A re-armed with a single 20mm cannon.

the Heinkels of KG4 were detailed to bomb the airfields at Mildenhall and Honnington. The British force standing ready to oppose them consisted of just two Blenheim squadrons, No. 23 at Collyweston and No. 29 at Debden; two Spitfire squadrons were also on standby. By the end of the night the Luftwaffe had lost six Heinkels – but the RAF had also lost three Blenheims and a Spitfire. From small beginnings such as this, a picture of a better night fighter was evolved. The single-seaters proved that they could operate at night, though the difficulty of landing a Spitfire at night soon led to the Hurricane being the preferred aircraft.

The ability to carry heavy armament to destroy the raider with the first burst was quickly realized. After the first burst the bomber could take evasive action, and was then easily lost in the darkness of the night. In a prolonged battle, the four fixed forward-firing machine guns of the Blenheim were often not enough to overpower the defensive guns of the raider, and it would be touch and go which would be shot down. On that first night, three Heinkels were shot down by Blenheims, who were also themselves shot down by the defensive fire. A one-for-one loss rate was clearly unacceptable, especially as the

true figure was worse than that. One of the Heinkels also shot down a Spitfire that joined in the attack with a Blenheim, and another damaged a second Blenheim that had also been attacking.

Specification for a Dedicated Night Fighter

A new specification, F.18/40, was drawn up and issued in August 1940 for a dedicated night fighter. It required a two-seat aircraft armed with either four cannon and six machine guns, like the Beaufighter, or six cannon. It was to have a top speed of 400mph (644kph) at 20,000ft (6,000m), a service ceiling of 35,000ft (10,700m) and a three-hour patrol endurance. The fitment of a gun turret was not a definite requirement.

Fairey prepared a version of the Firefly to this specification, Gloster designed their G.39, Miles the M.22A, and Hawker their P.1008.

Boulton Paul's P.96

Boulton Paul's submission for Spec. F.18/40, the P.96, was virtually an enlarged Defiant, powered with either the 2,300hp

Napier Sabre NS6SM, or the 2,300hp Bristol Centaurus CE45M. It was offered in two distinct versions, with either a Type A Defiant turret, and the pilot operating the AI equipment, or without a turret and an AI operator beneath a long transparent canopy in the rear fuselage, facing forwards. With the turret, the aircraft would also be fitted with either two or four forward-firing cannon. The version without the turret would have six fixed forward-firing cannon.

The aircraft was thus not a 'turret fighter' in the same way as the Defiant or Roc, as the armament was to be split in the same way as the Hawker Demon's had been. The aircraft had an all-up weight of around 13,000lb (5,900kg) and the Sabre-engined version was estimated to have a top speed of 367mph (591kph) at 21,000ft (6,400m) with the turret, or 389mph (626kph) without. The estimates for the Centaurus-engined versions were 392mph (631kph) at 34,000ft (10,363m) with the turret, or an impressive 415mph (668kph) without.

A drawing exists of a standard Defiant equipped with six forward-firing cannon, to illustrate tests with three alternative fairings. Test one was with individual conical sleeves for each cannon; test two was

A model of the P.96B with the Napier Sabre engine, a Type A turret and two forward-firing 20mm cannon.

	P.96A	P.96B	P.96D	P.96D (no turret)
Technical Information for the Boulton Paul P.96				
Engine	Sabre	Sabre	Centaurus	Centaurus
Armament	6x20mm	4x20mm	6x20mm	4x20mm
	no turret	turret	no turret	turret
Top speed				
at 21,000ft	415mph	392mph	389mph	367mph
6,400m	668kph	631kph	626kph	591kph
Span	45ft 10in	45ft 10in	45ft 10in	45ft 10in
	13.97m	13.97m	13.97m	13.97m
Length	37ft 5in	37ft 5in	39ft 8in	39ft 8in
	11.41m	11.41m	12.09m	12.09m

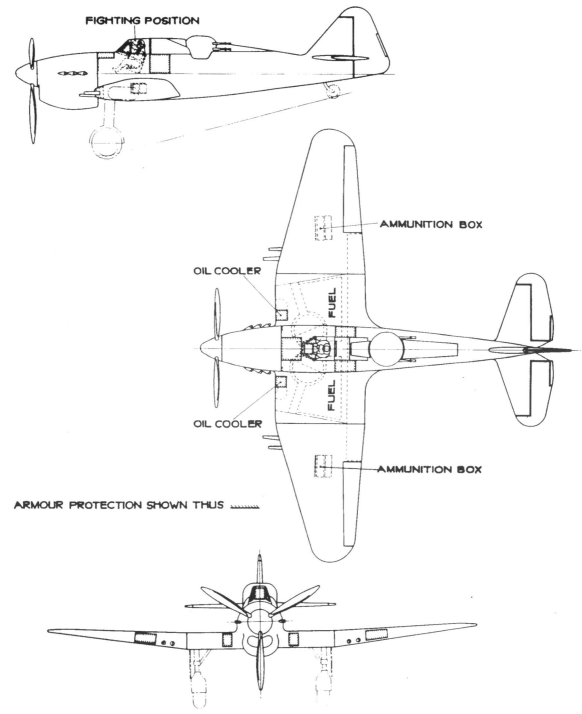

BOULTON PAUL AIRCRAFT LTᴰ. WOLVERHAMPTON.

FIGHTING POSITION

AMMUNITION BOX

OIL COOLER

FUEL

FUEL

OIL COOLER

AMMUNITION BOX

ARMOUR PROTECTION SHOWN THUS

A.M. SPEC. F.18/40

SINGLE ENGINE TWO SEATER NIGHT FIGHTER

I. NAPIER SABRE SERIES NS6SM ENGINE

BOULTON PAUL SERIES P96C

The Boulton Paul P.96.

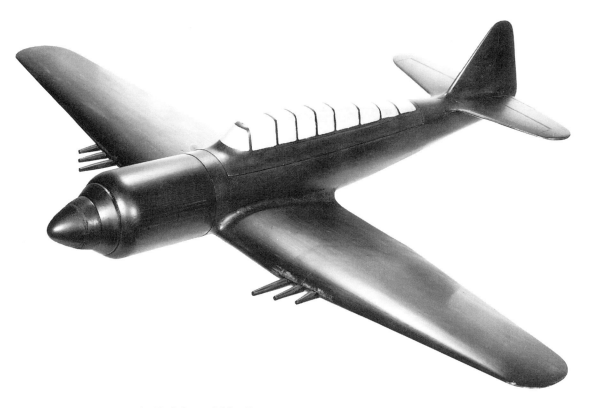

The Boulton Paul P.96D without a turret and with six forward-firing 20mm cannon.

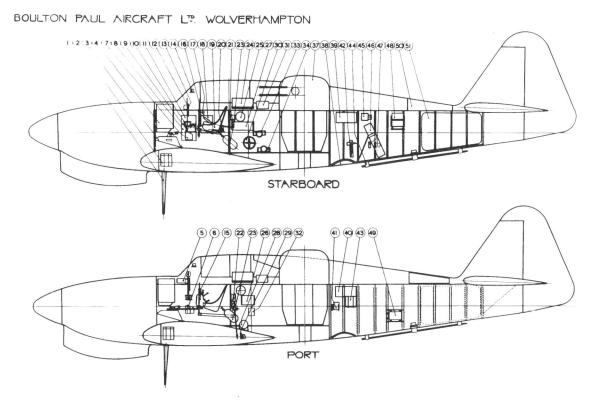

BOULTON PAUL AIRCRAFT Lᵀᴰ. WOLVERHAMPTON

STARBOARD

PORT

The Boulton Paul P.96C with a Napier Sabre engine.

SCALE IN FEET

The Centaurus-powered P.96 with a Type A turret and four forward-firing cannon.

The P.92/2 half-scale model of the proposed P.92 turret fighter, showing the slim lines of the fuselage.

An artist's impression of the P.96B head-on.

with tapered group fairings for each set of three cannon; and test three was with the cannon below the wings in a nacelle-like group fairing. The drawing does not indicate the nature of the tests or their date, but they were unlikely to be in the air; most probably they were wind-tunnel tests in connection with the P.96 project. They might also have been connected with the idea of building a single-seat Defiant armed with twelve machine guns or six cannon, an idea that was rejected at a special conference on 4 September 1940, on the basis that two-seat Defiants were needed and it would have been wrong to have disrupted their production.

Boulton Paul's P.97

The Air Ministry decided that single-engined aircraft could not have sufficient performance to meet the specification, and so Boulton Paul designed a twin-engined aircraft, the P.97, with the same basic themes. The P.97 was a twin-boom design powered by two Napier Sabre NS.6SM engines, and fitted with a tricycle undercarriage. The specification called for

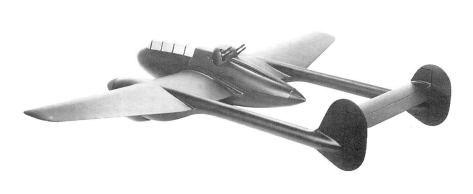

A model of the P.97B with the Type A gun turret as well as fixed forward-firing cannon.

fixed cannon armament plus a gun turret, which could easily be removed as required in service. In its P.97A version it was armed with six 20mm cannon with 900 rounds of ammunition, in a weapons bay on the underside of the fuselage pod and no turret.

There were two alternative positions for the AI operator: in the first he sat well to the rear of the pilot in a stepped-up posi-

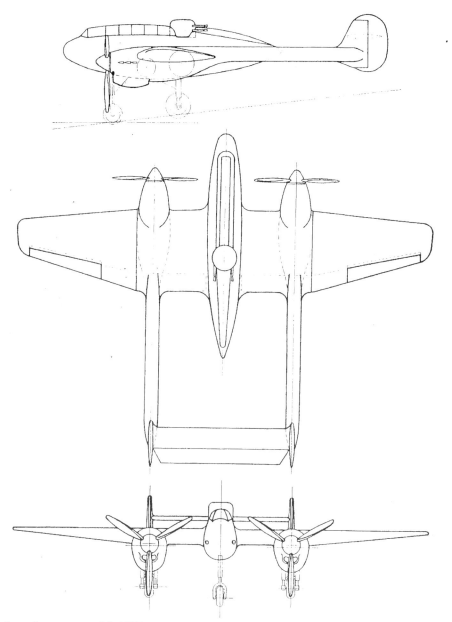

General arrangement of the P.97B.

tion, behind his own windscreen, and was provided with a revolving seat so he could have good all-round vision. This version covered the removable turret facility in its simplest form and without disturbing the aircraft's centre of gravity; however, it did not allow close access of the AI operator to the pilot, as required by the specification. As an alternative the AI operator would have been provided with an aircraft control unit connected to the automatic pilot, allowing him to control the aircraft in the last stages of an interception.

In the second version, the AI operator sat right behind the pilot beneath a long, flush-fitting canopy. He was also provided with a swivelling seat to provide rear warning, and this could be raised to give the AI operator a forward view. The top of his canopy folded forward to form a windscreen, in much the same manner as that of the rear seat of a Miles Master.

The P.97B version was equipped with two fixed cannon plus the Type A gun turret, and the radar was therefore operated by the pilot. The turret was the basic Type A with improvements, so that the guns could be depressed to 20 degrees below the horizontal, though this limited their elevation to 70 degrees. There was a retractable fairing to the rear of the turret in the manner of that on the Defiant, and the aircraft was also capable of carrying six cannon as well as the turret, thereby exceeding the specification requirements.

Two 500lb (227kg) bombs could also be carried in the weapons bay if four of the cannon were removed, giving the P.97 extra versatility as an intruder or ground-attack aircraft. The aircraft could be further modified by replacing the lower forward nacelle with a new unit containing a prone bomb-aiming position, and space for

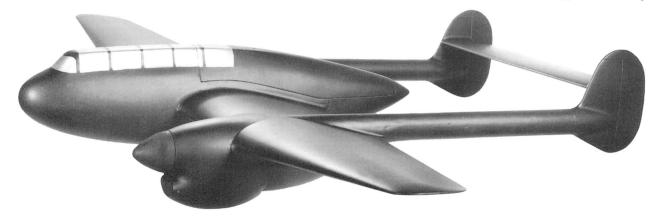

A model of the P.97A, with the radar operator in a cockpit just behind the pilot.

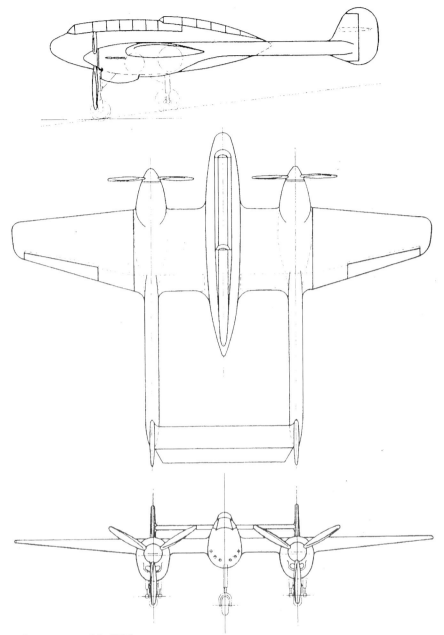

two extra 250lb (113.5kg) bombs, turning the aircraft into a conventional three-seat medium bomber. With both turret and AI position removed, the aircraft could be flown as a long-range, single-seat fighter.

The main fuel tanks were in the wing centre-section, with capacity for 520gal (2,360ltr). With the turret removed, overload tanks totalling 230gal (1,050ltr) would be sited in the turret bay, and just forward of it. For ferry flights, another 170gal (770ltr) jettisonable tank could be carried in the weapons bay on the bomb racks.

Using the P.97 as a basis, Boulton Paul also submitted a brochure for a pilot-operated movable cannon mounting. Slots on either side of the cockpit would contain 20mm cannon able to move in elevation only, in conjunction with a special gun-sight. This had echoes of the revolving Lewis gun barbettes on the second Boulton Paul Bittern prototype twelve years earlier, but this new cannon mounting could be depressed below the horizontal for ground attack, as well as raised for air-to-air firing, from beneath a target or across the arc of a turn in a dogfight.

The concept of attacking a surface target while flying straight and level was to re-emerge a few years later when the Boulton Paul Type L mounting was designed for the nose of the Shackleton, a very similar mounting as that envisaged for the P.97, but later altered, with the cannon much closer together for production; this was made possible by moving the Shackleton's radar from the nose, to a ventral position. The nose gunner was thus able to fire at a surface target as the Shackleton made a low-level bombing run, to suppress return fire.

General arrangement of the P.97A.

A head-on view of the P.97A, normally armed with six 20mm cannon.

BOULTON PAUL AIRCRAFT L™ WOLVERHAMPTON

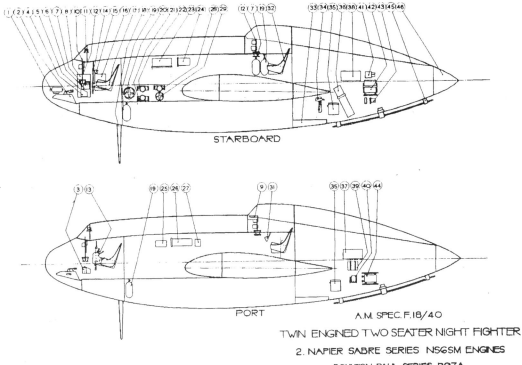

STARBOARD

PORT

A.M. SPEC. F.18/40

TWIN ENGINED TWO SEATER NIGHT FIGHTER

2. NAPIER SABRE SERIES NS6SM ENGINES

BOULTON PAUL SERIES P.97 A.

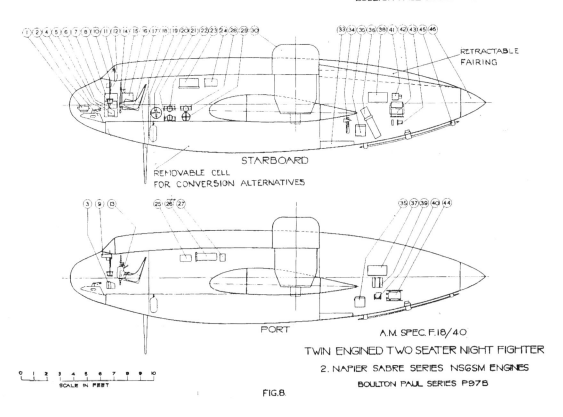

RETRACTABLE FAIRING

STARBOARD

REMOVABLE CELL
FOR CONVERSION ALTERNATIVES

PORT

A.M. SPEC. F.18/40

TWIN ENGINED TWO SEATER NIGHT FIGHTER

2. NAPIER SABRE SERIES NS6SM ENGINES

BOULTON PAUL SERIES P.97 B

SCALE IN FEET
0 1 2 3 4 5 6 7 8 9 10

FIG.8.

The fuselage of the P.97, showing the equipment layout.

(Left) A sketch of the use of the nose-cannon mounting for ground attack – a mounting designed with the P.97 in mind, which came to fruition with the Shackleton nose mounting.

Interestingly, the considerable amount of work that Boulton Paul had done with regard to the use of plastic materials in aircraft, with many Defiant panels being redesigned in the material, led the company to claim that much of the P.97, including the tail booms, tailplane, fin, rudder, outer wings and gun doors would be made of this material once the P.97 was in production. The company had first used plastic in aircraft as far back as 1919, when the P.10 biplane exhibited at the Paris Salon d'Aeronautique had fuselage panels of Bakelite-Dilecto.

The ML Night Fighter

A similarly powered twin-boom fighter was also designed to Spec. F.18/40 by R. Malcolm Ltd, of Slough. It was designated the ML Night Fighter, using the initials of its designer's name, Marcel Lobelle. M.J.O. Lobelle had been a Belgian refugee during World War I, and had become Fairey's chief designer in 1924, joining R. Malcolm Ltd just before the war.

The ML Night Fighter was submitted for consideration in January 1941, and had a far more radical engine and armament layout than the P.97. The Napier Sabre engines were in push/pull arrangement at each end of the central pod, and there was only a single fin and rudder placed centrally on the tailplane in the slipstream of the engines. The pilot sat in the port boom/fuselage. The armament was carried in two gun turrets at the front of each boom: the port turret was fitted with the specified six .303in machine guns with 6,000 rounds, and the starboard one with two 20mm cannon and 150 rounds. The gunners could thus only fire over the forward hemisphere. In addition there were two fixed forward-firing 20mm cannon and 150 rounds in the wings, fired by the pilot.

The technical details submitted by the company mentioned a nose-wheel undercarriage, but the photographs of a model attached to the proposal showed a tail-wheel, with the leg attached to the central fin.

Technical Information for the Boulton Paul P.97

Engines	2 x Napier Sabre NS.6SM, 2,235hp	
Span	58ft 6in (17.86m)	
Length	45ft 6in (13.87m)	
Wing area	525sq ft (48.77sq m)	
Aspect ratio	6.5	
Loaded weight	19,586lb (8,840kg) (P.97A); 19,232lb (8,723kg) (P.97B)	
Fuel capacity	520gal (2,363ltr)	
	P.97A (without turret)	*P.97B (with turret)*
Top speed		
at 20,000ft	404mph	398mph
(6,000m)	(650kph)	(640kph)
at 22,500ft	419mph	413mph
(6,860m)	(674kph)	(665kph)
at 34,000ft	425mph	418mph
(10,360m)	(684kph)	(673kph)
Rate of climb		
at sea level:	3,520ft/min	3,560ft/min
	(1,073m/min)	(1,085m/min)
Time		
to 20,000ft	6.7min	6.6min
(6,100m)		
Ceiling	39,500ft	39,500ft
	(12,040m)	(12,040m)
Range	1,430 miles	1,430 miles
	(2,300km)	(2,300km)

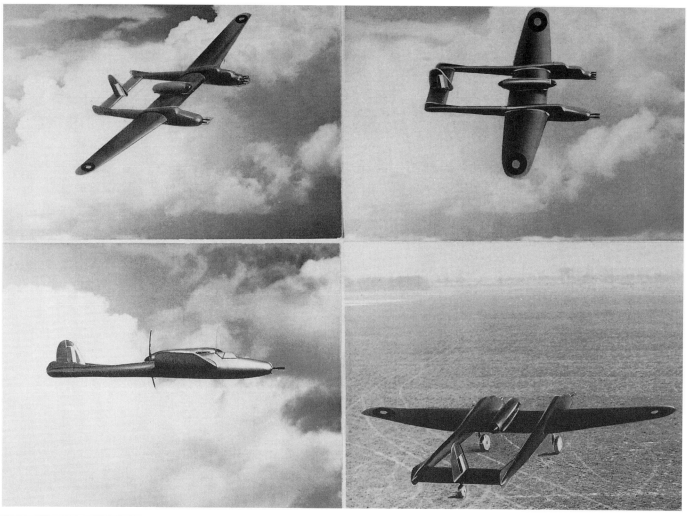

(Above) Four views of a model of the ML Night Fighter, showing a tail-wheel undercarriage.

Technical Details for the ML Night Fighter	
Engines	2 x Napier Sabre NS.6SM, 2,235hp
Span	66ft (20m)
Length	8ft (14.6m)
Wing area	600sq ft (58sq m)
Aspect ratio	7.25
Airscrew dia	14ft (4.3m)
Loaded weight	1,500lb (9,750kg)
Top speed:	
at sea level	362mph (582kph)
at 5,000ft (1,500m)	386mph (621kph)
at 10,000ft (3,000m)	382mph (615kph)
at 15,000ft (4,500m)	400mph (644kph)
at 19,000ft (5,800m)	425mph (684kph)
at 25,000ft (7,600m)	414mph (666kph)
at 30,000ft (9,100m)	404mph (650kph)
Climb to:	
10,000ft (3,000m)	3.2min
15,000ft (4,500m)	4.9min
20,000ft (6,000m)	6.8min
25,000ft (7,600m)	9.4min
30,000ft (9,100m)	12.7min
Service ceiling:	38,500ft (11,735m)
Range:	4hr at 225mph (362kph)

The Gloster Reaper

The Boulton Paul P.97 was considered too radical by the Air Ministry, and so the highly unusual ML Night Fighter stood little chance of acceptance. The preferred fighter to emerge from the F.18/40 specification was entirely conventional, but had started life as a turret fighter: the Gloster F.34/35. Gloster had redesigned this aircraft to the F.9/37 cannon fighter specification, with the turret removed and five fixed forward-firing 20mm cannon fitted, two in the lower forward fuselage beneath the pilot, and three in the upper rear fuselage where the turret had been. Two prototypes of the F.9/37 design were built, one with Bristol Taurus engines, and one with Rolls-Royce Peregrines, the powerplant of the successful F.9/37 design, the Westland Whirlwind.

Anxious not to abandon a promising

design, Gloster adapted it in 1939 with Merlin engines, one or two crew, and the heaviest armament then considered for a fighter: four 20mm cannon in the lower forward fuselage, and a tray of eight .303in machine guns beneath the fuselage where the turret had been. This design was called the Gloster Reaper, and the Air Ministry considered it would form the basis for an excellent solution to the F.18/40 specification. Boulton Paul were given instructions to help Gloster with the detail design of this fighter, but when it became clear, first, that the Reaper would not be available for production until well into 1942, and also that the de Havilland Mosquito would form the basis for an excellent night fighter with even better performance, the Gloster Reaper was cancelled.

The Beaufighters

The adaptation of an existing design to take a gun turret was an alternative to the design of a brand new airframe. In March 1941 two Merlin-engined Beaufighter Mk.IIs, R2274 and R2306, were adapted on the production line to take a Boulton Paul Type A four-gun turret, sited immediately behind the pilot's cockpit. The turret was equipped to elevate the guns from a minimum of 21 degrees to 84 degrees, clearing all parts of the aircraft's structure. The small observer's canopy normally fitted was replaced by a flush metal panel. The six wing-mounted machine guns and two of the fuselage cannon were also deleted. In this form the aircraft was re-designated the Beaufighter Mk.V.

One of the aircraft, R2274, went to Boscombe Down for brief handling trials and to investigate the effects of speed on the turret operation. It was found that at speeds of 400mph (644kph) achieved in a dive, turret rotation remained within 1 degree per second of the normal average. At this speed there was some vibration in the cupola panels, and the turret was found to be very draughty when the guns were pointed forward. The rotation of the turret did not affect the handling of the aircraft.

Both Beaufighters were sent for trials with No. 406 Squadron at Acklington, and later by the RAF's premier night-fighter squadron, No. 29. The arrangement was found to have three significant merits. First, it was easier to engage a slow-moving target, which could easily be over-shot in a normal fixed-gun approach, and then lost in the darkness. Second, it

enabled the crew to make the best of a bad approach, letting the gunner open fire even when it would be impossible for the pilot to place his sights on the target. Lastly, it let the Beaufighter approach from beneath the target, which was more visible from below on dark nights. These advantages were something the Defiant crews already knew about.

No more Beaufighters were fitted with the turret because it reduced the top speed of the aircraft too much, from 303mph (488kph) at 15,000ft (4,500m) to 272mph (438kph). Also, the turret blocked the pilot's emergency exit, a hatch in the floor immediately behind his seat.

The Fraser-Nash Havoc

The major advantage of the turret fighter in night fighting, the ability to approach and attack the target from below, was now widely recognized, and in March 1941 Frazer-Nash adapted a Douglas Havoc, BD126, to take movable, upward-firing guns. Six .303in machine guns were fitted in two rows of three behind the pilot's cockpit. They could move in elevation from 3–50 degrees, and in traverse 19 degrees either side of the centreline. Their movement was controlled by a gunner seated in the glazed nose of the aircraft with a remote sight and a clear vision panel in the roof. The mounting was designated the FN.71, and was inspected at Tolworth on 2 April 1941. The 'field of search' for the gunner was criticized, and this was modified by Frazer-Nash; the mounting was then re-designated the FN.72.

The Havoc was delivered to the Fighter Interception Unit on 24 July 1941 for trials, and later also went to No. 85 Squadron, an operator of standard Havoc night fighters. Although both of these found the installation very effective, no more Havocs were converted, firstly because putting the gunner in the nose left no room for forward-firing guns, and also because the Havoc was considered too slow for further development.

The Mosquito

When the Mosquito came into service as a night fighter during the summer of 1941, it provided an airframe that was not too slow; a proposal to adapt the aircraft to take a Bristol Type B.XI Mk.I four-gun turret was therefore accepted. One Mosquito,

W4050, was completed with a dummy turret on 24 July 1941; two more airframes, W4053 and W4073, were then fitted with the turret at Salisbury Hall, and flew out on 14 September and 5 December 1941. The reduction in the top speed of the aircraft with the turret fitted once more ended any further development, especially as the normal Mosquito night fighter with fixed guns was by now achieving satisfactory results.

Finding a Defiant Replacement

The project to find a turret-fighter replacement for the Defiant was still on the agenda, however, and on 24 April 1942 a conference looked at three new alternatives. The first was a Defiant fitted with a Merlin 61 engine, that would give it a top speed of 321mph (516kph) at 26,000ft (7,900m), a ceiling of 35,500ft (10,800m) and an endurance of 3.19hr.

The second was a new airframe with a Bristol Centaurus engine: this would have a top speed of 368mph (592kph) at 22,500ft (6,850m), a ceiling of 31,500ft (9,600m) and an endurance of 3.8hr. Whether this was the Boulton Paul P.96 is not clear, though the P.96 is quoted as having a better performance than these figures suggest. The third option was an aircraft powered by two Rolls-Royce Griffon engines, with a top speed of 385mph (619kph) at 27,000ft (8,230m), a ceiling of 36,100ft (11,000m) and an endurance of 4hr. Again, whether this scheme was related to the Boulton Paul P.97 is not clear. The conference decided that none of these options provided sufficient performance, and the project to find a Defiant replacement was dropped.

In the USA

Though a turret fighter to follow the Defiant did not come to fruition in Great Britain, it did on the other side of the Atlantic. As reports of British experience against German night-bombing raids began to filter through to the Americans, it became clear that a dedicated night fighter was required. The ad hoc use of standard day fighters at night, which had been the usual practice of most air forces up to then, was clearly not acceptable. Although Britain led the world in airborne radar, in 1940 the Americans were already working on air-to-air radar, and it was also clear that a modern night fighter required the ability to carry an AI set and a radar operator. The successful use of the Defiant during the early months of the Blitz also suggested the use of a gun turret, British experience during the Blitz having shown that speed was not of prime importance. Sufficient speed to overtake raiders was obviously required, but too much speed could be an embarrassment, leading to overshooting, and losing the target. Long endurance was of far more importance – the ability to loiter aloft until vectored onto an intruder – as was a very heavy armament to destroy a target in the first quick burst, before evasive action could be taken by the target.

Northrop P-61 Black Widow

Late in 1940 the Northrop Aircraft Corporation began to design a dedicated night fighter that would incorporate the elements suggested by British experience: sufficient performance, heavy armament incorporating a turret, long endurance, and a radar operator with the best AI radar available. Northrop looked at different configurations, for a while considering two gun turrets, one on the nose and one on the dorsal position; this would have required a crew of four: two gunners, a pilot and an AI operator.

The Army Air Corps was happy to back Northrop's interest in the project, and on 11 January 1941, two prototypes of the Northrop design were ordered as the XP-61. Two months later a static test specimen and thirteen pre-production YP-61s were also ordered. On 1 September 1941, nearly six months before even the prototype XP-61 had flown, 150 production examples were ordered by the United States Army Air Corps. Such was the USAAC's desperate need for night fighters that on 12 February 1942 another 410 P-61s were ordered. Fifty of these aircraft were to be assigned to the Royal Air Force – though in the event Britain only ever received one P-61, for evaluation. It was, incidentally, flown by the Boulton Paul test pilot, Robin Lindsay Neale, on a 30min flight from Boscombe Down, on 6 September 1944. The Mosquito proved to be effective and available sooner, so much so that American night-fighter squadrons in Europe were equipped with Beaufighters and Mosquitos while they awaited deliveries of their own P-61s. The first XP-61 finally flew for the first time on 21 May 1942.

The aircraft that emerged bore a strik-

ing resemblance to the Boulton Paul P.97 project, with very similar armament, power, size and performance. It was a twin-boom aircraft powered by two 2,250hp Pratt & Whitney R-2800 Double Wasp radials. The fuselage pod contained a crew of three: pilot; radar operator, in a raised position with his own windscreen; and a gunner facing aft in the rear of the fuselage nacelle, who operated the remote-control dorsal turret containing four 0.5in Browning machine guns. These could be fixed to fire forwards, together with the four forward-firing 20mm cannon in the lower fuselage. Like the P.97, the P-61 could also carry two 1,000lb (454kg) bombs under the outer wings.

The first detailed designs for a turret fighter to Spec. F.9/33 had produced aircraft as big as medium bombers, such as the Boulton Paul P-74. Ten years later the last detailed designs for turret fighters, such as the Boulton Paul P-97 and the Northrop P-61 Black Widow, had also produced aircraft as big as medium bombers. The circle was complete.

The P-61 Black Widow goes into Production

Flight testing of the first aircraft revealed tail-buffeting problems when the turret was operated, so this was deleted on the first production batch of P-61s, which were given the name 'Black Widow'. In any case, the same basic turret was being used on the Boeing B-29, which had priority. Deliveries of production P-61As commenced in October 1943, followed by the P-61B in July 1944 to the Pacific theatre, where the Black Widow recorded its first

victories. From the 201st production example of the P-61B, the gun turret was reintroduced. A new General Electric turret with a redesigned fire control system was fitted. A total of 250 turret-equipped P-61Bs were built, and then they were supplanted on the Northrop production lines by the P-61C, with turbo-charged R-2800 engines giving 2,800hp, which gave a greatly increased performance to the aircraft. Maximum speed was increased to 430mph (690kph) at 30,000ft (9,000m), and the service ceiling was raised by 8,000ft (2,430m) to 41,000ft (12,500m).

Although it was the last turret fighter to go into service, the P-61's turret was only used in the fixed forward-firing position. The turret fighter's ability to attack from beneath or on the beam was not exploited. In part this was due to improvements in airborne radar, which made approaches from the rear of a target easier to co-ordinate. By the time the P-61 entered service there were very few targets, and the bulk of the work undertaken by the P-61 squadrons was intruding, usually ground attack.

At the same time that the P-61 Black Widow was entering service with a turret that would only be used to fire straight ahead, and the RAF had abandoned night fighters with turrets, the Luftwaffe was fitting its night fighters with upward-firing guns, albeit fixed at a steep angle. The system was called Schräge Musik (Sloping Music), the German for 'jazz', and it enabled German night-fighter pilots to attack the unprotected undersides of RAF heavy bombers with a great deal of accuracy. They were often able to aim specifically for the fuel tanks or engines, so that the bomber would explode before the crew

Comparison between the Boulton Paul P.97 and the Northrop P-61		
	Boulton Paul P.97	Northrop P-61B
Type	Night Fighter	Night Fighter
Layout	Twin booms	Twin booms
	Nose-wheel u/c	Nose-wheel u/c
Crew	Two	Three
Engine	2 x Napier Sabre 6SM	Pratt & Whitney R-2800
Power	2,235hp/ea	2,250hp/ea
Fixed armament	6 x 20mm cannon	4 x 20mm cannon
Turret armament	4 x .303in	4 x 0.5in
Span	58ft 6in	66ft
	(17.83m)	(20.12m)
Length	45ft 6in	48ft 11in
	(13.87m)	(14.93m)

Northrop P-61 Victories during World War II

Pacific/Asia

	Victories	Probables
5th Air Force (3 squadrons)	37	4
7th Air Force (3 squadrons)	22	3
13th Air Force (2 squadrons)	6	1
10th Air Force (1 squadron)	0	0
14th Air Force (1 squadron)	5	1

Europe/Mediterranean

9th Air Force (2 squadrons)	53	7
12th Air Force (4 squadrons)	5	0
Total	128	16

even knew they were under attack.

On the night of 30/31 March 1944, 781 Lancasters and Halifaxes set out for Nuremberg expecting cloud cover, but finding instead clear skies. A total of ninety-five of the bombers failed to return, ten more were destroyed in crashes on their return, and 440 aircrew were killed, with 148 more taken prisoner. A great number of the aircraft shot down succumbed to the Luftwaffe's 'sloping music', and the sky over Germany was lit again and again by exploding bombers, which horrified the other crews and led to a rumour of a secret German weapon. But it was no secret to the crews of the Defiant turret fighters who had used the same attacking technique three years previously.

Air-to-air shot of the Northrop P-61C Black Widow with the turret locked to fire forward.

CHAPTER SEVEN

Further Night Fighting

Flt Lt Deanesley/Sgt Scott of No. 256 Squadron received the DFC and the DFM respectively, the squadron's first honours. But on the following day, 17 May, Deansley was brought back down to earth, literally, when he hit the tea van while taxiing. There was slight damage to the aircraft but the tea van was wrecked, though the occupants escaped unhurt.

On the night of 22nd/23rd, No. 256 Squadron had one more success: Flt Lt Coleman/Flt Sgt Smith took off at 20.55hr, and just half an hour later shot down a Junkers Ju 88 at 21.30hr, near Oswestry in Shropshire.

No. 151 Squadron had one success in June when Edmiston/Beale shot down a Ju 88 over Yarmouth; but during July, August and September the only successes achieved were by the redoubtable Plt Off Richard Playne Stevens, now flying a cannon-armed Hurricane. By July, No. 96 Squadron, which had taken to using Honiley as a forward base, had achieved a sixth night-time victory with its Defiants. On 10 June, Sqn Ldr Burns/Fg Off Smith were circling the 'Sardine' focal point, one of several such holding points to which they could be assigned by ground control, when suddenly they spotted a Ju 88 on their port side and only 100ft (30m) below. Smith fired a 1sec burst, and the Junkers' pilot put his nose down and went into a tight turn. Burns banked with him, and Smith got in a second burst from 70yd (64m) range down to 40yd (37m). Burns now managed to get below the bomber and Smith fired two more bursts, sending the bomber to its destruction.

Four 264 Squadron air gunners by a Defiant night fighter; left to right: Flt Sgt Chandler, Sgt McNair, Sgt Fred Barker, Sgt Croucher.

The Night-Fighter Squadrons are Reorganized

It was time for a reorganization of the night-fighter squadrons. In June No. 141 Squadron began converting to Beaufighters, and flew its very last Defiant patrols on the 4 August. The crew of Plt Off

After the burst of activity in May, the Luftwaffe turned its attention to Russia, and the short summer nights saw very few raiders over Britain. In June, July, August and September No. 264 Squadron achieved no interceptions, and the only excitement was when they were filmed by Movietone News in June. Wing Commander A.T.D. Sanders, who had taken over command of No. 264 from George Garvin the previous November, was posted to command No. 86 Squadron in June, and was replaced by Sqn Ldr P.J. Sanders, who was no relation, and had commanded No. 92 Squadron during the Battle of Britain. He had been recovering from injuries received after his Spitfire was hit in an air battle on 20 September 1940 and he was soaked in petrol. He had lit a cigarette on landing, and his flying suit had caught fire.

For their exploits in May of shooting down four German bombers, the crew of

Houghton/Sgt Ferguson made the last Defiant operational landing by the squadron, at 06.00hr in T3928.

Beaufighters began to equip No. 255 Squadron in July and No. 307 Squadron in August, the latter flying their last Defiant patrol on the 15th. These three Defiant squadrons were replaced by four new ones, all with Commonwealth connections. The first was No. 125 (Newfoundland) Squadron that formed on 16 June at Colerne. A number of Defiant aircrew posted from other squadrons formed the nucleus of the squadron, including Eric Barwell, Desmond Hughes and Fred Gash. Barwell had changed his gunner a month before this move: instead of Sergeant Martin, who had been with him for a year, he crewed up with Plt Off Martin, no relation and a much older man, who had been a fighter pilot during World War I. In that war he had been shot down and taken prisoner, but had escaped from the prisoner-of-war camp at Holzminden. He had joined the Indian Forestry Service between the wars. He did not go with Barwell to No. 125 Squadron because he wanted to see some action and knew that the new squadron would be some time working up. Even with No. 264 Squadron, things went very quiet during the summer, and so Martini, as he was called, volunteered for a couple of trips in the turret of a Wellington bomber – and on the second of these his aircraft was shot down and he was killed.

No. 125 Squadron's build-up was in fact very long and slow, and they were not declared operational until 27 September; they were then based at Fairwood Common in South Wales.

No. 125 Squadron aircrew lined up in front of a Defiant, with Eric Barwell to the right of the propeller.

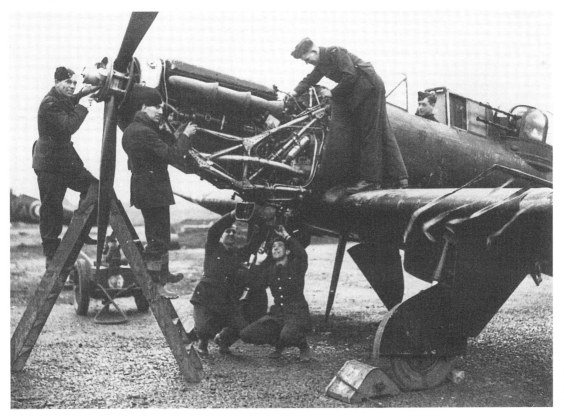

A No. 125 (Newfoundland) Squadron Defiant being serviced, probably at RAF Colerne.

Boulton Paul Defiant N3378

On 23 August 1941 No. 255 Squadron was declared non-operational while they completed their conversion to Beaufighters. The twelfth Beaufighter had arrived on 1 August, and the first four Defiants left on the 21st, three of them going to No. 409 squadron. Six more Defiants left over the next two days, three of them going to No. 151 Squadron and three to 46 MU. One of the Defiants left at Kirton-in-Lindsey was N3378, a Defiant with three victories to its name. It had flown its last operational patrol on 18 August when Plt Off Clarke/Sgt Allen took off at 22.50hr, landing back just after midnight. Its last attempted interception had been on 8 August, when Plt Off Ballantine/Sgt Bayliss were vectored after a raider but were unable to find it.

Now that it was non-operational, a number of the squadron's personnel were granted leave, and Plt Off James Craig was allowed to take N3378 up to Edinburgh where his parents lived. He gave a lift to LAC George Hempstead, who also lived in Scotland. They set off for their return from Turnhouse at 08.08hr on 29 August. About half an hour later Craig contacted Kirton-in-Lindsey to let them know he was returning to base, but he never arrived.

James Craig (right) on leave at his parents' house in Edinburgh, before his return to No. 255 Squadron in N3378.

The following day the squadron sent up nine Beaufighters and a Defiant to search the route he would have taken, but they found nothing. Further searches were made on the 31st, but on 1 September the weather was too bad. On 2 September three aircraft once more searched the route, but nothing was found. It was not until 23rd that the fate of N3378 was discovered: two shepherds found the crash site of the Defiant, and the two crewmen huddled alongside. They had survived the crash, but had died of their injuries and of exposure whilst awaiting rescue. The aircraft had crashed near the top of Bleaklow Moor in the Peak District, only a few feet from a summit known as Near Bleaklow Stones. They had been well off course, which was why the searchers had been unable to find them. Their bodies were taken down to Glossop Police Station, and Plt Off Craig was buried at Kirton-in-Lindsey on 26 September.

Personnel from No. 10 Barrage Balloon Unit visited the site, where little of the wreckage was recovered. They sent a message to the squadron stating that there seemed to be many bullet holes in the aircraft, suggesting that the crash had been due to enemy action. However, there had been no recorded German activity over the North on that day, and so the possibility of the Defiant having been shot down by Spitfires operating from one of the nearby airfields was also postulated.

No proof of a 'friendly fire' incident has ever been discovered, but another possible reason for the Defiant being off course was also raised: James Craig's wife was living in Wakefield with her parents at the time, and her house was only 15 miles from the crash site. It would not have been the first time that a pilot had got into trouble flying low over a loved one's house.

Whatever the reason for the loss of N3378, its wreckage lay on the Dark Peak as a silent memorial to the two men who had died there. Over the years a number of enthusiasts carried down bits of the wreckage as souvenirs, including the fin brought down by a Cheshire man who had worked at Northern Aircraft during the war, making Defiant fins. In 1993 the Boulton Paul Association in Wolverhampton began collecting Defiant parts, acutely aware that the last surviving complete example was far away in the RAF Museum, Hendon.

They soon learned about N3378, and began tracking down and acquiring those parts of the aircraft that had been brought down off the moor, which included the almost complete rear fuselage/tail. Further parts were carried down off the moor by association members. Such was the poor condition of many of the pieces that restoration would have meant throwing away much of the surviving structure and building new, and so the wreckage was displayed in a re-creation of the crash site, as a memorial to James Craig and George Hempstead, and a successful turret fighter, Boulton Paul Defiant N3378.

The formation of one night-fighter squadron with North American connections, No. 125, was followed by two new Canadian Defiant squadrons, No. 409 and No. 410. The first, No. 409 (Nighthawk) Squadron, was formed at Digby on 17 June, with thirteen Defiants, all arriving on 9 July. No. 410 (Cougar) Squadron was formed on 30 June at Ayr, with its first five Defiants arriving on 8 July. The fourth new Defiant squadron to be formed in the summer of 1941 was No. 456, an Australian squadron that formed at Valley on 30 June, its first seven Defiants arriving on 2 July. For a brief period in August there were thus eight Defiant night-fighter squadrons, the highest number to be achieved.

Two of these squadrons did not keep their Defiants for very long. No. 409 Squadron flew its first patrol on the 3 August, and was declared fully operational

on 20th; however, it did not make any contacts, and began to convert to Beaufighters the following month. No. 456 Squadron flew its first operational patrol on 5 September, but began to convert to Beaufighters the same month.

Disaster for N1569

No. 456 Squadron suffered one very unusual accident before the changeover was complete. On 26 July 1941, on only his second night flight on the Defiant, a

Two aircrew of No. 456 (Australian) Squadron at RAF Valley.

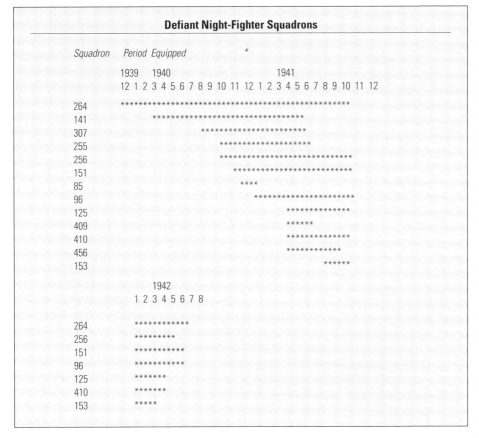

Defiant Night-Fighter Squadrons

Squadron	Period Equipped		
	1939	1940	1941
	12	1 2 3 4 5 6 7 8 9 10 11 12	1 2 3 4 5 6 7 8 9 10 11 12
264		**	
141		********************************	
307		************************	
255		*******************	
256		****************************	
151		**************************	
85		****	
96		**********************	
125		**************	
409		******	
410		**************	
456		************	
153		******	

Squadron	1942
	1 2 3 4 5 6 7 8
264	*************
256	*********
151	***********
96	***********
125	*******
410	*******
153	*****

new member of the squadron, Bryan Wild, with Sgt Walker as his gunner, was making a normal landing at RAF Valley when just prior to touchdown at 110mph (120kph) at about 12ft altitude (3.65m) there was a sudden loud bang: obviously they had hit something. Wild had to make an instant decision: whether to carry on with the landing, or to try and go round again. He reasoned that if he opened the throttle, any propeller damage might result in disaster, and he did not fancy climbing away in the darkness of the night in a damaged aircraft.

The landing continued normally until the starboard wing began to settle, and it soon became clear that there was no undercarriage on that side. Wild quickly switched everything off, and pulled his canopy back. The starboard wing-tip hit the runway with a loud scraping noise, and then the port undercarriage leg collapsed and shot up into the wing. The aircraft slewed to starboard and slid into the sand dunes, which brought it to an instant stop. Wild and Walker scrambled from the wreck but there was no fire. All that remained was to find out what they had hit.

It turned out to have been a mobile cookhouse, being towed by a tractor to a dispersal site across the runway in use, despite the red light showing. The starboard undercarriage leg remained embedded in it, but luckily the two airmen with it were riding on the tractor, and were unhurt.

The Defiant was none other than N1569, the one that Plt Off Jim Bailey had force-landed on top of a Kent hedgerow on 26 August 1940, having been hit by a Bf 109. It had only arrived at 24 MU after repair by Reid & Sigrist from that experience on 16 May 1941, and had been issued to No. 456 Squadron on 4 July. As related previously, N1569 was a redoubtable Defiant, and was once again repaired, going subsequently to No. 256 Squadron (as did Bryan Wild), then to Nos 287 and 289 Squadrons, being finally abandoned in the air in June 1942.

By the autumn of 1941 there were therefore six Defiant squadrons waiting to meet the return of the Luftwaffe as the nights grew longer: No. 96, No. 125, No. 151, No. 256, No. 264 and No. 410.

New Tactics

During the summer, not only was there a reorganization of the Defiant force, but new tactics were tried out. The bizarre Turbinlite experiment was expanded to include Defiants from No. 264 Squadron in June, and No. 151 Squadron in August. The Turbinlite flights were equipped with Douglas Havocs with a large searchlight in the nose where the armament would normally be. The Havoc would track a raider with its radar, and at the crucial moment illuminate it with the searchlight. A Hurricane flying in formation beneath the Havoc, using light-coloured strips on the underside as a reference, would then move forward and shoot the raider down. At least that was the theory.

The Turbinlite Havocs had been co-operating with Hurricane squadrons for some time when it was decided to try them

Sgt A.D. Lofting in the cockpit of his No. 264 Squadron Defiant.

with Defiants, but these had no more success than the Hurricanes had. It was found that on the few occasions when targets were actually illuminated they showed a marked reluctance to stay in the searchlight beam, which only served to warn the bomber of the night-fighter's presence and gave its gunners something to aim at. Furthermore, once the raider had slipped out of the beam, it was found that the brightness of the light had destroyed the night-vision of all concerned, and he invariably escaped.

Coincidentally, a 'turret fighter' had been engaged in operations with an airborne searchlight during World War I. An FE.2B, A781, was fitted with a searchlight with a Lewis gun coupled on each side, so that the gunner could aim the searchlight and fire the guns at the same time. The searchlight was powered by a small propeller-driven generator located under the nacelle. Carrying the armament and searchlight in the same aircraft would seem to be a better scheme, but this installation had no more success than the Turbinlite Flights.

No interceptions took place while No. 264 and No. 151 were co-operating with the Turbinlites, except on the night of 22 October 1941, when Plt Off Stevens in his Hurricane was a Havoc's partner: he was so frustrated that he broke away, found a German bomber by himself and shot it down. This was as great a testament to the failure

of the Turbinlite experiment as could be envisaged!

If this were not enough, No. 151 Squadron was also assigned to co-operate with the 'flare-burning tactic' from December 1941 into 1942. In this scenario a Havoc would drop a parachute flare over a low-flying raider, and the Defiant or Hurricane would then move in and shoot it down. The Defiant night-fighter force was better served, in being re-equipped with Mark II Defiants and the installation of pilot-operated radar.

The Mark II Defiants

The first production Mark II, AA370, was delivered to Boscombe Down on 20 August 1941, and No. 264 Squadron was the first to receive the more powerful aircraft; its first four Mark IIs arrived on 29 August, and the squadron was completely re-equipped by the end of September. Only one of the other Defiant squadrons re-equipped with the Mark II before the end of the year, No. 151, which starting receiving them in September. Success

A No. 151 Squadron Defiant.

The prototype radar-equipped Defiant AA370 at Boscombe Down.

with the Mark II Defiants began on 31 October, when Plt Off McRitchie/Plt Off Sampson intercepted four Ju 88s 25 miles (40km) east of North Yarmouth, destroying one and damaging the other.

On 15 November, Plt Off McRitchie was successful again, this time with Sgt Beale as his gunner, when they destroyed another Ju 88. Set against this, on the same night Sgt Jee/Sgt Bainbridge went missing over the sea flying AA423, and could of course have been a victim of aerial combat, though there is no evidence to support this.

The Fitment of Radar

Preparations for the fitment of radar to the Defiant were made in the autumn of 1940. Boulton Paul received details of the equipment that needed to be fitted, and they prepared installation drawings. A Defiant belonging to the Special Duties Flight, N1553, was delivered to the company on 11 November, and the installation of the AI Mk IV set was undertaken. The cathode ray tube display was sited to the pilot's left, with the controls to the right. The receiver, control box and power pack were

behind the pilot's seat, and the transmitter in the rear fuselage. The arrow-like transmitter aerial was on the starboard wing, with twin poles on the port wing. The H-Type receiving aerials were on the fuselage sides just in front of the pilot's cockpit.

The aircraft was designated the Mk IA with the radar fitted, but the extra drag of the aerials affected the aircraft's performance, and the outer-wing fuel tanks of the Mark II could not be fitted to the Mark I because of the aerials. The aircraft was

sent back to the Special Duties Flight on 23 April 1941, but technical problems delayed its operational use until August. By then the Mark II aircraft with its extra power was becoming available, as was the new Mark VI radar set, with extra band width. The first radar-equipped Mark II was AA372, of the Telecommunications Flight.

The first squadron to receive radar-equipped aircraft was No. 96, with three Mark IAs arriving in November 1941. It

A radar-equipped No. 96 Squadron Defiant operating over Crewe in a co-operation exercise, with Army anti-aircraft gunners. The pilot was Flt Sgt Cornwell, the gunner Flt Sgt Heycock.

A radar-equipped Defiant at the Boulton Paul Factory.

was to be the sole user of the Mark I equipped with radar, the conversion of which was largely done by Boulton Paul themselves. Conversion of the Mark IIs was done by No. 32 MU at St Athan, and No. 264 Squadron received the first radar-equipped Mark II in January 1942, with No. 151 and No. 256 receiving radar aircraft in April 1942.

The radar was a mixed blessing in the Defiant. Using it rather destroyed the pilot's night vision, and he could not position the aircraft for his gunner to fire unless he could actually see the target. In the end, very little success was had through using radar. The only victory No. 264 Squadron ever had using the radar set was on the night of 17 April 1942 when Plt

Off Stuart/Fg Off Maggs destroyed a Heinkel He 111 south of Beachy Head. Mervyn Maggs had been a Royal Flying Corps pilot during World War I, the third Defiant gunner to be so; the others were Carlin and Martin – but unlike them, Maggs survived his second war.

A Winter of Little Activity

This success followed another winter of little activity, though there was one bizarre success on 12 October 1941 when Plt Off Gray chased a Dornier Do 217 without ever being able to get his Defiant in a position to fire. Nevertheless the Dornier crash-landed, and was duly claimed by the squadron.

No. 256 Squadron also had a victory in October, their last flying the Defiants. Flt Sgt Smith/Plt Off Kilpatrick shot down a Ju 88 over Coventry, flying T3995.

In December and January there were also no interceptions, but on the 18 December, No. 264 Squadron was invited to the Boulton Paul factory to receive a silver salver to commemorate the destruction of 100 German aircraft while flying Defiants. Flt Lt A.S. Thomas received the salver from the company chairman Lord Gorell, even though they had only actually claimed the destruction of ninety-six enemy aircraft at the time. After the presentation at the factory, members of the squadron were entertained for dinner, each with one of the female employees for

A No. 256 Squadron Defiant coded JT-J, crewed by Flt Sgt Ray Jeffs (RNZAF) and W/O Derek Hollinake undertaking formation flying practice.

A formation flight by radar-equipped No. 264 Squadron Defiants.

The presentation of a silver salver by Lord Gorell, chairman of Boulton Paul Aircraft, to Flt Lt S.R. Thomas, celebrating No. 264's 100th victory, even though they had not quite made that score. Wearing the trilby hat on the right is J.D. North.

company. Such was their consumption of the free beer continually set in front of them, there were almost no airmen present when Lord Gorell stood up to praise them for their combat record – they were all visiting the toilets!

Accidents such as the Defiant/Botha collision over Blackpool provided the only damage to the routine of No. 256 Squadron flying at Blackpool through the summer and autumn of 1941. Christopher Deanesly took over command of the squadron, and in January they flew their first ever convoy patrols over Liverpool Bay.

Catalogue of Accidents

The month of February 1942 was to prove the unluckiest the squadron had experienced. On the 7th, Plt Off Olney/Sgt Greenwood crashed in the sea in their Defiant, V1116, off Lytham Pier, and three

The Defiant/Botha Crash at Blackpool

The worst accident of the war involving a Defiant took place over the centre of Blackpool on the afternoon of Wednesday 27 August 1941. Three Defiants of No. 256 Squadron from Squires Gate were practising formation flying. One of them was N1745, crewed by Sgt L.J. Ellmers as pilot and Sgt N.A.J. Clifford. Both men were twenty-three years of age, and both were New Zealanders.

As the Defiants were flying at 2,000ft (610m) over the sea in a north-easterly direction they saw a Blackburn Botha, L6509, of No. 3 School of General Reconnaissance, also based at Squires Gate. It was flying roughly in the same direction but 1,000ft (300m) lower, over the centre of Blackpool. The crew on board were Plt Off A.A. Horne, Plt Off K.J.A. Sale, and a civilian mechanic from Brooklands, Frank Longson.

The Defiants turned and dived, as if making a dummy attack on the Botha. The first two flashed by the Botha, which then began a turn to starboard – and this manoeuvre probably caused the collision, as the third Defiant, N1745, struck the Botha amidships, cutting it in two, and itself losing a wing. The tail of the Botha fell in the sea, but the main part plummetted through the main entrance hall of Blackpool's Central Station, the nose striking the ground only a few yards from

the bookstall. There was a huge explosion and a column of black smoke billowed into the air.

The Defiant crashed to the ground on a house in Regent Road near to the police station. The gunner, Sgt Clifford, tried to bale out and did in fact fall away from the doomed aircraft, but he was too low, and crashed into Regent Road with his parachute unopened.

The booking hall at the station was devastated. Several died instantly and many were severely injured, others fled the station with their clothes on fire. The fire brigade and ambulances rushed to the scene, but their efforts were hampered by crowds of people rushing from the promenade to the scene of the crash. Despite there being a war on, it was Blackpool in August, and the promenade was crowded.

All five men in the two aircraft died, plus eleven people in the station. There were also thirty-nine people injured, seventeen serious enough to be detained in hospital. In fact these figures could have been worse, as the London train had left only ten minutes earlier, and if the crash had taken place just before then, the death toll might have been huge.

No. 256 Squadron air gunner, Sgt Squires in his 'office'.

A No. 256 Squadron Defiant at Squires Gate in the winter of 1941/2.

tions at Cranage, and on 21 October 1941 it moved its fourteen Defiants and two Hurricanes to Wrexham, which had paved runways. Shortly afterwards, on the 25th, there was a bizarre incident when Defiant T3999, crewed by Plt Off J.J. Phoenix/Sgt Les Seales, took off from Wrexham. They suffered undercarriage damage on take-off and were ordered to bale out, but Phoenix had trouble releasing himself from his harness. Seales thereupon climbed out of his turret onto the wing, and, edging forwards gripping whatever he could, he reached the pilot's cockpit and helped release Phoenix from his harness; they then both parachuted to safety. As a result of this feat Les Seales acquired the nickname 'Dizzy'. Over fifty years later, at the age of eighty-one, he returned to his wing-walking career when he answered the call from the 'Utterly Butterly' team for wing-walkers for their Boeing Stearmans. Despite having lost a leg in a road accident some years before, he flew strapped to the wing of one Stearman while his grand-daughter flew on another. He was somewhat miffed to discover that there had been an older wing-walker in America, so waited two years and then did it again, so he could claim the title of 'Oldest Wing-Walker in the World'. He proclaimed: 'I love doing it, and I've no intention of stopping now!'

Defiants in Trouble

No. 96 Squadron had a particularly bad night on 3 November 1941. Sqn Ldr Burns/Fg Off Smith suffered the dreaded wireless failure in T4008 flying over North Wales. Completely lost and with their fuel running out, they baled out and the aircraft crashed near Rhayader. Once the aircraft became overdue, and of course with no radio contact, the squadron sent up two Defiants to search. One of these, N1575, with Flt Lt Verity/Sgt Armstrong, soon had engine trouble, and they, too, were forced to bale out. And unbelievably, the other one developed engine trouble; furthermore, Sgt Scott had taken a ground-crew corporal as his observer, and it turned out that the corporal did not know how to use the parachute! Scott was therefore obliged to stay with the aircraft, and in fact pulled off a creditable forced landing; neither pilot nor observer suffered injury, and the aircraft was eventually recovered and repaired.

The 96 Squadron Operations Book

days later when a Court of Inquiry was being held into this crash, Defiant T4041 taxied into a car on the perimeter track, causing the death of Sgt Carr. The following day, 11 February, Plt Off Harrison-Yates and Sgt Woodford baled out of their Defiant after undercarriage trouble, and another Defiant force-landed on the airfield. Finally, on the 26th of the month, Sgts Joyce and Walden were killed when their Defiant, T3995, crashed on the airfield.

During the summer, 'A' Flight of No. 256 was moved to Ballyhalbert in Northern Ireland, and on 24 October this unit was formed into a new squadron, No. 153, which became fully operational in December; but the following month it began re-equipping with Beaufighters without its Defiants having seen any combat. One of the gunners who had been with No. 256 Squadron was Sgt R.T. Adams: with his pilot Flt Lt West, he had shot down two German aircraft during 1941, and only missed a third because his guns had refused to fire. He did not want to retrain as an AI operator, saying that he loved the Defiant, and wished to remain an air gunner. Like many Defiant gunners he was transferred to bombers; sadly he was shot down over Germany.

Dizzy the Wing-Walker

No. 96 Squadron had suffered throughout the summer from the poor airfield condire-equip with the radar-equipped Defiant II; however, they were to have no combats with these aircraft, though they did record one 'victory' when they shot down a stray barrage balloon. On 13 April the first of a few Oxfords arrived for twin-engined training, largely carried out by Sqn Ldr Haine himself. The first Merlin-engined Bristol Beaufighter II arrived on 2 May.

On the evening of 19 February between 18.42hr and 19.20hr, four Defiants of No. 151 Squadron were vectored against five German raiders approaching a convoy off the Norfolk coast. Sqn Ldr Smith/Sgt Beale found and attacked a Dornier Do 217 at 20,000ft (6,000m) and shot it down in flames. Just afterwards they were attacked from astern, and then a Junkers Ju 88 flew right above them, overshooting in the usual fixed-gun night-fighter fashion. As it did so, Sgt Beale opened fire and saw clear hits on the undersides; but then they lost it, and could only claim it as damaged.

Two other crews, Sgt MacPherson/Sgt Tate and Plt Off Wain/Plt Off Lynes, also saw Do 217s and opened fire, claiming damage to the German bombers, but their Defiants were too slow to catch the Dorniers to complete the job. Nevertheless, the German bombers had been driven away from attacking the convoy.

'Goodbye Old Faithfuls'

It was clear that a faster night fighter was needed, and on 6 April No. 151 Squadron received its first Mosquito. The following day all the Canadians were posted to No. 410 (Cougar) Squadron at Drem, despite vigorous protest. On the 27th, the No. 151 Squadron Defiants had their final success when on a Fighter Night over Norwich a Ju 88 was chased out to sea where it crashed – even though it had not been fired on.

On 23 May, the squadron's Operations Book recorded that 'The Defiants are now definitely "off the board" for 151 Sqd. Goodbye Old Faithfuls'. These were rather different sentiments than those expressed by No. 151 Squadron's pilots when the Defiants first arrived, when they were determined to prove that the Hurricane was a better night fighter. Only the extraordinary Richard Playne Stevens could be said to have done this; and he had died on an intruder mission over Holland on 15 December 1941, still in his Hurricane.

Up north, No. 410 Squadron had had a not uneventful winter, with quite a cata-

An all-New Zealand No. 256 Squadron Defiant crew. On the left is Sgt Derek Hollinake wearing his gunner's parasuit, and Sgt Ray Jeffs.

records another amusing incident, when Plt Off Ritchie had to bale out over North Wales because of engine failure. A farmer approached him suspiciously when he landed, and asked him where he had come from. 'Up there,' replied Ritchie, pointing to the clouds. 'Where's your aircraft?' asked the farmer, even more suspiciously. 'I left it up there!' replied Ritchie.

On 7 January Sqn Ldr R.C. Haine assumed command of No. 96 Squadron, which then had on strength thirteen radar-equipped Defiant 1as, fifteen standard Defiant 1s, and four Hurricanes, although the single-seaters finally left in February. Shortly afterwards they began to

A No. 410 Squadron Defiant coded 'RA-H' in the winter of 1941/2.

A group of No. 264 Squadron aircrew gathered by one of their Defiant night fighters.

logue of crashes in the bad weather and mountains of Scotland and northern England. But its Defiants had never made contact with the enemy, and in April they, too, began converting to Beaufighters.

The following month No. 256 began converting to Beaufighters, and on 30 May No. 96 Squadron stood down as an operational Defiant unit, continuing with preparations to introduce the Beaufighter II, and transferring its gunners to Bomber Command. The last Defiant fighter squadron to convert was No. 264, which interestingly had also been the first. They began converting to Mosquitos after two years and five months' flying the Defiant. During that time they had claimed ninety-eight German aircraft destroyed, for the loss of twenty-six Defiants shot down by the enemy, though of course many more were destroyed in accidents. They said farewell to their very last Defiant in July 1942.

Night-Fighter Successes by Type 1941–42

29 May to 2 July 1941

Type	Destroyed	Probable	Damaged
Beaufighter	24	2	4
Defiant	2	-	2
Havoc	2	2	2
Hurricane	5	-	1
Spitfire	-	1	1

3 July to 8 October 1941

Type	Destroyed	Probable	Damaged
Beaufighter	24	3	-
Blenheim	3	-	-
Defiant	-	2	3
Havoc	3	2	3
Hurricane	9	1	-
Spitfire	1	-	1

9 October 1941 to 28 February 1942

Type	Destroyed	Probable
Defiant	4	
(other figures not available)		

1 March to 29 July 1942

Type	Destroyed	Probable
Beaufighter	69.5	17
Defiant	1	2
Havoc/Boston	1.5	3
Mosquito	12	1
Spitfire	2	1

Top-Scoring Defiant Crews

Defiant pilots were unusual in that they could become 'aces' without ever having fired their guns in anger. It was the essence of the turret fighter that it was the team that secured the victories, rather in the way that McDonnell F-4 Phantom crews scored victories in Vietnam with the back-seater firing the missiles. The following are the scores of the top-scoring crews when flying Defiants. Some pilots went on to score victories flying other aircraft, or even came from single-seaters to the Defiant, but those victories are not included. The total scores are those victories claimed, adding up all the fractions of shared victories, but not including probables and damaged aircraft. In most cases the team remained the same, but in some cases a pilot acquired a new gunner, and the total is that for the pilot. The rank given is the rank at the time of the last victory flying a Defiant.

Sgt E.R. Thorn/Sgt F. Barker   (No. 264 Squadron)

Total 12 $^1/_2$ (1 at night) (4 x Bf 109E, 2 x Ju 87,
Bf 110, 2 $^1/_2$ He 111, Ju 88, 2 x Do 17)

Sqn Ldr P.A. Hunter/Sgt F.H. King   (No. 264 Squadron)

Total 9 $^2/_3$ (5 x Bf 109E, Bf 110, 2 $^1/_2$ He 111, Ju 87,
$^1/_6$ Ju 88)

Flt Lt N.R. Cooke/Cpl A. Lippett   (No. 264 Squadron)

Total 9 $^1/_6$ (2 x Bf 109E, Bf 110, 5 x Ju 87, $^2/_3$ x Ju 88,
$^1/_2$ x He 111)

Flt Off M.H. Young/LAC S.B. Johnson   (No. 264 Squadron)

Total 9   (1 at night) (2 $^1/_2$ Bf 109E, Bf 110, $^1/_6$ x
Ju 88, $^1/_2$ x He 111)
With Sgt L.P. Russell as gunner (Bf 109E,
Bf 110, He 111, $^2/_3$ x Ju 87, $^1/_2$ x Ju 88)

Flt Off E.G. Barwell/Plt Off J.E.M. Williams   (No. 264 Squadron)

Total 7   (1 at night) (2 x Bf 109E, 2 x Ju 87, He 111)
With Sgt A. Martin as gunner (Bf 109E, He 111)

Flt Lt T.D. Welsh/Sgt L.H. Hayden   (No. 264 Squadron)

Total 6 $^1/_2$ (1 at night) (Bf 109E, Bf 110, 2 x Ju 87,
Ju 88, 1 $^1/_2$ x He 111)

Plt Off G.H. Hackwood/LAC P. Lillie   (No. 264 Squadron)

Total 5 $^1/_2$ (Bf 109E, 1 $^1/_2$ x Bf 110, 1 $^2/_3$ x Ju 87,
1 $^1/_3$ x He 111)

Fg Off F.D. Hughes/Sgt F. Gash   (No. 264 Squadron)

Total 5   (3 at night) (2 x Do 17, 3 x He 111)

Plt Off D. Whitley/LAC R.C. Turner   (No. 264 Squadron)

Total 4 $^5/_6$ (3 x Ju 87, Ju 88, 1/2 Bf 110, $^1/_3$ x He 111)

Sgt V.B.S. Verity/Sgt F.H. Wake   (No. 96 Squadron)

Total 4   (at night) (2 x Ju 88, 2 x He 111)

Flt Lt E.C. Deanesly/Sgt W.J. Scott   (No. 256 Squadron)

Total 4   (at night) (2 x He 111, Do 17, Ju 88)

Top-Scoring Defiant Crews *continued*

Sgt H.E. Bodien/Sgt Jones   (No. 151 Squadron)

Total 3   (at night) (2 x He 111, Do 17)

Flt Lt D.A. McMullen/Sgt Fairweather   (No. 151 Squadron)

Total 3   (at night) (3 x He 111)

Sqn Ldr G. Garvin/Flt Lt R.C.V. Ash   (No. 264 Squadron)

Total 3   (3 x Ju 88)

Thus eight Defiant crews can justifiably be called 'aces' in that they destroyed five or more enemy aircraft in action – that is, if we include Whitley/Turner, whose bits and pieces add up to 4 5/6 victories (plus one probable). It is often said that all victory totals in air fighting are probably unintentionally exaggerated, but it is rarely pointed out that in some cases totals might well be less than they should be. Who is to say that Sqn Ldr Hunter/Sgt King did not shoot down the Ju 88 they were chasing when they were last seen, or that some of the night-time probables not recorded here, did not crash in France, or in the North Sea?

Victories and Losses

Trying to keep 'score' in aerial combat situations is a minefield of contention. Not only are victories hard to pin down for the reasons already given, but losses can be equally ambiguous. When Defiant N1569 was shot down on 28 August 1940 and was force-landed by Jim Bailey on top of a Kentish hedgerow, who could have begrudged the German pilot adding one to his victory score? Yet neither Defiant crewman was hurt, and the Defiant was repaired and went on to serve with No. 456, No. 256, No. 287 and No. 289 Squadrons, and was finally abandoned in the air over the Moray Firth on 19 June 1942, nearly two years later. Thus the only 'loss' was the cost of the repair work at Reid & Sigrist. A number of the German bombers claimed as 'probable' or 'damaged' might well have arrived back at their base with far more actual damage and with dead or dying crewmen aboard. One of the No. 141 Squadron Defiants not usually included in the 'shot down' category on 19 July 1940, was L6983. Though it was forced-landed after the action, after the gunner had baled out and was posted missing, it was repaired, but only ever served as an instructional airframe subsequently, and probably never flew again.

The following figures are therefore open to all kinds of interpretation. I do not claim they are anything but a guide to the performance of the Defiant squadrons in aerial combat, my personal estimate of their achievements.

Squadron		Victories	Defiants Lost in Aerial Combat
264	day	83	25
	night	15	1
141	day	4	6
	night	10	-
96		6	-
151		15	-
255		7	-
256		9	1
307		3	-
277		-	1
515		-	2
54 OTU		-	1
Totals		152	37

CHAPTER EIGHT

Radar Countermeasures

A publicity photograph of a No. 264 Squadron Defiant over Biggin Hill.

Since the beginning of the war, the Telecommunications Research Establishment had been preoccupied with countering German bombing aids and perfecting British radars, but by November 1941 details of the German Freya radar were well known, and the famous Bruneval Raid on the night of 27/28 February 1942 secured actual hardware from the Wurzburg radar.

Two electronic counters to the German ground-to-air radars were designed. One was a jamming system codenamed *Mandrel*, which would be carried up by an aircraft to orbit in a sector where a British bombing raid was planned, jamming the frequency of the Freya radar in that sector, with other aircraft jamming Freya in other sectors so that the Germans would not know from which direction the raid was approaching.

The other system, which was not a jammer, was first suggested in July 1941. It was designed to lure German fighters away from a real raid by staging an apparently much larger raid in another sector. This equipment was codenamed *Moonshine*, and worked by picking up the Freya signal and retransmitting it exactly in phase. One Moonshine set was able to affect one-eighth of the Freya frequency; however, two sets could not be carried on the same aircraft because of mutual interference. A formation of eight aircraft would therefore be required, and would give the appearance of a much larger formation on the German radar screens. Because formation flying would be required, the Moonshine system could only be used in daylight.

It was planned that the Moonshine aircraft would be joined by squadrons of fighters as they crossed the Channel. It would appear to the Germans as if a large bomber formation were being joined by escorting fighters, against which they would hopefully commit a large proportion of their interceptors. As the British formation approached France, the Moonshine aircraft would dive for home, leaving the fighters to battle it out with the Germans.

There was a marked reluctance to use either Mandrel or Moonshine because to do so would quickly reveal its existence to the Germans, and encourage their own adoption of radar countermeasures. However, on 11 February 1942 the German battlecruisers *Scharnhorst* and *Gneisenau*, with the heavy cruiser *Prinz Eugen*, made their 'Channel dash' from Brest back to Germany. This daring scheme was aided by the German jamming of British coastal radars, showing that the Germans were operational with their own electronic countermeasures. And so the green light was given to the exploitation of Mandrel and Moonshine.

Mandrel and Moonshine for Defiant

On 11 May 1942 a conference was held at Uxbridge attended by representatives from the Air Ministry Signals Department, No. 11 Group, and No. 80 Signals Wing from Radlett. It was agreed to deploy Defiants as the electronic countermeasures aircraft, as the Defiant night-fighter squadrons were all in the process of being re-equipped, freeing large stocks of aircraft, and crews experienced in night-flying operations, important in the case of Mandrel.

It was agreed that a unit of eighteen Defiants would be required, nine equipped with one device, and nine with the other (both could not be carried on the same aircraft because of mutual interference). The aircraft would be the longer-range Mark IIs fitted with the standard AI racks and wiring, and with the old-type retractable radio aerial masts. It was suggested that one Defiant night-fighter squadron should be transferred to the new task, but AVM Sholto Douglas preferred a new unit to be formed, so as not to interfere with the planned re-equipment of the night-fighter force with Beaufighters and Mosquitos.

This new unit was known initially as the Defiant Flight, and began to receive its aircraft from 7 May 1942; but from 28 May it was officially called the 'Defiant Special Duties' Flight', and was set up at Northolt attached to the Station Flight. Two Defiants were delivered shortly afterwards for initial trials of the equipment, AA631 and AA443, the former originally from No. 96 Squadron, and the latter from No. 264 Squadron; these served as the prototypes for the Moonshine equipment. The trials continued until 24 May, and with the system proven, fourteen more Defiants were delivered in June. Many of the crews came from night-fighter squadrons, such as Flt Sgts Lewis and MacCauley from 96 Squadron, and especially the gunners who were not being retrained as AI operators, such as Fred Gash, a veteran of No. 264 Squadron. Many others were newly trained aircrew.

On the 4 June, one Defiant was sent to Hatfield to be fitted with the prototype Mandrel equipment, manufactured by General Electric nearby. The Mandrel set consisted of a T1408 transmitter, a Type 68 modulator, a Type 300 power unit and a transmission mast. On the 13 June, Sir Henry Tizard took the decision to use Moonshine as soon as possible, but to hold Mandrel back until a really big operation came along.

For the first month the crews practised with their new aircraft, and then on 20 July, eight aircraft flew up to Drem for the first trials of Moonshine. A mobile GCI unit was sent there, and modified to transmit the usual Freya frequencies (Drem, north of Berwick, was sufficiently far away for the Germans not to pick up the transmissions). After these successful tests it was decided to test the equipment on the Germans.

The 6 August 1942 was the date chosen to operate electronic countermeasures against the German radars for the first time, and nine Defiants took off at 14.00hr; however, AA435 developed engine trouble and had to force-land at Middle Wallop, and the operation was cancelled. Later in the day, at 18.55hr, nine Defiants took off once more and flew a holding pattern off Portland Bill, retransmitting the Freya signals. After five minutes they set off towards Cherbourg, maintaining radio silence and with their IFF sets switched off, turning back when they were 35 miles (56km) from the

French coast, and therefore out of range of the Wurzburg radar, and landing back at base at 20.55hr. The Germans raised their balloon barrage and scrambled twenty-six fighters. On 11 August nine Defiants took off to fly an identical test, but they were recalled because of bad weather, and were only in the air for thirty-four minutes.

On the following day, 12 August, an identical operation was flown, with Moonshine not being used. There was no reaction from the Germans, and the equipment had proven itself. During this operation Plt Off Wingfield/Plt Off Simmonds also developed engine trouble and crash-landed at Tangmere. On 14 August there was a further flight, with ten Defiants taking off at 15.05hr and landing back at Tangmere at 16.50hr.

Circus Operations

The first major operation for Moonshine was on 17 August when the Defiant Flight took part in *Circus 204*. The *Circus* operations were primarily fighter sweeps designed to draw as many German fighters into action as possible, and usually involved a small number of bombers on a real raid. In the case of *Circus 204*, twelve Boeing B-17 Fortresses took part in a

A low pass of the same Defiant across Biggin Hill.

bombing raid on Rouen, with the Defiant flight helping to make it look like a much larger raid. Eight Defiants, together with a ninth aircraft acting as a monitor, took off from Northolt at 16.27hr. They were joined by three Spitfire wings and the Fortresses over Walton-on-Naze, and flew to a point 25 miles (40km) east of North Foreland. The Defiants then dived for home at zero feet, leaving the Spitfires to pounce on more than 144 German fighters that were drawn into the air.

On 19 August, the Defiant flight took part in *Circus 205*, with three Typhoon squadrons as part of the air cover for the Dieppe raid; the following day they were part of *Circus 206*, a repeat of *204*, except that the destination of the B-17s was Amiens. Also there was a massive German response, with nearly 300 fighters being scrambled.

On 21 August they were part of *Circus 207*, with twelve B-17s heading for Rotterdam, covered by ten squadrons of fighters. The Defiant flight was a whole hour within range of the German radars, and more than 144 fighters were scrambled. On the 27th there was an exact repeat of this operation, but only just over fifty German fighters took the bait.

On 28 August the Defiants helped twelve B-17s to bomb Meaulte as part of *Circus 210*; but then in the first few days of September there were four operations recalled by radio when the Defiants were already in the air. *Circus 214* on 5 September was the biggest yet, with twelve Bostons bombing Le Havre, and thirty-six B-17s bombing Rouen, escorted by a vast fleet of fighters that tackled the 250-plus German fighters that were scrambled.

No. 515 Squadron in Action

On 1 October the Defiant flight was redesignated No. 515 Squadron, and moved to Heston. It was found that eighteen Defiants were required to ensure that eight would be available for an operation, with an extra one or two normally going along as monitors.

The Moonshine Defiants were also used on the operations codenamed *Ramrod* and *Rodeo*. On 11 October, for instance, ten aircraft, with six squadrons of fighters, took part in *Rodeo No. 101*, flown in four parts over four different days. Then on 22 November eleven Defiants took part in *Ramrod No. 38* against Lorient, with two

squadrons of fighters escorting sixty-eight B-17s and eight B-24s.

Defiants equipped with Mandrel had been available as from August, but had not been on the unit's strength until the use of Mandrel was authorized. Analysis of eleven operations aided by the use of Moonshine showed that the average of 107 aircraft taking part drew a response of eighty-six German fighters scrambled, whereas the main raids for which they were forming the diversion had 153 aircraft taking part, but drew only sixty-four German fighters into the air. Moonshine was used operationally a total of twenty-nine times.

his Defiant at night within 5 miles of his assigned spot: with Mandrel switched on it was not possible to use the aircraft's radio, so dead reckoning had to be used, and the IFF could not be switched on, so there was always a slight threat from British defences.

The first use of Mandrel became typical of all such operations. Three Defiants were moved for refuelling to West Malling, three to Coltishall and two to Tangmere. At their designated times they began orbiting over a specific spot, calculated to be most ideal to jam a Freya sector. The Defiants were normally able to maintain this location for about half an hour, after

No. 515 Squadron Moonshine Operations			
Date	No of Aircraft	Time	Details
6.8.42	9	14.00	Recalled (AA435 engine trouble)
6.8.42	9	18.55-20.55	Total success 26+ German fighters scrambled
11.8.42	9	12.00-13.15	
12.8.42	9	11.00-12.50	AA525 crash-landed at Tangmere
14.8.42	10	15.05-16.50	
17.8.42	9	16.20-17.55	*Circus 204* with 3 Spitfire wings and 12 B-17s bombing Rouen, 144+ fighters scrambled
19.8.42	9	11.00-12.30	*Circus 205* with 3 Typhoon Squadrons. Diversion for Dieppe raid
20.8.42	9	16.00-18.20	*Circus 206* with 3 Spitfire Wings and 12 B-17s bombing Amiens. 287+ fighters scrambled
21.8.42	9	08.50-10.20	*Circus 207* with 10 fighter squadrons and 12 B-17s to Rotterdam. 144+ fighters scrambled
27.8.42	9	15.35-17.05	Repeat of *Circus 207* with 3 Spitfire Wings, 51+ fighters scrambled
28.8.42	9	11.25-13.50	*Circus 210*, with 12 B-17s to Meaulte
29.8.42	8		Recalled by radio
4.9.42	9		Recalled by radio
4.9.42	8		Recalled by radio
4.9.42	9		Recalled by radio
5.9.42	9		*Circus 214* with 12 Bostons to Le Havre and 36 B-17s to Rouen, 250+ fighters scrambled
6.9.42	9		
7.9.42	9		
2.10.42	9		
11.10.42	9		*Rodeo 101* with 6 fighter squadrons. 1 aircraft aborted
25.10.42	10		
6.11.42	10		
7.11.42	10		From Exeter
8.11.42	9		
22.11.42	11		Div. 10 Grp *Ramrod No. 38* on Lorient with 68 B-17s and 8 B-24s

Mandrel was first used on the night of 5/6 December 1942. The Air Ministry refused to supply enough Defiants to jam the whole of the Freya radar chain, and so normally just eight positions were targeted, with extra Mandrel being used on the ground in the area of the Channel. It required a very experienced pilot to orbit

which they returned, the bomber stream hopefully having cleared the danger areas.

During December there were seven more similar Mandrel operations, using the same three airfields as forward bases; but on the third operation, in 1943, Manston was used for the first time, and on 14 January Bradwell Bay was also used.

That night two of the Defiants returning to Tangmere after the operation, AA576 and AA581, succeeded in colliding on the ground; Flt Sgt Neale suffered head injuries in AA581, which was deemed too damaged to repair.

On 23 January, the three Defiants operating from West Malling were forced to return after mud thrown up by the wheels had clogged their radiators, causing the engines to overheat. This was a frequent problem in Defiants on wet airfields, and there were warnings in the Pilot's Notes against taxiing too fast in such conditions. The same thing happened again on 5 February when one Defiant was forced to return to West Malling with its radiator clogged.

Although No. 515 Squadron's crews were flying rather tedious missions, they were occasionally broken by moments of excitement. On 13 February, Flt Lt Macauley/Sgt Jordan took off from Tangmere for a routine Mandrel operation. While on station they were attacked by a Bf 110 night fighter. Jordan got in three bursts of fire at their attacker, and then their assailant disappeared.

On the 25th, AA629, operating from Coltishall, was also attacked by a German night fighter, and the gunner fired 400 rounds in their defence, without being able to claim any hits. Again their assailant disappeared, and they returned early from the operation.

The threat was not always from the Germans. On 3 April, Flt Sgt Moule/W/O Whitmill were operating from Bradwell Bay. At around 22.00hr there was intense anti-aircraft fire because of a German aircraft in their vicinity. Moule took evasive action from 7,000ft (2,000m) down to around 1,500ft (450m), and then asked control for a vector back to base. Shortly afterwards the Defiant hit a balloon cable, and the starboard wing caught fire. Both men bailed out, but Warrant Officer Whitmill died.

Bomber Command requested that the Mandrel aircraft be kept on station for two hours, but the Defiants only had the range to manage half an hour at some orbit stations. Plans began to be made to re-equip the squadron with Beaufighters, which not only had more range but also had more room to accommodate other pieces of equipment. On 5 May 1943 an Airspeed Oxford was delivered to the squadron, to be used for twin-engined training by the pilots.

On 21 May AA658, flown by Flt Sgt T.J. Macauley/Sgt M.C. Wilmer, was declared missing; MacCauley was one of the longest-serving pilots and a veteran of No. 96 Squadron. Why the aircraft did not return was never confirmed, but there was known to be an enemy aircraft in the area at the time.

Continuing Mandrel Operations

The pattern of Mandrel operations continued, with sorties on twenty-two nights in April, seventeen in May and twenty-four in June, involving between one and eight aircraft each night. The squadron began to start suffering from a shortage of spare parts, and during May more and more operations were abandoned because of malfunctions. It did not help that small numbers of Defiants were being parked outside on forward airfields, where facilities for maintenance were difficult. The squadron was even beginning to have to wait for an aircraft to crash to cannibalize it for spares. On 1 June the base for operations had been moved to Hunsdon in Hertfordshire.

Operating well-worn, single-engined aircraft out over the North Sea was a risky business. On one Mandrel patrol, Flt Lt S.R. Thomas, a veteran of No. 264 Squadron's early days, suffered total instrument and electrical failure while off the Dutch coast near Den Helden. There was 10/10 cloud cover below them. He turned for home, and when he thought he was probably over land he offered his gunner the chance to bale out, an offer that was politely declined. With little fuel left, they gingerly descended through the cloud, and eventually broke into the clear at 1,500ft (450m). They flew on looking for familiar landmarks, and then saw a flashing Chance light, which turned out to be that of Coltishall, the airfield from which they had taken off. They flashed the downward recognition signal and came into land, the engine cutting dead as the wheels touched the ground.

The Germans had responded to the Mandrel jamming by creating new Freya wavelengths outside its capabilities. The Defiants flew seventy-three more sorties during July, with the last four on the 17th. During this operation one of the four Defiants, AA651, crewed by Flt Lt Walters/Flt Sgt Neil, left Tangmere at 23.05hr and did not return. A Mosquito pilot of No. 256 Squadron saw an aircraft going down in flames in the general area that the Defiant was supposed to be operating, and also saw an FW 190 in the same vicinity, which he promptly shot down.

If the German fighter did shoot down the Defiant it was the last Defiant ever lost to enemy action, and on the very last operational sortie by a turret fighter.

Further Mandrel operations with the Defiants were planned but were all cancelled because of the weather and technical problems. Although No. 515 Squadron kept some of its Defiants until December, all further missions were flown by Beaufighters.

Defiants for Electronic Trials and Tests

After No. 515 Squadron had given up its Defiants, the type still had two roles to play in the electronic countermeasures war. Firstly the Defiant TT.1, DR936, was used for IFF trials at the A & AEE Boscombe Down, late in 1942. Identifying friend or foe was becoming an essential ingredient of the electronic war. Then the Telecommunications Research Establishment developed a device for homing in on the German night-fighter radar emissions, codenamed *Serrate*. To test this and other devices in the air, the Radar Development Flight was formed at Drem, late in 1942. It acquired the brand-new Mark II Defiants, AA580, AA654, AA659 and AA660, on 18 October 1942. They were equipped with transmitters that worked on the frequencies used by the German air-to-air radar.

These Defiants served as targets to train Beaufighters equipped with the Serrate device, initially from Nos 141, 169 and 239 Squadrons. The first of these to become operational with Serrate, in June 1943, was No. 141 Squadron, an old friend of the Defiant. They began intruder missions over the Continent, hunting down the German night fighters by homing in on their radar emissions. The hunter had become the hunted. By the end of September the squadron had despatched 233 intruder sorties

Also in June 1943 the Radar Development Flight was re-designated No. 1692 Flight, with Flt Lt Ian Esplin in command, and in January 1944 it acquired six more Defiants, enabling more and more Serrate squadrons to be trained and to operate

No. 515 Squadron Mandrel Operations

Date	No. aircraft	Airfield	Notes
6.12.42	3	West Malling	
	3	Coltishall	
	2	Tangmere	
9.12.42	2	Tangmere	
	3	Coltishall	
	2	West Malling	
11.12.42	1	West Malling	
	3	Coltishall	
13.12.42	3	Coltishall	
14.12.42	3	Coltishall	
17.12.42	3	Coltishall	
	2	Tangmere	
	3	West Malling	
20.12.42	3	West Malling	
	2	Tangmere	
	3	Coltishall	
21.12.42	3	Coltishall	
2.1.43	2	Tangmere	
	2	West Malling	
3.1.43	2	Tangmere	Recalled, but AA651 did not hear
8.1.43	3	Manston	
	3	Coltishall	
9.1.43	2	Tangmere	
	3	West Malling	
	3	Coltishall	
11.1.43	3	West Malling	
	1	Tangmere	
13.1.43	3	West Malling	
	3	Coltishall	
	2	Tangmere	
14.1.43	2	Bradwell Bay	
	3	Tangmere	2 collided on landing
	2	Coltishall	
15.1.43	3	Coltishall	
	2	Bradwell Bay	
	1	Tangmere	
20.1.43	3	Coltishall	
21.1.43	2	Coltishall	
	2	Tangmere	
	3	West Malling	
23.1.43	2	Tangmere	
	3	West Malling	Returned, mud-clogged radiators
26.1.43	3	Coltishall	
	2	Bradwell Bay	
27.1.43	3	Coltishall	
2.2.43	1	Northolt	
	1	Coltishall	
3.2.43	1	Bradwell Bay	
4.2.43	1	Bradwell Bay	
	2	Coltishall	
5.2.43	2	Coltishall	
	1	Bradwell Bay	Returned, mud again
7.2.43	2	Tangmere	
	3	Bradwell Bay	
	3	Coltishall	
11.2.43	1	Manston	
	3	Coltishall	
13.2.43	1	Tangmere	Fired at Bf.110
	2	Coltishall	
	1	Bradwell Bay	
14.2.43	2	Tangmere	
	3	Coltishall	
	2	Bradwell Bay	
15.2.43	3	Coltishall	
	2	Tangmere	
	1	Bradwell Bay	
16.2.43	3	Tangmere	
	1	Bradwell Bay	
18.2.43	3	Coltishall	
	3	Tangmere	
	2	Bradwell Bay	
19.2.43	3	Coltishall	
	1	Bradwell Bay	
24.2.43	1	West Malling	
25.2.43	3	Coltishall	Exchanged fire with night fighter
26.2.43	1	West Malling	
	2	Tangmere	
28.2.43	3	Coltishall	
	1	West Malling	
3.3.43	1	Coltishall	
	3	West Malling	
4.3.43	3	West Malling	
	2	Tangmere	
	3	Coltishall	
5.3.43	3	West Malling	
	3	Coltishall	
8.3.43	2	West Malling	
	2	Tangmere	
9.3.43	2	West Malling	
	2	Tangmere	
10.3.43	3	West Malling	
	2	Coltishall	
	1	Tangmere	
11.3.43	1	Tangmere	
	3	Bradwell Bay	
12.3.43	3	Coltishall	
	1	West Malling	
13.3.43	3	West Malling	
	2	Tangmere	
	3	Coltishall	
	1	Heston	Monitoring flight
14.3.43	1	Heston	Monitoring flight
26.3.43	2	Tangmere	
	3	West Malling	
27.3.43	2	West Malling	
	1	Tangmere	
	3	Coltishall	
28.3.43	2	Tangmere	
	2	West Malling	
29.3.43	1	West Malling	
2.4.43	4		
3.4.43	4	Bradwell Bay	AA542 hit balloon cable evading AA fire
4.4.43	5 + 1 Monitoring flight		
5.4.43	4 + 1 Monitoring flight		
6.4.43	5		
8.3.43	7 + 2 Monitoring flights		
9.4.43	8		
10.4.43	8		
11.4.43	7 + 1 Monitoring flight		
13.4.43	8 + 1 Monitoring flight		
14.4.43	8 + 1 Monitoring flight		
15.4.43	9		
16.4.43	8		
17.3.43	8 + 1 Monitoring flight		
18.4.43	8 + 2 Monitoring flights		
19.4.43	3		
20.4.43	8		
24.4.43	3		
26.4.43	8		
27.4.43	5		
28.4.43	5		
30.4.43	2		
May 1943	99		Operational flights over 17 nights
June 1943	118		Operational flights over 24 nights (AA572 Missing)
July 1943	73		Operational flights to 16th
17.7.43	4		Last Defiant operational sorties, AA651 missing, possibly shot down

with the bomber streams over Europe, increasingly equipped with Mosquitoes. The electronic countermeasures' war, started in such a small way by the Defiants of No. 515 Squadron, developed into a whole group, No. 100, formed in December 1943. By July 1945, No. 100 Group had eleven squadrons, five equipped with Mosquitoes, two with B-17 Fortresses, three with Halifaxes and one with a mixture of aircraft. They were involved not just in jamming and spoofing German radars, but also in electronic intelligence-gathering, and hunting down their German equivalents in their own skies. It was a massive new component of modern warfare, all begun when nine aircraft of the Defiant Flight took off and headed for the French coast on 6 August 1942.

Air-Sea Rescue Defiants

The dedicated air-sea rescue squadron came into being as a direct result of the British situation after Dunkirk, when the war was being fought across the Channel and the North Sea, and aircraft were increasingly required to search for airmen who had baled out or ditched in the sea. The obvious candidate was the Supermarine Walrus, because it could actually land and rescue men from the water in calm conditions; however, it was more usual for a search aircraft to direct a rescue launch or lifeboat to a downed airman. The aircraft chosen initially was the Westland Lysander which, although it was found wanting in its army co-operation role, was nevertheless endowed with excellent qualities for visual search. Lysanders were normally equipped with four M-Type dinghies on their bomb racks, which could be dropped near airmen in the water whilst they awaited the arrival of surface craft. In the winter of 1941 four new air-sea rescue squadrons were formed, numbered 275–8, and equipped with a mixture of Lysanders and Walrus amphibians.

It was proposed shortly afterwards that the Defiant would make a useful air-sea rescue aircraft, as it would have a much faster transit time to a search area, and also greater ability to defend itself in areas where German interference was likely. In February 1942 Boulton Paul carried out a trial installation on AA326 – a new Defiant Mk1 held at 46 MU – of a cylindrical M-Type dinghy on each of the light-duty bomb racks that the Defiant was designed to carry. The M-Type dinghy was an automatically inflating, three-man dinghy. Drop trials were carried out successfully, and on 29 March 1942 a new Defiant-equipped ASR squadron was formed, receiving its first aircraft, T4000 (that had previously been at the RAE, Farnborough) on 3 April. The squadron received eight more Defiants to provide ASR cover for No. 13 Group in the North of England and Scotland. Strangely, T4000 was the newest aircraft it received; the oth-

The trial installation of the Type M dinghy on a Defiant at Boulton Paul.

ers were all ex-54 OTU, 60 OTU, 410 Squadron or 125 Squadron, and therefore well used examples.

No. 277 ASR Squadron was the first to actually receive a Defiant – N3398 – on 30 March 1942; it was assigned the code letters BA-A, and in April, after a short spell with No. 96 Squadron, the original trial ASR Defiant, AA326, went to this squadron for comparison with the Lysander in the air-sea rescue role. On 16 April, after some local flying, a practice rescue was carried out. The satisfactory result of this trial meant that the four original ASR squadrons began to receive Defiants, although they also kept both their Lysanders and the Walrus amphibians, using whichever aircraft was most appropriate for a particular search and rescue.

ASR Defiants in Action

The No. 10 Group ASR Squadron No. 276 was the first to receive Defiants in any numbers. It was based at Harrowbeer in Devon, with detachments all over the South-West, and its first two Defiants, AA352 and AA353, arrived on 3 May. These were both ex-96 Squadron aircraft, and it was to be a feature of the Air-Sea Rescue Squadron re-equipment that as the night-fighter squadrons gave up their Defiants in the spring and summer of 1942, they would be re-assigned to the ASR squadrons. By the end of May, No. 276 had received ten more Defiants, most of these being ex-96 Squadron, some having to go via St Athan to have their radar removed.

No. 276 operated sea searches over the Western Approaches, the Bristol Channel and St George's Channel, with detachments at Fairwood Common, Perranporth,

Roborough, Portreath and Warmwell, as well as Harrowbeer itself. The Defiants were used for just over a year until June 1943, with Spitfire IIAs arriving to supplement them and the Lysanders and Walruses. Twenty different Defiants passed through their hands over this period, but only two were lost in service.

On 7 November Defiant N3516, crewed by Flt Sgt T.A. Vaux/Sgt C.G. Cave, took off at 13.15hr to search for a Spitfire pilot reported to have baled out 30 miles (50km) off Dodman Point in Cornwall. During the search the Defiant was reported to have crashed into the sea. Another Defiant, T3999, crewed by Fg Off Seabourne and Flt Sgt Poxton, took off at 14.00hr to search for both the Spitfire pilot and the Defiant crew. They landed again at 16.05hr having found nothing, refuelled and took off again at 17.20hr. They were recalled twenty minutes later and the search was resumed by a Walrus, but nothing was found.

A couple of weeks later Seabourne was to take the same Defiant – T3999 – on a search 75 miles (120km) out across the Channel, so near to the French coast that two Spitfires were sent to escort him. During the search an enemy aircraft was reported to be approaching, but was not seen by the three fighters, and nothing had been found when they returned.

Though most searches for men in the water proved to be fruitless, occasionally they were successful. On 9 December 1942 Flt Sgt Davies and Sgt Bain in Defiant T3999 searched for a downed Whitley bomber 5 miles (8km) off Bude. They succeeded in finding the dinghy and dropped another, and a smoke-float, and continued to orbit until low on fuel, waiting for a boat to arrive.

On 22 January 1943, Flt Sgt K. Hall/Flt Sgt W. Elder baled out of Defiant T4051 when lost in bad weather. The aircraft crashed at Stafford Farm, West Stafford, Dorset.

No. 275 squadron provided air-sea rescue coverage for the Irish Sea, and the seas off Northern Ireland. It was based at Valley in Angelesey, with detachments at Eglinton in Northern Ireland and on the Isle of Man. It received three Defiants on 5 May 1942, and was in fact only to receive five in total, mostly ex-255 and 256 Squadron aircraft. The squadron kept Defiants until August 1943, the last one – T3920 – departing on the 22nd.

ASR Squadron No. 277

The busiest ASR squadron was No. 277, operating over the English Channel and the southern part of the North Sea. Based at Stapleford Tawney, it had detachments at Martlesham Heath, Hawkinge, North Weald and Shoreham. It was also to be the largest ASR user of Defiants, having acquired thirteen before the end of May 1942, and having thirty-one pass through its hands before giving them up in June 1943.

The first thirteen Defiants were mostly received directly from No. 264 and No. 410 night-fighter squadrons as they were given up; but practice flying with these war-weary aircraft began to show problems almost straightaway. For instance, on 12 May, N3421 suffered a forced landing at Fairoaks after engine failure on a training flight from Stapleford Tawney, and had to be sent to Reid & Sigrist for repair. On the 18th, N3443 was in such need of overhaul it, too, was sent away; it was eventually struck off charge without further use. On the 25th, N1561 stalled on approach to Croydon in bumpy weather and crashed, killing the crew, Flt Lt G. Grant-Govern and Mr D.W. Mouri, and a civilian on the ground.

The following month the squadron began to receive more well-used Defiants from No. 60 OTU, as that unit ceased training Defiant night-fighter crews. The first operational search was carried out on 19 June from 14.05hr to 14.45hr by N3392, but nothing was seen. The following day, three Defiants – N3392, AA398 and AA3421 – were scrambled to search for aircrew 10 miles (16km) south of Dover. This time they spotted a parachute

A No. 276 (ASR) Defiant, T3997, formerly of No. 96 Squadron.

in the water and escorted a launch to the scene.

The 13 June 1942 might be cited as a typical day for No. 277 Squadron. From Martlesham Heath a Walrus flew a routine patrol, and two Defiants, V1117 and N3392, were given air tests. At Hawkinge, Lysanders took off on two operational flights but were then recalled, and another undertook a sea search for a downed aircrew along with Defiants T3994 and AA302. A third Defiant was taken on a solo local flight, presumably with ballast in the turret, and was then flown to Biggin Hill. Defiant N3398 flew back to Stapleford Tawney, returning later in the day with another Defiant, AA302.

Although the ASR Defiants primarily had a humanitarian function, they were still operational fighters, and this was brought home on 17 July when N3392, crewed by Plt Off Morrison/Sgt Burl, was scrambled from Martlesham Heath to intercept a German bomber off the coast; however, they were unable to find it. This may well have been the last ever attempted interception by a Defiant.

On 25 July, Flt Sgt J.S.B. Arundel/Sgt W.G. Bunn took off in Defiant V1117 on a sea search over the Channel. They were attacked by a FW 190 fighter about 4 miles (7km) north of Dunkirk, and were shot down, both men being killed. This was the last Defiant ever confirmed to have been lost to enemy action.

On 19 August 1942 No. 277 Squadron provided twelve Defiants and other aircraft as ASR cover for the Dieppe Raid. One downed pilot was rescued when W/O Knowlton/Flt Sgt Rose in Defiant BA-B saw him floating in a dinghy and directed a launch to him. Masses of oil patches, and wreckage from downed aircraft were also seen, and some Junkers Ju 88s were also spotted bombing a ship. One of the squadron's Walruses picked up a Boston crew, and one of the Lysanders was chased inland by a German fighter.

As noted earlier, from 11.00hr to 12.30hr on the 19th, No. 515 Squadron had nine Defiants in the air providing Moonshine ECM cover for a diversion to the Dieppe Raid. With two squadrons and twenty-one aircraft involved, this was the largest number of Defiants ever assigned to one operation.

Sometimes the Defiant ASR crews, flying war-weary aircraft on long sea patrols, became candidates for their own rescue organization. For instance, on 27 January 1943, W/O Greenfield/Flt Sgt Horan took off in Defiant N3392, on a sea search for a bomber crew downed in the North Sea. Twenty-five miles (40km) off the coast of Suffolk they experienced engine failure, had to ditch themselves, and were then rescued from the water. The Defiant ASR pilots had the standard K-Type one-man dinghies worn by Hurricane and Spitfire pilots on overwater operations, but the gunners had to clip one on, as there was no room in the turret to wear one.

ASR Squadron No. 278

The fifth and last Defiant ASR Squadron was No. 278, based at North Coates in Lincolnshire with detachments all over the east coast and in Scotland. Like the other original ASR squadrons, it began receiving Defiants in May 1942, the first six arriving on the 7th, all being ex-96 Squadron, having been to 30 MU to have their radar removed. No. 278 was to use a dozen in all, but unlike the other units, it would be for only seven months, giving up the last one on 12 December.

The only one lost while on No. 278 Squadron service was AA360, one of the ex-96 Squadron aircraft: it was hit by a Lockheed Hudson, while parked, minding its own business, on North Coates airfield on 29 July 1942, and had to be struck off charge.

After a year of flying Defiants, the other four ASR squadrons began to give up their Defiants in June 1943, replacing them mainly with Spitfires, which had proved to be quite capable in the ASR role. Just as the first fighter squadron to receive Defiants, No. 264, was also the last to relinquish them, the first ASR squadron to receive Defiants, No. 281, was also the last.

CHAPTER TEN

Training on Defiants

As indicated earlier, Boulton Paul began the design of a dual-control trainer version of the Defiant, with the turret removed and a raised instructor's position substituted; but the aircraft was so easy and pleasant to fly, this was not built. The first Defiant squadrons, No. 264 and No. 141, trained their own aircrew; but after that No. 5 Operational Training Unit at RAF Aston Down began to equip with a small number of Defiants, the first, L6991, arriving on 17 May 1940, and five more the following month, including K8620, the second prototype. A cowling blew off K8620 on 13 July, and the aircraft was written off during the following crash-landing at Porthcawl. The unit only ever operated twelve Defiants alongside its Hurricanes, and became No. 55 OTU later in the year.

In December 1940, a dedicated night-fighter OTU was created at Church Fenton, No. 54, equipped with both Defiants and Blenheims. In March 1941, No. 54 OTU had twenty-six Defiants and twenty-seven Blenheims on strength, as well as eleven Masters, five Oxfords, twelve Tiger Moths and two Fairey Battle target tugs. A total of thirty-nine Defiants went through No. 54 OTU's hands, and then a second night-fighter OTU, No. 60, was created at Leconfield in May 1941, also equipped with both Blenheims and Defiants. Though the two aircraft had a similar role, they were totally different in operation, and so it was decided to concentrate all the Blenheims (and later Beaufighters) in No. 54 OTU, and all the Defiants in No. 60 OTU.

No. 60 OTU: A High Accident Rate

No. 60 OTU moved to East Fortune in Scotland, and became one of the largest users of Defiants, with 106 going through its books over the next eighteen months. Not surprisingly there was a high accident rate, with at least twenty-four of these Defiants being written off, and many more

minor accidents. The highest number of accidents occurred during take-off or landing. For instance, on 19 July 1941, V1140, an almost new Defiant with only just over thirty-six flying hours, crashed on landing at East Fortune; and only ten weeks later a Defiant that had only just preceded it on the production line, V1138, crashed while on approach.

On 15 August, N1692 struck farm buildings on approach to RAF Drem. The pilot, Sgt F.G. Westray managed to gain enough height for his gunner to bale out, but died himself while attempting a forced landing.

On 30 December, N1680 struck the ground 50yd from Drem railway station in deteriorating weather conditions, killing the crew. No. 410 Squadron, based at Drem, had been grounded at the time because the weather was considered too bad for operational flying, but the OTU Defiants 5 miles (8km) away at East Fortune, as was often the case, kept flying. They were able to watch N1680 make three attempts to land at Drem, the trainee pilot obviously unaware that in Defiants, when the wheels were down, the undercarriage doors obstructed the coolant flow to the radiator. After three circuits with the wheels down all the time, the watching pilots saw the tell-tale stream of glycol vapour, and then the aircraft rolled onto its back and dived into the ground.

The Scottish weather was to claim several other No. 60 OTU Defiants. A veteran of all three OTUs, L7023, crash-landed at Eldershope, Selkirk, after running out of fuel when the crew were lost in bad weather. In an identical situation, N1799 crashed in January 1942, the crew having baled out after they had run out of fuel while lost over Pathhead, Midlothian.

Two No. 60 OTU Defiants, N1754 and V1172, were lost after an air-to-air collision on 11 December 1941, but luckily all four crew members were able to bale out safely. Another Defiant, N1705, may well have been involved in another mid-air collision on 8 February 1942. The crew

reported over the radio that they 'hit something solid in cloud', and then lost control and crashed on approach to East Fortune.

The something solid might also have been one of the Scottish hills, and other No. 60 OTU Defiants that flew into high ground were N1679, N1739 and N3495. The first of these three was flown by an all-Polish crew, Sgt Stanislaw Sadawa and Plt Off Wladyslaw Blasinski, both of whom had made a typical escape from the German occupation via Romania and France. Interestingly, Blasinski had been a pilot in the Polish Air Force, but was deemed below the minimum standards for the RAF and volunteered to become an air gunner. After taking off at 10.00hr, they flew south over the Cheviot Hills. After fifty minutes, disorientated or lost, Sadawa had made the fatal mistake of descending through cloud, and hit Dunmoor Hill in Northumberland at an altitude of about 1,800 ft (549m).

Two other aircraft were posted missing over the sea: T3914 and V1182. One aircraft, N1797, was written off after the brakes failed while taxiing at East Fortune, and it hit something unyielding. This problem was one that the Defiant pilot's notes warned about. A No. 410 Squadron Defiant pilot 5 miles (8km) away at Drem had a similiar accident when taxiing a Defiant from one side of the airfield to the other. A slow, idling propeller was not able to replenish the pneumatic reservoir, so that when he applied the brakes on arriving on the apron in front of the maintenance hangers at the bottom of the airfield, nothing happened. Inside the hangar he was aimed at, was a Whitley bomber that had been damaged by anti-aircraft fire over Germany and was being repaired by a party from Armstrong-Whitworth Aircraft. The Defiant hit the hangar door which, dislodged from its rollers, fell forward onto the Defiant. As the pilot ducked down into the cockpit, he just had the chance to see the white-overalled fitters running for their lives in all directions.

The door impaled itself on one of the Defiant's propeller blades, which had stopped in the vertical position, so the shame-faced pilot was able to squeeze out and explain himself.

Further South: No. 54 OTU

Further south, the OTU at Church Fenton in Yorkshire, No. 54, had a further hazard to contend with besides inexperienced pilots, bad weather and high ground: the possibility of meeting the enemy. On the 26 April 1941, Sgt F.C. Crozier/Flt Sgt S. Bell were on a night exercise. They crashed after hitting trees 5 miles (8km) north of the airfield, apparently while trying to avoid a German aircraft. Just over a month later, on the 29 May, Sgt D.A. Heggie, flying N1556, a Battle of Britain Defiant, crashed and died after a mid-air collision with a Bristol Blenheim, L8377; a German aircraft was also reported in the vicinity.

By the end of 1942 the need to train further Defiant pilots was beginning to diminish, since the aircraft's operational days were numbered. Those Defiant pilots still needed were thenceforth trained at No. 18 (Pilots) Advanced Flying Unit at RAF Church Lawford, near Rugby in Warwickshire.

Defiants for Gunnery Schools

The Defiant's turret made it an ideal aircraft on which to train air gunners for Bomber Command, as well as for the turret-fighter squadrons themselves. The company had devised a wheeled ground trainer for the Type A turret, with its own engine and electrical generator, and trainee gunners were able to operate these against low-flying targets, before moving on to air-to-air firing practice. These ground trainers were usually only fitted with one gun, and those in the air with only two guns, to conserve ammunition.

Four air gunners' schools were to receive Defiants in some numbers: No. 2 AGS at Dalcross, No. 7 AGS at Stormy Down, No. 10 AGS at Barrow-in-Furness, and the Central Gunnery School. In some cases these units had already used a Boulton Paul aircraft for gunnery training, as a handful of Overstrands received camouflage paint at the start of the war, and were very useful for training air gunners when there were few spare aircraft around

---

Overstrands in Gunnery Schools

No. 10 Bombing & Gunnery School, ex-No. 2 Air Observers School

K4551 - ex No. 101 Squadron.
K4557 - ex No. 101 Squadron, SOC March 1940.
K4563 - ex No. 101 Squadron, later 2174M, No. 12 STT, Melksham.
K8173 - ex No. 101 Squadron, crashed July 1940.
K8174 - ex No. 101 Squadron, disposed Henlow, January 1940.
K8176 - ex No. 101 Squadron, and Boulton Paul turret trials.
Later at Special Duty Flight and ACDU.

The self-contained ground turret trainer produced by Boulton Paul.

Trainee air gunners gathered round a Type A turret in a ground trainer.

A cadet gunner in an AGS Defiant: these were equipped with only two guns.

equipped with power-operated gun turrets.

No. 10 B & G School eventually became No. 10 AGS; located at Barrow, it became the largest user of Defiants, with 114 through its books. RAF Barrow was an airfield on a peninsular jutting out into the Irish Sea, which created its own problems if engine failure occurred on take-off. This happened to Defiant N3449 on 20 August 1942. The aircraft was ditched one mile north of Millom, but both crew members, Plt Off J.R. Mackie and LAC G. Bradshaw, were killed.

One Defiant, N3328, was lost while being ferried from Barrow to Walney Island on 24 October 1942. Sgt J.L. Coulter of the Royal Australian Air Force was flying it over the Peak District when he ran into a severe hailstorm. The aircraft stalled and crashed near Lower Clough Farm, Barnoldswick, and Coulter was killed.

Considering that the Defiant was a very easy aircraft to fly, with good visibility for the pilot (compared with a Spitfire or Hurricane), quite a few were lost while being ferried. For example, the engine cut on N3319 while it was being ferried by No. 14 Ferry Pilot Pool, and it crashed near Timperley in Cheshire; and N3371 also lost its engine on a delivery flight, and was force-landed near Dunbar in East Lothian. Another engine failure happened to N3444 while it was being delivered after an overhaul, and it dived into Harrowbeer airfield. Amongst other Defiants lost while being ferried were N3337 and T3927.

The second-largest user of Defiants amongst the Air Gunners Schools was No. 2 at Dalcross, where 108 were 'consumed'. Like No. 60 OTU to the south, there was a high accident rate due to the Scottish weather and mountains, and well worn aircraft. None of these reasons caused the loss of N1625 and T40032, however, which collided while formation flying over Dalcross on 29 December 1942.

Nor were the conditions to blame for the two accidents that befell T4101 at No. 2 AGS. On 3 November 1941 it hit the airfield Chance light after drifting on approach; and on 16 March 1943 it struck a tree while undertaking low flying near Nairn. Low flying was a particular temptation for many AGS pilots, whose daily job was just to drive aspiring gunners around while they blazed away at air or ground targets. Some of them, particularly the Poles, were known to improve 'their' pupils' score by flying nearer the target than briefed. Gunners with Polish pilots often found a towed target flapping just off the aircraft's wing-tip. Gunnery exercise over, the pilots would often indulge themselves in a little low flying or aerobatics, to the discomfort of their trainee gunner.

One well-known accident involved a No. 2 AGS Defiant ditching in the Moray Firth, though it is often attributed to Loch Ness. The eight-sixth production Defiant, L7035, had a short but troubled operational career. Issued to No. 307 (Lwow) Squadron on 14 September 1940, on 5 October it was landing at Kirton-in-Lindsey when the pilot retracted the undercarriage instead of raising the flaps. Repaired and put back into service with No. 307, it was landing at Jurby, on the Isle of Man, when it overshot, apparently because of oil on the windscreen. This time it went to Reid & Sigrist for repair, and on 8 November 1941 was issued to No. 2 AGS at Dalcross.

On 4 May 1942 it was being flown on a camera gun exercise by Flt Sgt Finney, with the trainee gunner, LAC Langley, part of No. 15 Course. On approach back to Dalcross the engine cut, and Finney was forced to ditch in the Moray Firth. Flt Sgt Sheppard was airborne in another Defiant and saw the ditching. He quickly landed, and climbed aboard the station's fire engine to race to the beach. He swam out to L7035 and assisted Finney ashore. Langley was left on the wing of the Defiant trying to blow up his Mae West, which had broken its valve during the ditching. He was a non-swimmer, and before help could reach him the Defiant had sunk, and Langley drowned.

The fact that this Defiant was so intact when last seen, and was also within swimming distance of the shore, has attracted a great deal of interest over the years from people anxious to increase the population of surviving Defiants. How much of the aircraft survives after sixty years of exposure to the full force of northern gales, in fairly shallow water and corrosive sea water at that, is another matter.

One other air gunners' school had ten Defiants: No. 1 Air Gunnery School at Bairagarh, near Bhopal, India. These were all target tugs – although that did not preclude them adopting more aggressive training roles than hauling an aerial target around: in May 1944 the T.T.1 AA371 was flown as the 'attacker' in an exercise with a Vultee Vengeance (AN766). The crew became lost and had to make a force-land-

Ground Instructional Airframes

As with many RAF aircraft, the final training role of several Defiants and Rocs was as ground instructional airframes, attached to technical training schools, and given new maintenance serials.

No. 5 Signals School, Malvern

2981M   Defiant N1681
2982M   Defiant N3394

No. 6 Signals School, Bolton

2975M   Defiant N1743
2976M   Defiant N1803
2977M   Defiant N3337

No. 7 Signals School, Science Museum, South Kensington

2983M   Defiant T3993
2998M   Defiant V1172
2999M   Defiant N1797
3000M   Defiant N3479
3006M   Defiant N1616
3007M   Defiant N1802
3008M   Defiant T4107
3009M   Defiant L6962

No. 1 School of Technical Training, Halton

2729M   Defiant N3377
3171M   Defiant L6976
3172M   Defiant L7023

No. 3 School of Technical Training

3196M   Defiant L6993
3197M   Defiant L6997

No. 4 School of Technical Training, St Athan

2732M   Defiant N1801
3210M   Defiant L6951
3211M   Defiant L7024
3212M   Defiant L7014

No. 5 School of Technical Training, Locking

2730M   Defiant N1621
2731M   Defiant N3307
3226M   Defiant L7036
3227M   Defiant L7012

No. 6 School of Technical Training, Hednesford

2436M   Roc   L3057
2733M   Defiant N1703
2734M   Defiant N3368
2783M   Defiant K8310
2980M   Defiant L6950
3240M   Defiant L6979

No. 7 School of Technical Training

3251M   Defiant L6988

School of Technical Training, Blackpool

2740M   Defiant N3445
2789M   Defiant N3370

No. 9 School of Technical Training

3198M   Defiant L6983
3199M   Defiant L6956

No. 10 School of Technical Training

3278M   Defiant L7033

No. 11 School of Technical Training, Hereford

3204M   Roc   L3122
3260M   Defiant N1611
3263M   Defiant L7000

No. 12 School of Technical Training

2982M   Defiant N3394
3262M   Defiant L7030
3279M   Defiant L6987
3280M   Defiant L6990

No. 14 School of Technical Training

3281M   Defiant L6989
3282M   Defiant L7008
3284M   Defiant L6984

No. 3 Air Gunners School, Stormy Down

2589M   Roc   L3111

No. 10 Air Gunners School, Barrow

3106M   Defiant L6957

In the case of one lucky Defiant, N3370 at Blackpool, the arrival of an 'M' number was not the signal for its demise. It was an ex-264, 456 and 125 Squadron fighter, and it was returned to effective status on 6 April 1942, going to No. 286 Squadron at Colerne. It was later converted to a target tug and was transferred to the Navy, being eventually struck off charge in December 1944.

Defiant L6983 was one of the nine aircraft in the first and only daylight engagement of No. 141 Squadron. Usually regarded as one of the seven aircraft shot down, its gunner, Sgt J.F. Wise, baled out and was not seen again; but the pilot, Plt Off I.N. MacDougall, then made a forced-landing. The aircraft was repaired at Reid & Sigrist and went to No. 27 MU, from where it was reassigned as an instructional airframe, 3198M, going to No. 9 School of Technical Training, and then No. 3 School.

Defiant N3315, coded UF-V, at 24 OTU Honeybourne. This was the aircraft in which Sgt Lipinski gained No. 307 Squadron's first victory.

ing at Sarangpur after running short of fuel.

Apart from the night-fighter OTUs and the air gunners schools, at least twenty-four other OTUs had one or two Defiants on strength. Most of them were bomber OTUs, and the Defiant was useful in that it was able to combine the roles of fighter affiliation with gunnery training in one airframe.

CHAPTER ELEVEN

Defiant Target Tugs

The Defiant was ideal for conversion to a high-speed target-towing aircraft, for which there was an increasing need during the war. The removal of the turret left the perfect place to site an observer to operate the winches and targets, for both air-to-air and ground-to-air firing exercises. The same was true of the Blackburn Roc, which had quickly been re-assigned to target-towing tasks, but the performance of that aircraft fell far short of what was required for realistic firing exercises. Although a proposal to utilize the Defiant as a target tug in 1940 had been discussed, the priority was then to produce enough fighter versions.

In July 1941, with supplies of fighter Defiants more than adequate to meet foreseen demands, the last thirty aircraft in the order for 300 placed in July 1940 (with serials beginning 'AA') were cancelled,

together with the entire following order for 298 Defiant IIs with serials beginning 'AV'. A new order was placed with Boulton Paul for 150 of a target-towing version of the Defiant Mark II, with the Merlin XX engine. This version of the aircraft was designated the T.T.I, and the prototype, DR863, was built on the Mark II production line, preceding eighty of the fighter version.

The Target Tug Prototype: Design Details

The turret was replaced by an observer's position, covered by a sliding glazed hood. There was a large drogue box beneath the rear fuselage, and a windmill projecting from the starboard side of the fuselage, pro-

viding electrical power to a Mk IIB winch for ground-to-air targets, and a Mk IIE winch for air-to-air targets. All standard targets then in use could be carried, including 3ft and 4ft sleeves, 4ft and 5ft 5in flags, 3ft astern attack targets, and high-speed flares.

The aerial mast was moved from beneath the fuselage to a more orthodox position between the two cockpits, and guard cables were fitted above and below the tailplane to protect the tail from damage from the winch cables. Surprisingly, even with the removal of the turret, the substantial weight of the winch and other equipment increased the loaded weight of the aircraft to 8,191lb (3,715kg), or 8,250lb (3,742kg) with tropical equipment and oil filter, and reduced its top speed to only 280mph (451kmph).

The prototype Defiant T.T.I, DR863, showing the wires protecting the tailplane, and the large windmill that powered the winch.

Outside the factory on 31 January 1942: a forward view of DR863.

The Defiant T.T.I prototype on test from Boscombe Down, with the observer's sliding hood open.

A production Defiant T.T.I, DR972, outside the factory showing the yellow/black stripes on the undersides.

Ready for Test-Flying

The prototype, DR863, known as the 'tow-target' Defiant in the factory, was ready for test flight in January 1942. The next one, DR864, followed the fighters off the production lines in May. But the need for an even higher-speed target tug prompted discussion of a version of the aircraft fitted with the 1,620hp Merlin 24 engine, and a rigorous weight-reduction effort with the aim of reducing the all-up weight to around 7,500lb (3,402kg). This version, designated the T.T.II, was not proceeded with; instead, late in 1941, it was decided to convert surplus Mark I fighters, which were being replaced by Mark IIs in the night-fighter squadrons.

The aircraft assigned as the prototype of this conversion was N3488, which had been experimentally fitted with extra fuel tanks, and was returned to Boulton Paul for conversion to target tug in December 1941. The structural conversion was essentially the same as that for the T.T.I, giving an all-up weight of 8,227lb (3,732kg), but with the lower-powered engine of the Mark I, its top speed was only 250mph (402kph). This version of the Defiant was designated the T.T.III, and N3488 was returned to

The Defiant T.T.III prototype conversion, N3488, at Boscombe Down.

Boscombe Down for testing on 26 May 1942.

Go-Ahead for Conversion

An initial order was placed with Reid & Sigrist at Desford for the conversion of a further 150 Defiants to T.T.IIIs. Reid & Sigrist continued to be the major contractor for all Defiant overhauls and repairs, both from battle-damaged and crashed examples. The vast majority of Defiants ended up at the crowded little Leicestershire airfield at some time during the war, many of them more than once. The exact number of T.T.IIIs eventually produced by Reid & Sigrist is unknown, but it is

An air-to-air shot of the T.T.I, DR863, showing the underfuselage drogue box.

certainly in excess of 224. They were then awarded contracts for the conversion of Mark II fighters to target tugs, becoming T.T.Is, and at least 149 of these were produced in addition to the new-build aircraft manufactured by Boulton Paul; these eventually totalled 140, the final ten being cancelled.

The total produced is confused by the fact that most of the anti-aircraft co-operation units that operated Defiants also flew fighter versions, for affiliation exercises. Just like the air-sea rescue squadrons, there were five anti-aircraft co-operation squadrons, one attached to each group of Fighter Command, with detachments throughout the group area as necessary. No. 287, the No. 11 Group AAC Squadron, was the first to receive a Defiant, N1726 arriving on 18 February 1942. It was based at Croydon, and was to have forty Defiants pass through its 'books' from then to October 1943, when the Defiants were given up. Many of these were fighter aircraft, but target tugs arrived as they became available.

A production Defiant T.T.I on the compass-swinging circle at Boulton Paul.

Equipping the Squadrons

No. 285 and No. 288 Squadrons, the AAC units for No. 9 and No. 12 Groups respectively, based at Wrexham and at Digby, received a number of fighter Defiants in March 1942 for anti-aircraft affiliation exercises. No. 286, the No. 10 group AAC unit, was based at Filton, and received its first Defiant on 2 April 1942. The AAC squadron for No. 13 Group in Scotland was No. 289 Squadron, and it became the biggest user of Defiants amongst all of these five AAC units: based at Kirknewton, it was to get through forty-nine Defiants between March 1942 and July 1943.

In addition, two AAC Flights received aircraft: No. 1479 at Peterhead, which acquired four Defiants; and No. 1480 at Newtownards, rather more with fourteen. No. 1479 Flight eventually became No. 598 Squadron, and still had a Defiant on strength at the time, but No. 1480 Flight had given up all its Defiants by the time it was re-designated No. 290 Squadron.

Each of the Bomber Command groups had a bomber (gunnery) flight, to give their gunners air-to-air practice: they were numbered 1482–5, and they also acquired Defiant target tugs as part of their equipment. The No. 4 Group TTGF Flight No. 1484 at Driffield received the most, having twenty different Defiants through its hands. No. 1484 Flight provided gunnery practice from Binbrook and Lindholme for No. 1 Group, and had six Defiants.

Two of the many anti-aircraft co-operation flights, Nos 1622 and 1631, were based at Gosport, but with detachments wherever they were needed along the south coast; they merged on 1 December 1943 to become No. 667 Squadron. They already operated Defiant target tugs before merger, and as a squadron were to receive more than any other anti-aircraft co-operation unit, a total of fifty-two.

In the same way, the anti-aircraft co-operation flight based at Roborough, Plymouth – No. 1623, originally C Flight of No. 2 AACU – was upgraded early in 1943 to squadron status as No. 691 Squadron, as part of No. 70 Group Fighter Command. At the time the unit had a complement of four Defiant target tugs, five Hurricanes, two Oxfords and a Blackburn Roc, so that in this unit the two turret fighters served together, but without their turrets. No. 691 Squadron continued to operate a variety of aircraft, including Barracudas and the mighty Vultee

Vengeance; but Defiants remained a feature of its strength, a total of thirty-four passing through its books. In 1945 the unit moved to Harrowbeer, a welcome improvement on the very small field at Roborough. Soon afterwards the Defiants were all finally replaced by the Vengeance.

Target Tugs the World Over

Defiant target tugs were shipped through-

out the world, fitted with tropicalization kits in most cases, most visibly the large oil filter scoop beneath the engine. No. 22-anti-aircraft co-operation unit in India received as many as fifty-four Defiant target tugs, and they were detached to airfields right across the sub-continent.

In Africa, No. 21 AACU operated six Defiants at Takoradi on the Gold Coast, No. 25 AACU had ten in Kenya, No. 23 AACU had a couple in Aboukir, but No. 26 AACU in Egypt had the most, with up

Three Defiant T.T.Is of No. 777 FRU, Hastings, Sierra Leone.

A Defiant T.T.I making a low pass across the Algerian airfield of Blida, still towing the drogue.

A Fleet Requirements Unit Defiant T.T.I.

An FRU Defiant T.T.I operating over Algeria.

to thirty on detachments throughout North Africa.

Large numbers of target-tug Defiants were transferred to the Fleet Air Arm for use by fleet requirement units all over the world. The exact number is unknown, as their RAF records are in some cases incomplete, and official naval records are almost non-existent. Some that were transferred to the Navy were then loaned right back to the RAF, to No. 667 and No. 691 Squadrons, who provided anti-aircraft for ships as well as army establishments. Other record cards show Defiants 'Returned to RAF Account', without mention of where they had been; or disappearing altogether, which probably means they went to the Fleet Air Arm. A total of 196 Defiant T.T.IIIs and ninety-one Defiant T.T.Is have been positively identified as being used by the Fleet Air Arm, but there were undoubtedly more than that.

An FRU T.T.III after suffering a forced landing at Hatston.

A Fleet Requirements Unit Defiant T.T.I.

A Defiant T.T.III after a forced landing in Ceylon.

141

CHAPTER TWELVE

Experimental Defiants

Defiants were found to be very useful for experimental work at Farnborough and Boscombe Down, because with the turret removed a flight-test observer could be carried.

Testing the Low-Drag Wing

For instance in February 1941 it was proposed to use a Defiant to test a special low-drag wing with a thickness of 18 per cent at the root and 9 per cent at the tip. The RAE sent a memorandum to Dr S.C. Redshaw at Boulton Paul on 6 February outlining the requirement. It was suggested that Defiant N3484, already at Farnborough for engine development work, should have its wings removed and be delivered to Boulton Paul to have the low-drag wing fitted, together with a suitable observer's position. It was intended that diving trials be undertaken at speeds of 500–550mph (805–885kph), and this would also require the strengthening of the aircraft's tailplane and the pilot's canopy. There would be no provision for fuel in the experimental wing, and so 50–60gal (230–270ltr) would have to be sited in the fuselage. Although the standard Defiant undercarriage would be used, smaller main wheels would have to be fitted. The new wing would have a smaller centre section than the standard Defiant wing, but larger outer wings, though the overall area would be reduced from 250sq ft (23sq m) to 232sq ft (21.5sq m).

Extra-thick duralumin skinning was to be used for the surface of the wings, so that fewer rows of countersunk rivets needed to be used. It was estimated that the drag coefficient of the aircraft with this new, low-drag wing would be 0.0202; that of the normal Defiant was 0.0273, and that estimated for Boulton Paul's P.94, the cleaned-up single-seat Defiant, would have been 0.024. In a meeting on 29 July, H.V. Clarke of the company's design department even suggested the use of plastic sheet to skin the wings.

Boulton Paul had already done a great deal of experimental work in the use of plastic panels to reduce weight on the Defiant, for example the gunner's lower fuselage escape hatch. The company had also in fact introduced plastic for aircraft skinning as far back as 1919, when their steel-framed P.10 biplane had fuselage panels of Bakelite-Dilecto. Mr Vesset of the RAE agreed to consider the use of plastic to cover a second wing if Boulton Paul provided a test specimen. In the event the whole programme was cancelled, but it presaged the intense effort that went into the attempt to produce a true laminar-flow wing.

Defiants Allocated for DTD Experimental Work 10 April 1941

K8310	Test of hood and seating for passenger compartment.
L6950	Rudder de-icing tests.
L6954	Tropical cowl trials.
N1550	Mass balance rudder and elevator tabs.
N1551	Flow test for Marston radiator.
N1553	A.I. wireless installation.
N1622	A.I. director aerial vibration test.
N3311	Operational trials in connection with gun turrets.
N3322	Vibration test at Rotol.
N3381	Vibration test at De Havilland.
N3397	Cannon turret torque trial.
N3488	Additional fuel tanks.
N3514	Vibration test at full service load.

Defiants to America for Trials

One Defiant, T4106, was shipped to America for trials in May 1941. It was an unused aircraft, and arrived at Wright-Patterson in July 1941. At around the same time, a number of Boulton Paul gun turrets were assigned to various American manufacturers to help with their own development of new turrets. The Defiant was listed as being inactive in July 1943, and was presumably scrapped.

Boulton Paul P.103

Boulton Paul's P.94 of 1940 had been succeeded by an even more advanced version of the Defiant tailored as a new carrier fighter to Spec. N.7/43, the P.103. The company offered it in two versions: the P.103A with the 2,100hp Rolls-Royce Griffon; and the P.103B, with the 2,300hp Bristol Centaurus. The aircraft was a very attractive-looking fighter with an all-round vision canopy. Its design was stuffed with advanced features, such as a contra-rotating propeller with a dive-brake facility, provision for rocket-assisted take-off, automatic electric trim tabs for the elevators, and a telescopic undercarriage, shorter when retracted.

Although the P.103 was not produced, the new naval fighter being the Hawker Sea Fury, the RAE was interested in many of these novel design features. It was decided to test them on a Defiant, and DR895 was assigned to be converted as a 'special features' Defiant. It would be fitted with the Griffon engine, with the 'dive-brake propeller', the telescopic undercarriage, main undercarriage doors that opened in flight to simulate bomb doors, and the electric trim tabs. As the aircraft would have to be flown onto an aircraft carrier to test many of the features in the environment for which they were designed, Captain Eric Brown, a naval test pilot, was assigned to check the basic aircraft's characteristics, and whether they were suitable for carrier operation. He passed the aircraft as suitable, despite slight reservations about the Defiant's stalling characteristics, as it dropped a wing with little warning.

In the end only two of the special features were tested on DR895: the long stroke undercarriage, which eventually found service on the Sea Fury; and the automatic electric trim tabs, which proved very satisfactory during the tests undertaken in June 1946 – however, they were rather overtaken by the use of power controls, Boulton Paul leading the way in this new field. Another Defiant, AA413, was assigned to Boulton Paul in June 1944 for the fitment of a contra-rotating propeller, but there is no further record of it until its disposal to Boulton Paul in 1948, together with DR895, supposedly for scrap – though a letter in *Air Pictorial* in 1952 refers to a Defiant at RAF Bridgnorth modified for deck landing with a strengthened undercarriage and an arrester hook. The Defiant at Bridgnorth has always been referred to as AA413, but this letter might well indicate that it was actually DR895, unless both aircraft went to Bridgnorth. To complicate matters further it is now known that a fighter Defiant stored in the flight sheds at Boulton Paul's factory in August 1948 also went to Bridgnorth.

Testing Ejection Seats

Early in 1944 the Ministry of Aircraft Production became concerned that the higher speeds being achieved by combat aircraft were making it difficult for the crew to bale out in an emergency: once their canopy had been jettisoned, the slipstream was pinning the crew in their seats, and if the aircraft were spinning or gyrating about the sky because of battle damage, the G-force was having the same effect. Figures were compiled to show that at speeds of up to 150 knots the crew had a 75 per cent chance of a successful bale-out, but at speeds over 290 knots their chances fell to only 2 per cent. The Royal Aircraft Establishment was therefore asked to investigate the problem.

In January 1944 the Air Ministry approached two engineering companies with a proven track record of aeronautical innovation to devise a suitable system to mechanically eject a pilot or crew-member from an aircraft operating at high speed. The two companies were Martin-Baker Aircraft Ltd at Denham where James Martin was the well respected chief engineer, and R.L. Malcolm Ltd at White Waltham, where Marcel Lobelle was chief engineer.

James Martin had already been working on the problem. After a meeting with Wg Cdr Jewell of Fighter Command in the summer of 1944 he had devised a swinging arm system. A spring-loaded arm would be sited on the upper fuselage, hinged near the fin and attached to the pilot's seat, ready to lift it from the aircraft in an emergency. He devised this method because he believed an emergency ejection system was required for existing aircraft such as

the Spitfire and Tempest – although measurements of the cockpits of those aircraft had shown that there was no room for any kind of self-ejecting seat. A model of his swinging arm was shown to ACM Sir Wilfred Freeman and Sir Stafford Cripps at the Ministry of Aircraft Production on 11 October 1944. Both were keen on the idea, and asked how they might assist in the further development of the scheme. Martin asked for a Defiant.

The Defiant, with its turret removed, was an ideal aircraft for the testing of the new ejection mechanism, which could easily be sited in the place where the turret had been. And unlike a trainer, for instance, the Defiant could operate at up to 300mph (482kph), for a more realistic testing programme. Shortly afterwards

Martin had further talks with representatives of Fighter Command, who made it clear that an ejection apparatus was not required for existing aircraft, but only for new designs such as the Meteor. Martin therefore immediately scrapped his swinging arm concept and began designing an ejection seat.

A Defiant T.T.I, DR944, was assigned to Martin-Baker, coming from the American Combat Crew Replacement Centre on 20 February 1945. It was found to be in a very dilapidated condition, and had to be overhauled by Martin-Baker. Two Defiants were assigned to R. Malcolm Ltd: a T.T.III, AA292, that arrived on 18 April 1945; and N3488 that arrived on 26 October 1945, apparently as a source of spare parts.

Bernard Lynch in the ground test rig for the Martin-Baker ejection seat. In the background can be seen the wings of Defiant DR944, awaiting the seat., its stars and bars still visible.

The first dummy ejection from an aircraft in this country, as the Martin-Baker ejection seat leaves Defiant DR944.

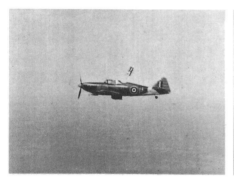

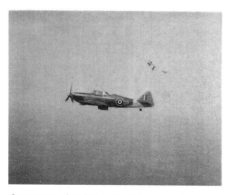
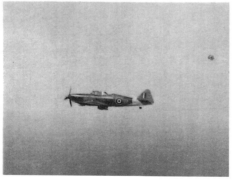

A sequence showing an ML Aviation ejection seat being tested from Defiant AA292 on 11 October 1945.

The Martin-Baker Seat

The Martin-Baker seat was ready in December 1944. It consisted of a seat sliding by means of four rollers on an H-section guide rail, with a telescopic cartridge-powered ejection gun. It was first tested on a 16ft (5m) high static rig, both with ballast and with volunteers, led by the renowned Bernard Lynch. The next step was to test it in the air. On 10 May 1945 the Defiant, fitted with the prototype ejection seat, was jacked into an 'in-flight' position, and loaded with sandbags that were then ejected into a catch-net. When this proved entirely satisfactory, the next step was to take the aircraft into the air. The following day the Defiant was flown to Wittering, and Rotol's chief test pilot, Brian Greenstead, flew DR944 with a dummy in the ejection seat: this was successfully ejected, the first such airborne ejection to take place over Great Britain. On 17 May, six further ejections of dummies were undertaken at speeds that were slowly increased to 300mph (482kph) (the Defiant's limit). After that, airborne test ejections were carried out in a modified Meteor.

The R. Malcolm Seat

The R. Malcolm seat was ready for airborne test on 1 October 1945 and, with a seat weight of 291lb (132kg), was ejected from Defiant AA292 at 250mph (400kph), with a 40ft/sec charge (12m/sec). Over the next few days, further ejections were made at different speeds and with the seat weight reduced to 251lb (114kg).

Although Martin-Baker became the standard ejection-seat supplier to the British armed forces, and indeed to those of most of the Western world, R. Malcolm Ltd, or 'ML Aviation' as they became (adopting the initials of their chief engineer), continued to develop their seats. These were test flown in a Meteor and a Wyvern, and then in the experimental Hawker P.1081. But this aircraft crashed, killing the pilot, who failed to eject, and so ML Aviation ceased their ejection-seat work.

CHAPTER THIRTEEN

Late Surviving Defiants and Rocs

L3084

Only a tiny number of Rocs continued in service into 1945, and none after the war ended. The only Roc that has any record of existence after the war is L3084, which served its whole service life as a target tug, including trials as a floatplane. It was noted without wings, fin or tailplane at the Victory Air Pageant, Eastleigh Airport, Southampton on 22 June 1946. It was nothing to do with the pageant, but stood 'in the long grass', having been in use as an engine test rig, with an 8ft (2.4m) diameter, four-blade airscrew inside a large cowl. As far as is known, this was the last surviving Blackburn Roc, presumably scrapped shortly afterwards.

The Blackburn Skua: L2940

The Roc's cousin, the Blackburn Skua, was also thought to be extinct until the remains of L2940 were recovered from the depths of Lake Grotli, Norway, where it had been landed (on the frozen surface) by its pilot, Major Richard Partridge, after damage from return fire from a Heinkel He 111 on 26 April 1940. The Skua was set on fire, and sank to the bottom of the lake when the ice melted. It was recovered and is displayed in its 'lake-bed' condition, at the Fleet Air Arm Museum, Yeovilton.

Defiants in Store

Only a handful of Defiants survived for more than a year or two after the war, though in January 1946 the total number of Defiants held by RAF storage units was eighty-seven. This was made up of thirty-eight F.Is, eighteen F.IIs, two T.T.Is, and twenty-nine T.T.IIIs. There were unlikely to have been any Defiants still in service with RAF units at this time.

Target Tugs: AA413 and DR895

As related previously, two target-tug Defiants, AA413 and DR895, were at Boulton Paul's factory after the war. They had been assigned for various experimental fittings for naval use, and were both sold to Boulton Paul in 1947, for reduction to produce. It appears that one or both of them went to nearby RAF Bridgnorth, and AA413 was recorded as being there in 1952. Certainly DR895 was being flown regularly before the end of the war, apparently as a communications aircraft – on one occasion on 6 April 1945, J.D. North was the passenger in a flight from Hendon, with Lindsay Neale at the controls.

There were a series of test flights with DR895 from January to the end of May 1946, presumably with the naval modifications specified. Interestingly, Lindsay Neale went through a deck-landing course on Seafires in November 1945, operating at East Haven and aboard HMS *Ravager*. Whether this indicated an intention for him to operate the Defiant with the new naval modifications on board a carrier is not known. The last recorded Defiant flight in Lindsay Neale's log books is the delivery of DR895 from Wolverhampton to Farnborough on 9 July 1946.

There is also a photograph of the Boulton Paul flight shed in August 1948 showing in the background a fighter Defiant with turret fitted, and a number of former employees remember it as having been there for some time. One of them, Bill Pauling, is certain that it, too, went to RAF Bridgnorth, but its serial is unknown.

The T.T.I Prototype, N3488

Another employee remembers seeing N3488, the T.T.I prototype, at the factory after the war, but the final record of this aircraft is on the scrap-dump at No. 31 MU. As this was an ammunition depot in a Welsh slate quarry, this may well be an error. Lindsay Neale's logbook records a twenty-minute test flight of N3488 on 11 November 1945, with a note that the engine seized. This was probably its last flight.

Boulton Paul Aircraft were offered a Defiant after the war, by the Air Ministry, as a token of the company's war effort. The offer was apparently refused by J.D. North, though his reasons have not been recorded. As related there were Defiants at the factory until at least the summer of 1948.

Defiants in Egypt

Some of the Defiants left in Egypt went into service with the Royal Egyptian Air Force. A report made in the summer of 1947 stated that the REAF's target-towing flight was still equipped with four Defiants, though these were all unserviceable (and likely to have remained that way). Other Defiant target tugs were still in use when the Indian Air Force was formed, and may well have been the last Defiants to fly.

The Career of N3430

In March 1952, N3430 was noted on the dump at Balado Bridge in Kinross. It is a pity that someone did not see fit to rescue this example, as it was a Defiant with a chequered career. It began its service at Rotol for propeller vibration tests, but was then issued to No. 141 Squadron as a night fighter. After an overhaul at Reid & Sigrist it went to No. 153 squadron in Northern Ireland for a short while, and was then issued to No. 276 on air-sea rescue duties. Converted by Reid & Sigrist to a target tug, it was transferred to the Navy and was used by the Flag Officer Carrier Training Flight at Fearn for a while; the rest of its Fleet Air Arm service being something of a mystery, before fetching up at Balado Bridge, where it was presumably scrapped.

The Complete Surviving Aircraft: N1671

The only complete Defiant that survives, N1671, has a similar sort of history, serving with two night-fighter squadrons, No. 307 and then No. 153, followed by No.

Defiant N1671 being assembled at RAF St Athan.

285 anti-aircraft co-operation squadron. It 'disappeared' after going to No. 52 MU in Cardiff, a packing depot, but a number of other aircraft there at the time were packed 'for museum purposes' so that it is very likely that N1671 was already allocated for museum display. It went from there to No. 82 MU, Lichfield for a while,

and then to No. 76 MU at Wroughton, stored in a single crate. When Wroughton closed, it is presumed to have gone to Stanmore Park because it did not appear in any other official records until November 1954 when it was listed as part of the Air Historical Branch collection of historic aircraft at Stanmore Park.

Defiant N1671 at the RAF Review at Abingdon in 1969.

N1671 in its original No. 307 markings in the Battle of Britain Museum at Hendon.

Over the next twenty years it shuttled between various RAF stations, appearing only at Battle of Britain open days, sometimes having been repainted, until it was finally assigned as one of the founding exhibits at the RAF Museum Hendon in 1971. It moved to the Battle of Britain Hall in 1978, and has remained there ever since.

Defiant Model L7005

The Boulton Paul Association in Wolverhampton began collecting Defiant parts in 1994, well aware that there was only one complete example. Their collection began with a wheel-brush, donated by former employee, Neville Webb. This was a curved brush that Defiants had fitted to their main undercarriage legs, to brush the mud off the main tyres as they retracted into the wings. Shortly afterwards the starboard tailplane and elevator of N3378 were acquired from collectors in Cheshire, and the association learned that the rear fuselage and other parts were still extant, having been brought down from the moors as souvenirs by various people over the years.

The rear fuselage was acquired from another collector in Oxfordshire, and piece by piece various other parts of the aircraft were tracked down and acquired, in a process that still continues. Restoration of the wreckage did not seem practical, as decades on the moors had corroded it to the point where most would have been thrown away and replaced by new material. The only part of the surviving wreckage to which paint still adheres is the fin, one of the first items brought down from the moor by a gentleman who had a particular interest in Defiant fins as he made them during the war at Northen Aircraft. The original intention of the association was to display the parts they had, mocking up the missing bits in between to

		Operational Record: Defiant N1671			
Date	Crew	Details	Date	Crew	Details
07.08.40		Delivered No. 6 MU Brize Norton.	11.05.41	Sgt Wisthal/ Sgt Stengierski	Night patrol.
17.09.40		Issued to No. 307 (I wow) Squadron, at Kirton-in-Lindsey, coded EW-D, A Flight.	16.05.41	Sgt Wisthal/ Sgt Stengierski	Night patrol, 1hr.
02.10.40		1 of 3 Defiants dispersed to Caistor.	19.05.41	Sgt Wisthal/ Sgt Wozny	Night patrol 25min.
27.10.40		Returned to Kirton-in-Lindsey.	21.05.41		Night patrol, 1hr.
07.11.40		Moved with whole Sqn to Jurby, Isle of Man	31.05.41	Sgt Bilau/ Sgt Wozny	Night patrol 15min.
15.11.40	Gp Cpt Tomlinson/ Fg Off Karwowski	Air-ground firing practice.	09.06.41		Two morning patrols.
22.11.40	Sgt Joda	Taxi aircraft to Shawbury to fetch Miles Magister.	09.06.41	Sgt Bilau	Dispersed to Church Stanton, 10min flight. A/c swung on landing Cat.3 damage.
30.11.40	Gp Cpt Tomlinson	Night-flying test.	14.06.41		To Reid & Sigrist for repair.
12.12.40		First operational flight. Daylight patrol and RT practice flight 1hr 35min.	08.10.41		To 46 MU Lossiemouth.
			31.10.41		Issued to No.153 Squadron, Ballyhalbert.
18.12.40	Sgt Dukszte	Convoy patrol, 1hr 10min, red section fired on by a ship in the convoy.	31.12.41	Sgt Luxford	Sole operational patrol with No. 153, 1hr 10min. TOTAL operational time, 15 sorties, 13hr 35min.
01.01.41		15min patrol over Jurby.			
14.01.41		To 6 MU to fit IFF and VHF.	22.06.42		To No. 285 (Anti-aircraft co-operation) Squadron, at Wrexham, coded VG.
13.03.41		Return to No. 307 Sqn now based at Squires Gate.			
26.03.41		Moved with squadron to Colerne.	22.02.43		To Reid & Sigrist for overhaul.
08.04.41	Sgt Piwko/ Sgt Trawacki	First night patrol. A 20min. flight at 9,000ft.	16.05.43		To No. 10 MU, Hullavington.
15.04.41	Sgt Wisthal	Night patrol 1hr 15min at 12,000ft. Sighted a/c which opened fire. Illuminated by searchlight beams, lost visual contact.	08.09.44		To 52 MU Cardiff (Packing Depot) possibly 'for Museum Purposes'.
			11.54		Listed as part of the Air Historical Branch Collection at Stanmore Park.
16.04.41	Sgt Wisthal/ Sgt Stengierski	Night patrol 1hr 10min.	07.57		Stored at Wroughton.
			00.58		Stored at Fulbeck.
21.04.41	Flt Lt Paul Patten	Short flight.	09.60		Displayed at RAF St Athan.
23.04.41		Night patrol 1hr 25min.	06.68		At Royal View at Abingdon.
26.04.41		Moved with squadron to Exeter.	07.68		Moved from Abingdon to Finningley.
05.41		Week's detachment at Pembrey. 2 night patrols flown.	01.04.71		To RAF Museum, Hendon.
			00.78		To Battle of Britain Museum Hall.

The remains of Defiant N3378 in a re-creation of the crash site, in the Boulton Paul Aircraft heritage project.

give the external impression of a whole Defiant, perhaps just from one side.

This scheme has now been superseded by displaying the wreckage in a re-creation of the crash site, as a memorial to the two men who died in the crash, while still adding to the conglomeration of Defiant parts. Alongside this a full-scale model of a Defiant is being built, with Alclad skin on a wooden frame, using many original parts like the wheels. This Defiant will be painted as L7005, the No. 264 Squadron Defiant being flown by Sgts Thorn and Barker when they won bars to their DFMs during the Battle of Britain, shooting down three German aircraft during one sortie, including the Bf 109 that shot them down.

T3955

Alongside the wreckage of N3378, the Boulton Paul Association displays the remains of another crashed Defiant, T3955. This was a No. 256 Squadron Defiant based at Squires Gate, and coded JT-R. It took off on a training flight on 15 May 1941, and crashed at Nether Kellet, Bolton-le-Sands, just over 2 miles (3km) from Carnforth in Lancashire. The two crew-members died in the crash. The Pennine Aviation Museum excavated the crash site in 1983, and came upon only a few battered fragments, up to 14ft (4m) down, which showed that the aircraft had hit the ground with some force. These fragments were donated to the Boulton Paul Association in the year 2000.

Surviving Turrets

Apart from the complete turret on the RAF Museum's N1671, there are very few surviving Boulton Paul Type A Mk. II gun turrets, the type fitted to the Defiant and the Roc. The Boulton Paul Association has parts of the turret from N3378, including the drive ring, with the cupola and other parts from other turrets, but is a very long way from having a complete turret. The only other known complete turret, apart from two of the different marks of Type A turret that were fitted to bombers, is an example found in a Florida scrapyard in the year 2000 by a turret enthusiast from Stone Mountain, Georgia. Though suffering from decades of exposure to the weather, it is missing only the glazing, and one of the doors.

It is unlikely to have come from the Defiant allocated to America, T4106, because in the same scrapyard was a Boulton Paul Type C turret, the one fitted in the nose of the Halifax, and the dorsal position of the Lockheed Hudson and Ventura. They were probably some of the examples of Boulton Paul turrets sent to American manufacturers to aid their turret development.

Surviving Engines

The other significant surviving Defiant relics in this country are engines recovered from Defiant crash sites. The most complete is the engine and bent propeller from N1766, Paul Rabone's No. 96 Squadron Defiant that crashed at Rowlees pasture, in the Peak District. It was excavated by a local group of enthusiasts, and spent some time in the Manchester Museum of Air

The Boulton Paul Association's Defiant full-scale model; it will represent L7005 when finished.

Operational Record: Defiant L7005

The Boulton Paul Association has chosen a very appropriate Defiant as the subject of their full-scale model: L7005, the top-scoring aircraft. Its crews claimed twelve German aircraft destroyed, plus a share in the destruction of two others, and won a DFC and three DFMs flying it. The aircraft saw action over Dunkirk and in the Battle of Britain, including four sorties in one day on 24 August 1940, and it flew at least three night patrols. It was also flown into action by five 'ace' crews, Cooke/Lippett, Welsh/Heydon, Hughes/Gash, Young/Russell and Thorn/Barker. The aircraft was a real star.

Date	Time	Crew	Details
24.05.40	Delivered to No. 264 from 10 MU, coded PS-X.		
27.05.40	08.30-10.20	Cooke/Lippett	Patrol Dunkirk.
27.05.40	11.20-13.10	Cooke/Lippett	Patrol Dunkirk one-third share in He 111 shot down.
28.05.40	11.40-12.55	Cooke/Lippett	Patrol Dunkirk.
28.05.40	15.45-17.05	Cooke/Lippett	Patrol Dunkirk.
29.05.40	14.30-16.25	Cooke/Lippett	Patrol Dunkirk 2 x Bf 109E and Bf 110 shot down, 1 third share in 2 x Ju 88 shot down.
29.05.40	18.55-20.40	Cooke/Lippett	Patrol Dunkirk 5 x Ju 87 shot down. FLt Lt Nicholas Cooke awarded the DFC, Corporal Lippett the DFM
21.06.40	02.55-13.40	Thorn/Barker	Night patrol.
22.06.40		Stokes/Commer	Night patrol.
04.07.40	12.40-13.05	Welsh/Heydon	Night patrol.
18.07.40		O'Malley/O'Connell	Convoy patrol.
19.07.40	06.30-08.45	Hughes/Crook	Convoy patrol.
19.07.40	09.40-11.40	Welsh/Heydon	Convoy patrol.
19.07.40	12.35-14.40	Knocker/Murland	Convoy patrol.
19.07.40	17.00-17.05	Hughes/Heydon	Convoy patrol. Recalled (141 Sqn debacle).
21.07.40	06.10-08.15	Welsh/Heydon	Convoy patrol.
21.07.40	14.00-15.40	Welsh/Heydon	Convoy patrol.
29.07.40	11.00-11.30	Banham/Baker	Convoy patrol.
30.07.40		Welsh-Heydon	Convoy patrol.
24.08.40	08.00-09.45	Hughes/Gash	Patrol Manston.
24.08.40	11.30-12.30	Young/Russell	Patrol Manston.
24.08.40	12.40-13.35	Young/Russell	Patrol Manston.
24.08.40	15.40-16.55	Young/Russell	Scramble Hornchurch; He 111 shot down.
26.08.40	11.45 -	Thorn/Barker	Scramble Hornchurch 2. Do 17 and Bf 109E shot down over Herne Bay. L7005 forced landing and written off. Sgt Roland Thorn and Sgt Fred Barker awarded bars to their DFMs.

and Space before being donated to the Night-Fighter Preservation Team at Elvington, Yorkshire.

Another Defiant engine is on display in Werkendam, Holland, a relic of the Defiant's first defeat on 13 May 1940. It is from L6958, Plt Off Thomas/LAC Bromley's aircraft. After shooting down two Ju 87s, they were attacked by Bf 109s and their Defiant was set on fire. Thomas baled out, but Bromley was probably killed by the fighter. The aircraft crashed near Breda, and the engine and other small parts were dug up by the Dutch Aircraft Recovery Team in the 1980s. The engine was split down the middle by the impact of the crash, and a special stand was built to display it.

A Merlin XX engine from the crash site of Defiant II, AA377, is on display at the Norfolk & Suffolk Aviation Museum at Flixton, near Bungay in Suffolk. This was a No. 264 Squadron Defiant that crashed 2 miles (3km) south of Leysdown, Kent, at 10 o'clock in the morning on 26 April 1942 during an air-to-ground firing exercise. The aircraft was at 2,000ft (610m) when the port wing was seen to drop, a sign of the Defiant's stall, and dive with the pilot only partially pulling out before hitting the ground. The engine was found by an aircraft archaeology group, 15ft (4.5m) down in a marshy ground.

Operational record - Defiant N3378

Date	Time	Crew	Detail
08.01.41	21.10-22.35	Trousdale/Chunn	Night patrol.
09.01.41	22.15-23.20	Trousdale/Farnes	Night patrol.
03.02.41	18.30-19.10	Trousdale/Chunn	Night patrol.
10.02.41	21.17-21.40	Heyton/Cutfield	Night patrol.
11.02.41	00.05-02.15	Heyton/Cutfield	Night patrol.
14.02.41	18.30-19.50	Trousdale/McChesney	Night patrol.
15.02.41	23.50-01.05	Trousdale/Chunn	Night patrol.
16.02.41	02.50-04.45	Trousdale/Chunn	Night patrol.
25.02.41	23.20-23.55	Ballantine/McTaggart	Night patrol.
26.02.41	19.30-20.55	Trousdale/Chunn	Night patrol.
12.03.41	23.11-00.57	Trousdale/Chunn	Night patrol.
13.03.41	19.58-21.36	Trousdale/Fitzsimmonds	Night patrol.
14.03.41	21.50-23.15	Trousdale/Fitzsimmonds	Night patrol.
19.03.41	00.20-01.20	Smith/Bayliss	Night patrol.
21.03.41	01.51-02.09	Smith/Bayliss	Weather test.
30.03.41	22.22-23.30	Smith/Bayliss	Night patrol.
05.05.41	01.05-02.52	Smith/Farnes	Shot down Ju 88 east of Donna Nook.
08.05.41		Trousdale/Chunn	Patrol at 20,000ft, saw e/a, could not catch it.
09.05.41	01.40-	Trousdale/Chunn	Shot down 2 x He 111.
16.05.41	23.25-00.25	Trousdale/Chunn	Night patrol.
29.05.41	01.11-02.42	Trousdale/Fitzsimmons	Night patrol.
12.06.41	01.13-02.11	Trousdale/Chunn	Night patrol.
17.06.41	23.54-01.19	Trousdale/Chunn	Night patrol.
21.06.41	23.44-00.26	Trousdale/Chunn	From Driffield.
30.06.41	01.52-03.10	Dale/Henderson	Over Yorks. 3x attempted interceptions.
04.07.41	00.35-01.27	Ballantine/Henderson	Patrol base.
08.07.41	00.05-01.21	Ballantine/Henderson	Patrol Donna Nook & Skegness
14.07.41		Bartlett/MacKenzie	Patrol S.Humber
18.07.41		Craig/Bayliss	Patrol, return with radiator trouble.
20.07.41		Ballantine/Henderson	Night patrol.
23.07.41		Ballantine/Henderson	Night patrol.
25.07.41		Ballantine/Bedford	Mablethorpe out to sea, bomber escort.
08.08.41	23.20-00.59	Ballantine/Bayliss	Vectored after e/a, which disappeared.
17.08.41		Plt Off Clarke/Sgt Allen	Patrol Flamborough Head.
18.08.41	22.50-00.10	Sgt Turner/Bedford	Night patrol.
29.08.41		Craig/Hempstead	Crashed en route Edinburgh to Hibaldstow.

The engine of Defiant L6958 on display at Werkendam in Holland.

The Kent Battle of Britain Museum displays the engine of L7026, shot down by Messerschmitt Bf 109s on 28 August 1940. The crew were Plt Off Peter Kenner and his gunner Plt Off Charles Johnson, and the aircraft crashed at Sillingbourne Farm, Hinxhill, Kent. The engine was discovered at a depth of 14ft (4.5m). The museum also has a display board featuring small items from the crash site of Defiant N1574, 'Bull' Whitley/Sgt Turner's aircraft that was shot down on the same day, crashing at Kingswood, Challock Forest, Kent.

CHAPTER FOURTEEN

Conclusions

Only two turret fighters went into production, the Defiant and the Roc, and only the Defiant saw significant action. The Northrop P-61 Black Widow was born in the midst of continuing British enthusiasm for the concept, but was never used as a turret fighter would expect to be used. Other fighters, such as the Blenheim, Bf 110 and Ju 88, had dorsal guns on movable mountings, but these were strictly defensive in nature, and there was no way they could be called turret fighters. Nevertheless it was possible for them to act like turret fighters: Guy Gibson in his book *Enemy Coast Ahead* described a Hampden formation that was attacked after bombing shipping off Norway:

> the Germans were flying in Messerschmitt 110 fighters, which had one gun which could fire sideways. Their mode of attack was to fly in formation with the Hampdens, perhaps fifty yards out and slightly to the front, and pick off the outside man with their one gun, aiming with a no-deflection shot at the pilot. The bomber boys could do nothing about it, they just had to sit there and wait to be shot down. If they broke away they were immediately pounced upon by the three Messerschmitt 109s waiting in the background. If they stayed the pilot received a machine gun serenade in the face. One by one they were hacked down from the wingman inwards.

This is a description of a perfect turret-fighter attack as envisaged by Air Commodore Higgins seventeen years before, and endorsed by all advocates of splitting the responsibility of aiming and firing the guns from flying the fighter. Things did not happen exactly as Gibson described them, however. The action took place on 12 April 1940, and twelve Hampdens took off from Waddington to attack shipping off Kristiansand, seven from No. 44 Squadron and five from No. 50 Squadron, under the command of Sqn Ldr J.J. Watts. After bombing the shipping in clear blue skies, Watts saw the German fighters closing in and took his formation down to sea level.

One Hampden, L4099, had been damaged by anti-aircraft fire and lagged behind. It was pounced on by the Messerschmitts and shot down. It may be that Bf 110s did make beam attacks with the free gun as described by Gibson, but it is also true that the single-seat Bf 109s – from II/JG 77 – also took advantage of the known Hampden blind-spot and flew parallel to the Hampden formation before turning in and attacking from the side. Although one Bf 109 was shot down by the dorsal gunner of L4074, the ventral gunners were entirely useless because the formation was so near the sea. The navigator of L4154, Sgt Clayton, was so overcome from the feeling of helplessness as the German fighters came in from the beam unopposed, that he took the Vickers K gun from the nose of the aircraft, and opened the astro-hatch. He then proceeded to fire at the attacking fighters, holding the machine gun as if it were a rifle. He won the Distinguished Flying Medal for this brave action.

Only four of the Hampdens returned to Waddington, and two others landed elsewhere, heavily damaged. This action has been used to illustrate how the turret fighter concept could have succeeded; but what it really shows is that single-seat fighters were perfectly capable of exploiting blind-spots in a bomber formation's defensive fire, and attacking from the flank. Nevertheless, it is undoubtedly true that a turret fighter would have been very successful against an unescorted formation of Hampdens, as the Defiants were when No. 264 Squadron met unescorted formations of Heinkel He 111s and Junkers Ju 87s near Dunkirk.

Against more heavily armed bombers, with power-operated dorsal turrets and beam guns, the story might have been very different, as the Luftwaffe found against large formations of Boeing B-17s and Consolidated B-24s. Even fleeting high-speed attacks by Bf 109s and FW 190s could be perilous activities, forcing the German fighter pilots to resort to head-on attacks

with closing speeds of nearly 500mph (800kmph), and firing times of only a couple of seconds.

The real problem for the turret fighter concept was that its protagonists did not envisage bomber formations being escorted by single-seat fighters. This had not happened during World War I, and long-range, single-engined fighters were not part of any air force's armoury. The operation of short-range fighters like the Bf 109 over London had been inconceivable when Specification F.9/35 had been issued, and so was the size of the attacking bomber formations. As Douglas Bader's 'Big Wing' showed, formations as large as three squadrons of single-seat fighters could attack in formation without much danger of collision, splitting the defensive firepower they faced, and delivering shattering attacks themselves. The very tight fighter formations envisaged during the 1930s were just not used during the Battle of Britain in the initial attack, after which the fighters tended to operate by themselves.

The one area where the turret fighter found a successful niche was at night. Always envisaged as a night fighter, the turret fighter operated individually after dark, and fully exploited its ability to home in on a bomber, either underneath or to the beam, and to deliver a sudden and highly accurate concentration of fire from short range, often aimed at specific targets such as the engines or crew compartment.

Even these advantages were negated once airborne radar had improved to the extent that night fighters could be placed in position behind their quarry with greater accuracy, and fixed-gun armaments, with four 20mm cannon as well as batteries of machine guns, had increased to such an extent that one burst of fire could overwhelm and destroy a target. The Northrop P.61 Black Widow vividly illustrated this change. Designed with the ability to make Defiant-like attacks from underneath, in practice they never did. Their advanced SCR-720 AI radar could place them directly behind a target so that their four cannon, and the four heavy machine guns in the turret, fixed to fire forward, could then destroy it with one burst. The turret fighter's time had come and gone, and it had only encompassed the months of the Blitz.

The concept of separating the responsibility for operating the aircraft's guns from that of piloting it resurfaced during the 1960s with the birth of the helicopter gunship. Operating against ground targets, and often below tree-top height, a helicopter pilot could not be expected, with the technology of the time, to fly his aircraft as well as to aim and fire his guns. The nose turret for heavy-calibre weapons, with a separate gunner to aim and fire them, was born, and the Bell Hueycobra, Hughes AH-64 Apache and Mil 24 'Hind'

were designed. Of course, as tactical weapons for use against ground targets, primarily tanks, these could hardly be termed 'turret fighters' in the accepted sense of the word; but since part of their role would be to shoot down the other side's helicopter gunships, perhaps the 'turret fighter' has at last found a secure niche.

A rear gunner's view of five Defiants of No. 264 squadron.

Defiant Construction

The Defiant was not an all-metal aircraft like the contemporary Spitfire. Apart from the control surfaces being fabric-covered, the upper rear fuselage with its retractable fairings was made of wood, as were the undercarriage doors. A government booklet produced in 1942 entitled *Women in the Workplace* included an article with several photographs about the construction of these very items, all done by women.

Boulton Paul were, of course, pioneers in metal construction, and had been building all-metal airframes since 1919, including that of the largest British aircraft ever built, the R.101 airship; but all those aircraft were fabric-covered. The metal skin of the Defiant was to be their first, and they took particular note of American techniques. A set of photographs in their archives, for instance, shows all aspects of the construction of the Douglas DC-2.

The system of construction they chose was evolutionary rather than revolutionary. It was not a unitary stressed-skin construction like the Spitfire, but a conventional metal airframe onto which the metal skin was wrapped and rivetted. In this respect it was very simple, and was deliberately designed so that the aircraft consisted of a number of major components that could be easily subcontracted, and which were bolted together at final assembly.

The skin plates were drilled on the flat, two or three at a time, in boiler-plate jigs, using pneumatic drills. All holes were dimpled, as countersunk rivets were used throughout. Then 'Z'-section stiffeners were rivetted to the skins, and when the skins were wrapped round the structure it was these stiffeners that were rivetted to the frame.

The heart of the aircraft was the wing centre-section, built up in a vertical jig, with the upper surface rivetted with conventional rivets and the lower surface with Armstrong-Whitworth's pop rivets. The patents for pop rivets were pooled with Boulton Paul and Gloster in the Metal Construction Pool in the early 1930s, to exploit the three companies' metal construction techniques.

The two wing spars consisted of upper and lower extruded light alloy booms, 'I'-section for the centre wing, and 'L'-section for the outer wings; these were connected by a corrugated metal web. The leading edge was made in separate detachable units, with D-section ribs to which the skin, pressed to shape on a Pels folding press, was rivetted. The rear section of the wing was supported with an auxiliary spar held half-way between rear spar and trailing edge. The inner part of the centre section was composed of the undercarriage bays, and outboard of these were the main fuel tanks.

Once the centre section was completed, it was revolved to a horizontal position, and the centre fuselage bolted on top of it, so that the upper surface of the wing actually formed the floor of the pilot's cockpit. This section of fuselage consisted of a strong frame made up of four longerons, the lower ones bent to conform to the wing shape. At the front they were braced in a tubular frame that carried the engine bearers. The longerons were boxed in with light alloy side members shaped to the fuselage section, and braced with bulkheads and alloy tube, with a horizontal corrugated top deck in which were the openings for the pilot's cockpit and the turret.

A publicity shot showing a Defiant wing centre-section in its vertical jig, with a female 'worker' dressed in a pristine white coat and stiletto heels! Clearly a model brought in, with little idea what she should wear in an aircraft factory!

The camouflaged Boulton Paul factory with the flight sheds to the left, a Halifax outside the Bellman hangars.

A row of Defiant tailplane jigs.

A Type A turret under construction.

The rear fuselage consisted of two side panels of skin wrapped round five tubular rib structures, joined together at the bottom, and formed into the fuselage shape by a horizontal corrugated deck at the top, onto which the upper wooden fusulage fairings were fitted. At the very rear end was bolted a tailpiece, in which the tailwheel was carried.

The tailplane and fin were one-piece multispar units covered in overlapping skin strips. Once removed from their construction jigs the tailplane was bolted on top of the rear fuselage, and the fin was then bolted on top of that. The elevators were identical, i.e. with the tab mechanism on the top on one side, and underneath on the other. Like the rudder they consisted of a D-shaped metal leading edge, forming a spar, and metal ribs covered with fabric.

Once the fuselage and tail were attached to the wing centre-section, the Merlin engine was fitted to the front. The engine was encased in an upper panel and two side panels, attached by Zeus fasteners. The lower cowling also contained the oil cooler duct. The aircraft would now be standing on its Lockheed undercarriage legs, and the turret would be slotted in.

The final assembly work was attaching the outer wings and the separate metal wing-tips, bolted to the spars with four bolts. The joint between the inner and outer wing was sealed by a rubber strip that wrapped around the wing. Like the elevators, the Frise ailerons had a D-shaped metal leading edge, and fabric covering.

The Defiant consisted of a total of twenty-one major components bolted together, varying in size from the wing centre-section to the wing-tips, and not including the engine and turret. Most of these could be, and were, sub-contracted, though Boulton Paul themselves retained the capability to build the entire airframe.

On 31 October 1939, Reid & Sigrist at Desford were brought into the Defiant programme with an order for 100 centre-sections that were to be delivered by June the following year. At the same time the company obtained an order for the final assembly of 100 Defiants, which were to be undertaken at the rate of four per month by the end of November. This proved very optimistic and the first Desford-assembled Defiant was not delivered until 16 May 1940, with the second on the 29th. The third was delivered on 2 June, and the fourth four days later. The fifth was under AID inspection on 11 June when the roof of the assembly hangar collapsed, thus ending Reid & Sigirist's assembly programme.

In May 1940 it was decided that 50 per cent of the Defiant should be subcontracted, and orders and jigs were issued accordingly.

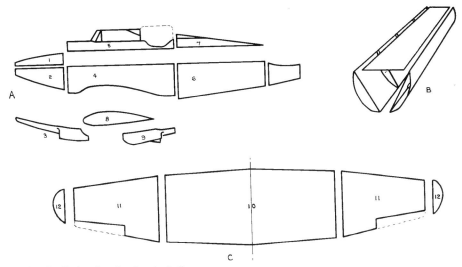

Boulton Paul's drawing showing the Defiant component parts.

Defiant Serials

Prototypes	2	K8310, K8620
Mark I	713	L6950 - L7036 Converted to - 238
		N1535 - N1582 T.T.III
		N1610 - N1653 (minimum)
		N1671 - N1706
		N1725 - N1773
		N1788 - N1812
		N3306 - N3340
		N3364 - N3405
		N3421 - N3460
		N3477 - N3520
		T3911 - T3960
		T3980 - T4010
		T4030 - T4076
		T4100 - T4121
		V1106 - V1141
		V1170 - V1183
		AA281 - AA330
		AA350 - AA362

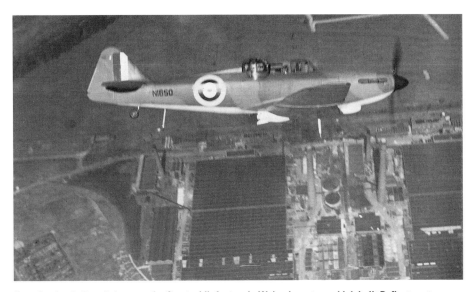

A production Defiant flying over the Courtauld's factory in Wolverhampton, which built Defiant centre-sections.

Six production Defiants outside the flight sheds.

Mark II	7	AA363 - AA36 Converted to 7 +
	200	AA370 - AA447 TT.I - 142
		AA469 - AA513 (Minimum)
		AA531 - AA550
		AA566 - AA595
		AA614 - AA633
		AA651 - AA670
T.T.I	140	DR863 - DR896
		DR914 - DR949
		DR961 - DR991
		DS121 - DS159
Total	1,062	

Location of Jigs for Final Assembly, 5.4.40

Item	Boulton Paul	Redwing Aircraft	Aero Engines	Hudswell-Clark	Northern Aircraft	Rollason Croydon
Ailerons	-	4				
Elevators	-		12			
Eng.mounts	2			6		
Fins	-				24	
Flaps	-					2
F'lage rear	8	8				
F'lage front	16	16				
F'lage complete	16	8				
Outer wings	12					12
Centre sect.	24		16			
Rudders	-		7			
Tailplanes	8				24	

Defiants Lost in Aerial Combat

Date	Serial	Squadron	Details	Date	Serial	Squadron	Details
13.05.40	L6958	264	Bf 109 attack over Holland		L7027	264	Bf 109 attack over Manston
	L6960	264	Bf 109 attack over Holland		N1535	264	Missing over Channel attacking a Ju 88
	L6965	264	Bf 109 attack over Holland					
	L6969	264	Bf 109 attack over Holland	26.08.40	L6985	264	Bf 109 attack over Herne Bay
	L6974	264	Bf 109 attack over Holland		L7005	264	Bf 109 attack over Herne Bay
	L6977	264	Bf 109 attack over Holland		L7025	264	Bf 109 attack over Herne Bay
28.05.40	L6953	264	Bf 109 attack over Channel	28.08.40	L7021	264	Bf 109 attack over Kent
	L6959	264	Bf 109 attack over Channel		L7026	264	Bf 109 attack over Kent
	L7007	264	Bf 109 attack over Channel		N1569	264	Bf 109 attack over Kent
31.05.40	L6961	264	Collision during Bf 109 attack		N1574	264	Bf 109 attack over Kent
	L6968	264	Bf 109 attack over Channel	08.10.40	N1627	264	Crashed on night patrol, cause unknown, possibly shot down
	L6972	264	Return fire from He 111					
	L6975	264	Bf 109 attack over Channel	07.05.41	N3500	256	Shot down by Ju 88 at night
	L6980	264	Collision during Bf 109 attack	29.05.41	N1556	54 OTU	Collision with Blenheim, e/a in vicinity
19.07.40	L6974	141	Bf 109 attack over Channel					
	L6995	141	Bf 109 attack over Channel	25.07.42	V1117	277	Shot down by FW 190 over Channel
L7001		141	Bf 109 attack over Channel					
	L7009	141	Bf 109 attack over Channel	21.05.43	AA658	515	Missing over Channel, e/a in vicinity
	L7015	141	Bf 109 attack over Channel					
	L7016	141	Bf 109 attack over Channel	17.07.43	AA651	515	Missing over Channel, FW 190 in vicinity
24.08.40	L6966	264	Bf 109 attack over Manston					
	L6967		264 Bf 109 attack over Essex					

Total 37

Defiant Victories in Aerial Combat

Date	Type	Squadron	Details	Date	Type	Squadron	Details
12.05.40	1x He 111	264	Fighter sweep over Holland	04.05.41	1x Ju 88	255	Night interception
	1x Ju 88	264	Fighter sweep over Holland		1x He 111	151	Night interception
13.05.40	4x Ju 87	264	Fighter sweep over Holland	05.05.41	3x He 111	141	Night interceptions, north-east
	1x Bf 109	264	Fighter sweep over Holland		1x Ju 88	256	Shot down over Wrexham
24.05.40	1x Bf 110	264	Fighter sweep over Dunkirk		1x Do 17	256	Shot down over Lancashire
27.05.40	2x Bf 109	264	Attacked over Channel	06.05.41	3x He 111	141	Night interceptions, north-east
	3x He 111	264	Broke up formation over Channel		1x Ju 88	96	Shot down over Lancashire
28.05.40	6x Bf 109	264	Attacked over Channel		1x He 111	96	Shot down over Lancashire
29.05.40	8x Bf 109	264	Fighter sweep over Dunkirk	07.05.41	1x He 111	141	Night interception, north-east
	7x Bf 110	264	Fighter sweep over Dunkirk		1x Ju 88	141	Night interception, Holy Island
	1x Ju 88	264	Fighter sweep over Dunkirk		3x He 111	256	Shot down over north-west
	21x Ju 87	264	Fighter sweep over Dunkirk		2x He 111	96	Shot down at Malpas and Wrexham
31.05.40	4x Bf 109	264	Fighter sweep over Dunkirk		1x Ju 88	96	Shot down over north-west
	4x He 111	264	Fighter sweep over Dunkirk	08.05.41	'Bomber'	264	Intruder operation over France
19.07.40	4x Bf 109	141	Attacked over Channel		1x He 111	264	Intruder operation over France
15.08.40	1x He 111	264	Night interception		1x He 111	255	Night interception
24.08.40	4x Ju 88	264	Sortie from Manston	09.05.41	1x Bf 110	264	Intruder operation over France
	2x Bf 109	264	Attacked over Kent		1x Ju 88	255	Shot down over Humber area
	3x Ju 88	264	Sortie from Manston		4x He 111	255	Shot down over Humber area
	1x He 111	264	Sortie from Hornchurch	10.05.41	1x Ju 88	151	Night interception
26.08.40	6x Do 17	264	Interception over Kent		1x He 111	151	Night interception
	1x Bf 109	264	Attacked over Herne Bay	11.05.41	2x He 111	264	Night interceptions
28.08.40	2x He 111	264	Interception over Kent		1x Do 17	264	Intruder operation over France
17.09.40	1x Ju 88	141	Shot down near Barking	12.05.41	1x He 111	307	Shot down near Exeter
16.10.40	1x He 111	264	Shot down over Brentwood	22.05.41	1x Ju 88	256	Shot down over Lancashire
22.12.40	1x He 111	141	Shot down near Beachy Head	10.06.41	1x Ju 88	96	Shot down over Cheshire
04.02.41	1x Do 17	151	Shot down over Weldon,Northants	22.10.41	1x Ju 88	256	Shot down at Coventry
12.03.41	2x He 111	264	Night interceptions	31.10.41	1x Ju 88	151	Shot down off Yarmouth
07.04.41	1x Ju 88	256	Shot down near Southport	15.11.41	1x Ju 88	151	Shot down on dusk patrol
08.04.41	1x He 111	264	Night interception	19.02.42	1x Do 217	151	Convoy patrol off Thames
	2x He 111	151	Shot down over Midlands	17.04.42	1x He 111	264	Shot down south of Beachy Head
09.04.41	1x He 111	264	Shot down over Godalming				
	2x Ju 88	151	Shot down over Midlands		Total 152		
	1x He 111	151	Shot down over Midlands				
10.04.41	1x Ju 88	264	Shot down over Beachy Head	Totals:	Heinkel He 111		52
	1x He 111	64	Night interception		Junkers Ju 87		25
	1x He 111	256	Shot down over Smethwick		Junkers Ju 88		28
12.04.41	1x He 111	307	Shot down over Dorset		Dornier Do 17		9
16.04.41	1x He 111	307	Shot down over Somerset		Dornier Do 217		1
02.05.41	1x Ju 88	151	Night interception		Messerschmitt Bf 109		28
03.05.41	1x Ju 88	151	Night interception		Messerschmitt Bf 110		9
	1x He 111	151	Night interception				

Index